SCOTLAND'S
NATURE IN TRUST

Manx shearwaters and kittiwakes

St Kilda

There are seven circles on St Kilda.
First, is the rim of the caldera
       which is the islands themselves;
Hirta, Soay, Dùn, Levenish and Boreray.
Second, are the steep hills
       that shelter Village Bay;
Mullach Sgar, Mullach Mór, Conachair and Oiseval.
Third, is the hill dyke that encloses
       the Village and the green inbye.
Fourth, is the Street:
       an indelible statement of empty houses.
Fifth, is the black tarmacadam,
       linking the base to the helipad:
a perforation on the landscape.
Sixth, is the saffron shore of Village Bay,
       borrowed each winter by the sea.
The seventh, and only unbroken circle,
       is that of the graveyard:
a grey wall carefully tended.

Glencoe: rocks in hanging valley with hikers

Glencoe.

SCOTLAND'S NATURE IN TRUST

The National Trust for Scotland and its
Wildlife and Crofting Management

J. Laughton Johnston

Illustrations by John Busby

T & A D
POYSER
NATURAL
HISTORY

Published in association with the
NATIONAL TRUST FOR SCOTLAND

Academic Press
24–28 Oval Road, London NW1 7DX, UK
http://www.hbuk.co.uk/ap/

Academic Press
A Harcourt Science and Technology Company
525 B Street, Suite 1900, San Diego, California 92101-4495, USA
http://www.apnet.com

ISBN 0-85661-122-0

A catalogue record for this book is available from the British Library

Typeset by Kenneth Burnley, Wirral, Cheshire
Printed in Italy by SFERA

00 01 02 03 04 05 SF 9 8 7 6 5 4 3 2 1

Contents

For Lillie and Betty

Foreword

The National Trust for Scotland is approaching its seventieth anniversary, in 2001, at a time when Scotland is changing quickly. The new Scottish Parliament is in its first year and there promises to be a period of rapid legislative change which will affect our land, the way it is used and looked after, those who live in the countryside and those who enjoy the wealth of landscapes Scotland has to offer for recreation and contemplation. In a world that grows ever smaller, with every remote corner becoming more accessible, our land and landscapes – especially those of the uplands and islands – take on more significance. An increasing responsibility therefore is placed on those who care for these areas. The National Trust for Scotland accepted this responsibility long ago: in 1932 when it accepted the gift of Burg on the island of Mull, and in 1935 when the first parts of the Glencoe property were purchased. Since then the Trust has become Scotland's second-largest private landowner, with nearly 75,000 hectares (185,000 acres) in its care. But what makes the Trust so special is not just the scale of its landholding but the commitment to care for it for the benefit of everyone – those who work on the land; local communities; visitors and tourists; mountaineers; biologists and naturalists; and those with an interest in the archaeology and buildings in the countryside.

Since the acquisition of Glencoe and Dalness in the 1930s, the Trust has always provided for public access, and in the early days perhaps saw little need to change other forms of management. Over the intervening years we have all become more aware of the special nature of the wildlife and wild places of our mountains and the need to protect these too. More recently we have come to appreciate the landscape as an archive of historical and prehistorical information, allowing us to learn, for example, about the lives of people who made shielings in which they could shelter while tending livestock in the hills. We are only now starting to understand how early settlers and prehistoric climate changes influenced the pattern of vegetation, particularly peatlands and woodlands. The conservation of all these features depends on the establishment of good management practices, and to achieve this the Trust needs the services of skilled staff and the support of local people.

This book traces some of the many changes in the Trust's management of a range of properties in the Highlands and Islands. It points to errors and problems, all part of the learning process we have shared with others over the last 70 years. We can be sure that the conservation tasks ahead will be no less difficult. The Trust still has the same commitment to Scotland's nature and land that first set us on our course, but now we also have the benefit of past experience. Laughton Johnston has provided us with a timely reminder of the importance of our heritage of wild nature, of its reliance on people and of the lessons the Trust has learnt. I hope you will enjoy reading this book, that it will inspire visits to properties in the Trust's care, and that it will remind policy-makers that our wild places and open countryside need our continued commitment to their protection.

Professor Ian Cunningham, CBE
Chairman of the National Trust for Scotland

Acknowledgements

Table 5.1	Courtesy NTS.
Table 10.1	Data courtesy Seabirds and Cetaceans Team JNCC.
Table 11.1	Data courtesy JNCC, FIBOT and SNH.
Figure 7.2	Courtesy NTS.
Figure 10.2	Courtesy Large Animal Research Group, Cambridge.
Figure 11.2	Courtesy Fair Isle Committee and Community Association, NTS and FIBOT.

Figures 2.1, 3.1, 4.1, 5.1, 6.1, 7.1, 7.2, 8.1, 9.1, 10.1 and 11.1 are based on the Ordnance Survey map, and reproduced with the sanction of the Controller of HM Stationery Office, Crown copyright reserved, Licence no. 542881.

Credits for the photographs are as follows:
NTS: pages 7, 10, 17, 23, 28, 31, 40, 42, 46, 62, 65, 70, 71, 86, 96, 101, 104, 114, 122, 124, 152, 158, 160, 161, 164, 167, 172, 176, 179, 187, 190, 194, 226, 228, 243, 250, 251.
R. Balharry: pages 13, 77, 83, 128, 136, 144, 148, 247.
A. Eckersall: page 185.
W. Fraser: pages 91, 97, 98.
L. Johnston: pages 21, 50, 54, 58, 142, 195, 196, 199, 202, 217, 225, 238, 255.
D. Mardon: pages 33, 37.
S. MacNally: pages 73, 74, 79.
S. Murray and the Institute of Terrestial Ecology: page 209.
A. Paterson: page 112.
R. Riddington and the Fair Isle Bird Observatory Trust: page 232.
I. Turnbull: page 108.

J. Laughton Johnston
March 1999

Author's Preface

Over the last thirty years or so I have worked for the Government nature conservation agency in its many guises – Nature Conservancy, Nature Conservancy Council, Nature Conservancy Council for Scotland, and latterly, on amalgamation with the Countryside Commission for Scotland in 1992, Scottish Natural Heritage. During that time I was involved directly or indirectly with several properties owned by the National Trust for Scotland (henceforward referred to as the Trust) – Fair Isle, Canna and Ben Lawers for example. I also followed closely the Trust's successful bid and subsequent management proposals for Mar Lodge Estate.

The average Scottish citizen probably perceives the Trust as a rather old-fashioned body influenced by landowning interests and supported by retired middle-class people, which looks after Victorian (and older) grand estate houses, their gardens and estates, left to it by impoverished aristocrats. Now, however, the Trust is becoming a more professional body undergoing changes in its structure and beginning to become aware of the full responsibilities it has assumed through ownership of countryside properties: responsibilities that have always been within its remit, but which previously have been rather neglected.

The involvement I had with the Trust during my career was in relation to nature conservation and the Trust's management of Ben Lawers in particular. During that time it became obvious to me that in some areas of the management of the natural heritage on Ben Lawers, the Trust was carrying through an innovative and exciting management agenda, even more radical and advanced than some of the recognised public and voluntary nature conservation managers on their own properties. On looking more closely at other Trust properties with which I was less familiar, I realised that several of those too were carrying out a level and quality of nature conservation management, and pursuing policies in relation to communities, that I had not associated with the Trust up to that point.

Few people are aware of the wide remit and responsibility of the Trust, but this has always been the case. One of the founders of the Trust, Sir Iain

Colquhoun of Luss, Bt, in the Foreword to the first book on the Trust's activities in 1939 (*Scotland Under Trust*), stated: 'I find that surprisingly few people are aware of the extraordinary interest and variety of the National Trust's possessions, and I, therefore, welcome the publication of *Scotland Under Trust* for, once the story of the Trust and its properties becomes more widely known so will its achievement be more valued and developed.' Sixty years on and with many more large countryside properties, the achievement and potential for the Trust in nature conservation management is still not widely known.

The initial impetus for this book was therefore a curiosity to see what the Trust was doing on its properties of nature conservation importance, and a desire to communicate this more widely, not just to Trust members, but to the general public. However, it quickly became apparent to me that a strict description and discussion of the Trust's nature conservation management alone, without taking into account much wider issues in the Scottish countryside, would be rather narrow and would not explain the interesting direction the Trust is now taking, nor from where it has come, or where its sights must be for the future. In addition, management of whatever kind requires groundwork, and in the case of the management of the natural heritage which is a living entity, it requires research, survey and monitoring. Much of this work is fascinating, but not readily accessible to the public, yet its results dictate, or at least influence, directions of management. It seemed therefore that there was a wonderful opportunity to discuss what lies behind the management of Trust countryside properties and to make that more accessible.

The Trust's natural heritage management, however, does not operate in a vacuum and it is inevitably involved in several universal 'conservation' issues that are, to some degree or other, controversial. It is important then to include discussion of these issues and the position the Trust takes on its various properties: issues such as deer management, native species forestry, fencing, footpaths and access, for example. At the same time the role of government agencies and the voluntary bodies in the countryside, not just in nature conservation but also in forestry and agriculture, is evolving into a wider community-support role: conservation cannot be divorced from community. This role has become increasingly important recently due to the growing problems of employment in the countryside and particularly in the 'marginal' natural resource economies of the Highlands and Islands, the crofting communities and hill farms particularly.

Two other potentially very important developments in the politics of rural Scotland which have been slowly simmering over many decades and are now coming to the boil must also be considered in this book in relation to the natural heritage management of the Trust's properties. These are, first, the level of involvement of local communities in decision-making, with much discussion of partnerships; and second, land reform and recent state support for the purchase of land by conservation bodies and communities themselves. The latter raises all sorts of issues for the Trust's 'inalienable' properties and both impinge on the approach to and control of the direction of management on these properties and the issue of national versus local interest.

It is probably important at this point to state what this book is *not* about! The issues above are best illustrated on a range of the Trust's large Highland and Island properties which exhibit a wide range of the Trust's environmental management. Since the main theme of the book is the Trust's management of the natural heritage, I narrowed the criteria for selection of properties to include only those with nature conservation designations. This book does not therefore include all of the Trust's Highland and Island properties. Additionally, on every property there is a whole range of management aims and prescriptions, and on the properties I have selected many of these are similar and do not require repeating for each. So I have not attempted to cover all of the management on each property. I therefore apologise to all Trust staff that, because of the constraints I have set myself in this book, I have had to omit some of the interesting and valuable work that they do. I regret also, that there has not been room in this book to acknowledge in full the contribution of Trust staff, such as the Rangers, the local offices and the backup expertise in ecology and archaeology, as well as the Trust members and volunteers, to the management of its properties.

In describing nature conservation management it is necessary to give some level of description of the geography, climate, geology and soils, species, communities and habitats for each property, but I have only included those elements necessary to illustrate particular areas of nature conservation management. This book therefore is not a definitive description of the landscape and wildlife of any of the properties, which are available in numerous and very accessible Trust publications.

The properties which met my criteria lie north of the Highland Boundary Fault and are, in the order they are dealt with: Ben Lawers, Canna, Torridon, Kintail and West Affric, Balmacara, Mar Lodge Estate, Glencoe, Ben Lomond, St Kilda and Fair Isle. It should be noted that with one of the properties, St Kilda, the natural heritage is actually managed by SNH for the Trust; however, the Trust remains the owner with overall responsibility, so by and large I have treated St Kilda as if it was managed by the Trust. What is most important about the Trust properties in this book, is the actual management that is being carried out on them – not necessarily who is actually doing that management or paying for it. I have tried to indicate who these other players are, but inevitably I will have omitted some and to them I also apologise.

The structure of the book is straightforward. The opening chapter briefly describes the Trust, its origin and the position it now occupies as a voluntary body and landowner in Scotland. The selected sites are then put into a geographical and biological context in relation to Scotland and to each other, and there is some discussion on conservation management issues which the Trust has to face on many of its properties. The next ten chapters are given over to the history and management of each site, using each to illustrate general issues and specific problems or challenges. The final chapter discusses some of the most interesting and sometimes controversial issues that have been raised in the preceding chapters, and the book closes with some thoughts on the future direction for the Trust in relation to the management of the natural heritage. There is often confusion between the terms 'natural heritage' and 'natural environment'. I shall use the term 'natural heritage' which is now in more common use and which here is meant to cover the solid geology, geomorphology, flora and fauna, and landscape.

The site visits were made through the summer months of 1998 from May to August. Although the weather was not always kind that summer, I had a wonderful time on the hill, island, shore and cliff, on the croft meadow, in the pinewood and on the moorland, often in the company of the Trust's local expert. In an attempt to convey the atmosphere of these wonderful places I have retained in the book the order in which I visited them, and my observations of each through the summer season. Except that is, for Ben Lawers, which I have commenced with, as this was the site which provided the inspiration for the book. The book therefore moves from Ben Lawers to spring in Canna in the Inner Hebrides and across the Highlands and Islands to early autumn in Fair Isle.

I took the idea of this book to Trevor Croft, the Trust's Director and, although I made it clear that I would write what I found, he generously and enthusiastically supported it. Without his support and that of every other member of the Trust's staff with whom I have been in contact, particularly the Rangers, the writing of this book would not have been possible. The Trust also gave me financial support, access to its Management Plans and relevant reports, the assistance of its staff, and the use of their and the Trust's wonderful collection of slides, for which I am extremely grateful. During the research for the book I visited the local Trust offices and each property in the company of the Ranger(s) as well as speaking to those associated with the management, monitoring and research on Trust properties, such as staff of SNH, RSPB, JNCC (Seabirds) and the Large Animal Research Group. The RSPB, SWT and SNH also kindly provided me with SSSI data. I also spoke to those who actually live on Trust property, and I am grateful for their patience and time in responding to my many queries. There are therefore many people who gave me their time and knowledge while carrying out their own busy schedules and I would like to thank them and those who read early drafts, made corrections and gave me useful comment. They are: Alexander Bennett, the late J. Morton Boyd, Anthony Bryant, Alan Bull, Margaret Fay Shaw Campbell, Hugh Cheape, Alister Clunas, Helen Cole, Mick Crawley, Stewart Cumming, Alasdair Eckersall, James Fenton, Dina Finan, Dougie Flynn, Willie Fraser, Ian Gardner, Phil Glennie, Brian Grainge, Mary Harman, Paul Harvey, Peter Holden, Michael Hunter, John Love, Richard Luxmoore, Dave Mardon, Stephen Mason, Roddy MacKerlich, Sharleen McLeod, Geraldine MacKinnon, Winnie MacKinnon, Seamus MacNally, Fiona Mitchell, Stuart Murray, Alasdair Oatts, Abbie Paterson, Josephine Pemberton, Richard Phillips, Nick Riddiford, Roger Riddington, Isla Robertson, Joy Sandison, Robin Satow, Alison Shaw, Anne Sinclair, Ian Stevenson, Eileen Stuart, Kate Thompson, Iain Turnbull, Robin Turner, Derrick Warner and Dave Wheeler. I am particularly grateful to those who also read later drafts, helped with production and suggested many amendments and improvements, and they are: Andrew Bachell, Dick Balharry, Ian Gardner and Paul Johnson.

I am also privileged that John Busby agreed to grace the pages with his evocative drawings of plants, birds, animals and places, and to him I am particularly grateful.

I have included four appendices. The first is Percy Unna's letter laying down the conditions, or principles, he set out concerning the properties whose acquisition he funded. The second explains a little more fully the confusing number of countryside designations that cover much of the Trust's countryside properties. The third covers all the equally confusing abbreviations that occur on almost every page, for which I apologise to the reader. For the sake of consistency I have used metric measures throughout, including hectares; but for those of imperial faith there is a brief conversion table in the fourth appendix.

In many places I have quoted from documents, and to distinguish the aims and objectives of Trust Management Plans for individual properties from other quotes, I have indented and italicised them. Finally, it is essential to note that *I* took the idea of this book *to* the Trust and that, in addition to their support, the Trust – trustingly – agreed not to impinge in any way on my editorial control. The ideas, comments, criticisms and support of the Trust's work in this book are therefore entirely mine. It is likely that the general reader, and the Trust, will disagree with a number of my opinions; but if the book sparks a debate, or at least spurs the Trust to look again at some of its natural heritage management, the rationale behind it and the balance of resources within the Trust that goes towards it, as opposed to other Trust responsibilities, I believe it will have achieved something.

Maps Legend

(See pages 29, 51, 69, 87, 105, 121, 153, 173, 191, 223)

National Trust Boundary

Site of Special Scientific Interest (SSSI)

National Nature Reserve (NNR)
(N.B. Also SSSI)

National Trust Sub Division

National Scenic Area

Candidate Special Area of Conservation

Environmentally Sensitive Area

Woodland Remnants (Kintail only)

Forestry Commission Boundary

Path

Chapter 1

General Issues

The general purpose of the National Trust for Scotland is stated in the 1935 Act:

> The National Trust for Scotland shall be established for the purposes of promoting the permanent preservation for the benefit of the nation of the *lands* and buildings in Scotland of historic or national interest or *natural beauty* and also of articles and objects of historic or national interest and *as regards lands for the preservation (so far as is practicable) of their natural aspect and features and animals and plant life* and as regards buildings for the preservation (so far as is practicable) of their architectural or historic features and contents so far as of national or historic interest. (my emphasis)

It is the aspect of the Trust's remit, set in italics above, concerning its management of the natural heritage of its properties which this book is all about (note that the word 'lands' was replaced by 'places' in the 1938 Act).

Much has been written elsewhere about the early history of the National Trust for Scotland (the Trust hereafter) and the debt it owes to the (English) National Trust and to the aims and purposes set out by the Trustees of Public Reservation in Massachusetts in the United States, which was established to protect its own natural and cultural heritage. Suffice it that the Trust had its Scottish origins in ambitious and energetic members of a propaganda body, the Association for the Preservation of Rural Scotland in the 1930s, which saw a pressing need to take Scotland's historical and landscape heritage in hand, i.e. under ownership, if it was going to be conserved for future generations. The Association however, under its constitution, was unable to hold land and buildings. The result was the formation of the National Trust for Scotland for Places of Historic Interest or Natural Beauty on 1st May 1931. Four years later, in 1935, the National Trust for Scotland Act was passed, making the Trust a statutory body and giving it powers to declare its

Facing page
Glen Quoich – Mar

land and buildings inalienable. Today, the Trust remains an independent body, the largest charity in Scotland, with a Council representative of a very wide range of Scottish interests.

Since its incorporation the Trust has been steadily accumulating properties of historical and landscape importance, including, quite early in its existence, sites such as Glencoe in 1935 and Kintail in 1943, which also had recognised wildlife interests. However, it was perhaps not until the purchase of Ben Lawers in 1950 that the Trust acquired a property primarily for its natural heritage value – its outstanding diversity of rare mountain and arctic-alpine plants.

Today, the Trust is the owner, on behalf of the Scottish people, of almost 80,000 hectares (800 square kilometres, or 300 square miles) which is 1 per cent of rural Scotland! How does this compare with other conservation-based 'not-for-profit' voluntary and public bodies and the largest private landowners in Scotland? In fact the Trust holds nearly 50 per cent of all 'not-for-profit' land managed for conservation in Scotland and more than twice as much as the next largest 'not-for-profit' conservation body, the RSPB. Discounting Forestry Commission (FC), with over 650,000 hectares, the Trust is possibly now the second-largest landowner in Scotland, with only the Duke of Buccleuch owning more!

This then is an enormous responsibility for the Trust, not just in terms of land management, but in terms of its responsibility to the people of Scotland – both the wider nation and the local communities – on whose behalf the land is held inalienably. Many of the buildings on this land, as one would expect, are recorded by the Royal Commission on the Ancient and Historical Monuments of Scotland (RCAHMS) on the National Monument Record of Scotland (NMRS). If one examines the percentage of Trust countryside properties that are designated as Sites of Special Scientific Interest (SSSI) for the national importance of their geology, landform and wildlife importance, it comes to approximately 45 per cent. The Trust also holds many areas designated for their landscape as National Scenic Areas (NSA). In several cases the natural heritage importance of the land has been further recognised as of international importance and designated as Special Protection Areas (SPA) and Special Areas of Conservation (SAC) by the European Union. In one instance (Fair Isle) a property has been given the European Diploma and in another (St Kilda), has been given the ultimate accolade by the United Nations as a World Heritage Site for its natural heritage.

How does the Trust measure up to the responsibility of this ownership and how does it manage these sites; for example, what management does it carry out? What aims and objectives are laid down in the management plans and on what information are they based? Does management on Trust property differ from that on land held by other conservation bodies, and what role has the local community? The Trust is far better known for its management of gardens and historic buildings, therefore with so much property covered by natural heritage designations, how much effort does the Trust now invest in the 'preservation of the natural aspect and features and animals and plant life' of these properties? These are just some of the questions raised in the following chapters.

Properties

I discussed the criteria for selection of the properties in the Preface to this book. Each is a large property, north of the Highland Boundary fault, and has at least one natural heritage designation as, or within, its boundary as shown in Table 1.1 (see Appendix II for explanations of designations).

However, before looking at the various properties in detail we need to put them in the context of Scotland's geography (see Figure 1.1), climate and geology so that we may appreciate their natural differences and better understand their management. We also need to be aware of the human history of Scotland which has had so much effect on its vegetation over a period of some 10,000 years, touching each of the properties in a slightly different way. And finally in this chapter we need to look at some of the current land management and natural process issues which are the subject of much debate, before we see how the Trust takes them into account in the management plans for its own properties.

Table 1.1   Countryside properties and their designations

Property name	Size (hectares)	SSSI	NNR	SPA	cSAC	NSA	MCA	OTHER
Mar Lodge Estate	31,376	✔	✔	✔	✔	✔		Ramsar/PNP#
Kintail/West Affric	10,712	✔*				✔	✔	
Torridon	6,515	✔	✔		✔	✔	✔	
Glencoe	5,829	✔			✔	✔		
Ben Lawers	3,452	✔	✔		✔	✔		ESA
Balmacara	2,274	✔			✔		✔	
Ben Lomond	2,195	✔				✔		ESA/PNP#
Canna	1,514	✔		✔		✔		
St Kilda	846	✔	✔	✔	✔	✔	✔	W. Herit./Biosph.
Fair Isle	1,089	✔		✔		✔		C. Europe/ESA

* very small part   PNP# Proposed National Park

Geography and geology

A number of attempts have been made to classify Scotland into bio-geographical zones using a variety of faunal, vegetational and climatic data.

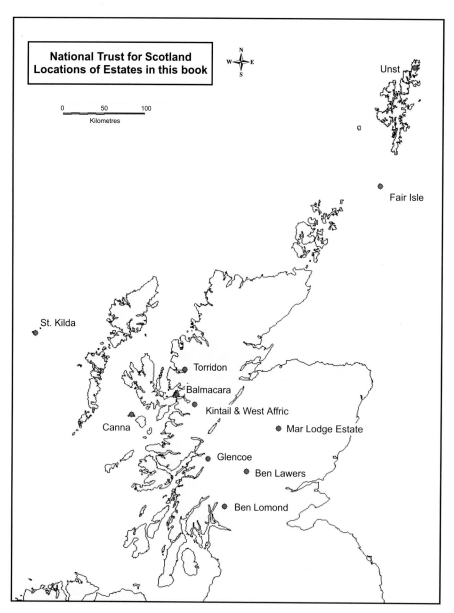

Figure 1.1
Map of Scotland
showing location of
Trust properties

One of the many problems met is that Scotland lies uncomfortably between the boreal coniferous and temperate deciduous zones of north-west Europe. There is also the fact that its climate is oceanic and therefore deteriorates rapidly with increasing altitude, which means that zones change on the vertical as well as horizontal plane. In addition the great variation in the geology and geomorphology can mean very local changes in vegetation. The Trust properties in this book are scattered across Scotland from the Central Highlands to the western and northern peripheries and therefore support a very wide and representative range of Scottish plant and animal communities.

Mar Lodge Estate and Ben Lawers lie in the Central Highlands, an area characterised by birds, vascular plants and bryophytes associated with the alpine zone and a relatively dry climate with relative extremes of temperature. Ben Lomond, Glencoe, Balmacara, Kintail and West Affric, and Torridon lie in the Western Mainland, another area of high relief, but with high rainfall and a milder climate, where species widespread in Western Europe overlap with those of strictly Atlantic distribution. Fair Isle lies in the Northern Isles, where much of the flora and fauna generally also occurs either on the coasts or the uplands of Scotland. Here the climate is relatively cool and damp, with strong winds, lowering altitudinal vegetation zones so that even at sea level the climate is equivalent to that at 350 metres in the Central Highlands. St Kilda, in the Western Isles, has a similar though slightly warmer Oceanic climate to the last two properties. Finally, Canna, another island property, lies at the southern end of the Western Isles and has the most mild and even climate of all the properties discussed here, reflected in the fact that several southern species of plants reach the northern limit of their world distribution in this area and are not found in the properties to the north. The ten properties therefore demonstrate a wide range of climates, even within such a small area as Scotland.

There is an immense variation in the geology of the properties which later we will see has a profound effect on the vegetation of each. To generalise – at one extreme are Mar Lodge Estate composed of mainly acidic and porous granites, and Torridon and Balmacara of acidic but impervious sandstones; while on the other are Ben Lawers of calcareous schists and Canna of basalts.

Crowded lay-by at Glencoe

Somewhere in between, in terms of the nutrient value of the soils formed from these rocks, are Fair Isle composed of Devonian sandstones, the metamorphic schists of Kintail and West Affric and the mica-schists of Ben Lomond. St Kilda is basically the rim of an extinct volcano, while Glencoe is a mixture of the ancient schists and more recent volcanic rocks.

Human history and its effect on Scotland's natural heritage

Twelve thousand years ago, and for tens of thousands of years before that of course, virtually all of what we now call Scotland was covered in ice, not re-emerging until the ice melted 12,000 Before Present (BP). Following a period of a few thousand years or so, as the climate improved and during which fellfield, tundra, scrub and finally woodland plant communities developed in succession, people gradually appeared in the landscape. Initially (Mesolithic), around 7–10,000 BP they were hunter-gatherers but then they gradually became the farmers (Neolithic). The earliest records of people in Scotland are in Lanarkshire some 10,000 BP. People probably entered Scotland after the last Ice Age from more than one direction; from the south and possibly from the east across the plains of the North Sea before they were flooded following the melting of the ice and the consequent rise of the sea level.

From those very early days people contributed to the natural changes taking place in the landscape – natural changes such as those brought about by climatic fluctuation and the appearance of new plants, animals and communities; for example turning tall-herb and woodland communities into grasslands and moorlands. As the human population increased and as their management methods became more sophisticated and widespread, their impact on the landscape grew. Today when we look around, we realise that very little of the original plant communities that evolved, due to a combination of climate, soils and wild herbivores, are now unmodified by people and their activities. Perhaps only cliff, mountain-top and deep peatland plant communities are as they would have been if people had never settled in Scotland.

But these communities, including their animal components, have, by and large, not only been modified by people: with few exceptions they have been impoverished. The exceptions include some of the semi-natural, herb-rich grasslands and moorlands created by well-managed grazing regimes (such as the machairs and limestone grasslands) and the wet grasslands and hay meadows found still in the crofting habitats. Losses, among many, include in excess of 95 per cent of the many varieties of native woodland communities which covered much of Scotland up to the tree-line, tall-herb and fern communities, the montane scrub and some of the sub-alpine communities

Sandy towards Canna

above. These diverse communities once covered a vastly greater area than any of the exceptions that have been created in their place and so their modification, if not destruction in many cases, has led to the loss of a great diversity of wildlife in Scotland, with its concomitant loss of the aesthetic contribution they made to the landscape. It has also led, we now realise, to the loss of a vast naturally renewable resource and to the present dilemma for conservation managers – should the present characteristic landscape of Scotland be conserved as it is, or restored to something like its diverse potential?

The much-quoted Fraser Darling wrote in the preface to his book *West Highland Survey*, 'And finally, the bald unpalatable fact is emphasized that the Highland and Islands are largely a devastated terrain, and that any policy which ignores this fact cannot hope to achieve rehabilitation.' It was Darling, and later Pearsall and others, who pointed to the damage to the soil, particularly in the wet climate and poor soils of the Highlands and Islands that is caused by the loss of trees and shrubs. The point about all the changes that have happened, is that the natural heritage of Scotland is a managed heritage, that most of the vegetation and soils are therefore only semi-natural, and that to restore or maintain diversity management needs to continue.

Communities

As Fraser Darling pointed out in the 1940s and 1950s, the land (and the sea) is the primary resource and only its sympathetic management will retain people in the Highland and Islands, however much money is invested in new

Croft land, Drumbuie

local industries or in the infrastructure – and that is still true today. In recent years a great deal of agricultural subsidy, both from Europe and the Scottish Office Agriculture, Environment and Fisheries Department (SOAEFD) has gone to farmers and crofters. Alas much of it, although giving critical support to those on the margin, has resulted through high sheep numbers, unnecessary reclamation and re-seeding – in damage to soils and semi-natural plant communities: the very resource upon which the whole agricultural structure and rural communities depend. At the time of writing it is quite apparent that some of this subsidy, particularly that for sheep, will be reduced. It will be tragic for rural communities and the land (and more expensive in the long run for the urban taxpayer) if support disappears altogether. What is wanted is a support system which will result in a more equitable balance between sheep and cattle which would be far better for the land. At the moment in many places there is over-grazing by sheep on the hills, and a turning over of once arable inbye fields to permanent grassland which are turning into monocultures, neither attractive to look at nor of benefit to our native wildlife.

If we are to retain communities and therefore management of the natural heritage in the crofting and other upland and marginal areas we must turn agricultural subsidy into community support and away from a hand-out that is ultimately destructive. What we need is positive management that allows a harvest of the sustainable potential of the land, while encouraging diversity of use, that creates a pleasing landscape in which to live and to visit and a variety of niches for wildlife, and that ultimately supports a thriving community. Such support must be seen and felt as encouraging primary production too and not simply as a service for tourists, naturalists and summer visitors. Today then, a great deal of natural heritage conservation activity, including that of the Trust, must be directed towards our understanding of the impact of our present and past management regimes and to the support of human communities.

In addition to crofting townships themselves, the Trust now owns major areas of Scotland's characteristic mountain, moorland, woodland and coastal habitats, of which many of the animal and plant communities have been reduced to remnants through thousands of years of exploitation. Much of the Trust's natural heritage management must then be to protect and extend these remnants. Natural heritage conservation today though, is not just about the saving of natural communities and species, but as we discussed above, about ensuring the place of people within the landscape. Not so long ago when conservationists used the term 'holistic' in relation to the natural environment, they meant to convey a concern not just for a single species but for the whole community of species and their interactions. They did not, however, include people and the cultural heritage in the way we do now when we recognise that our impact on the natural environment is so all-pervasive. The conclusion is that if we are to manage our natural environment to restore its diversity and productivity we must also support our rural populations, while at the same time we must promulgate the understanding of the regulation of 'natural' systems if we are to achieve this. Involving the community also raises the question of the balance between the local and the national, and sometimes international, interests. The Trust holds land 'for the nation'. Who are the nation, and has the Trust struck the right balance between the interests? We will look then at what the Trust is doing, particularly where there are crofting townships, at Kintail, Balmacara, Canna, Torridon and Fair Isle, where low-intensity agriculture is supporting whole communities; also at Ben Lawers and Ben Lomond where there are large farms.

Moorland management

Moorland is one of the most extensive of the semi-natural habitats in Scotland, which has largely been created below the tree-line by deliberate management over a long period of time. Upland moorland and associated grasslands form a large component of many Trust properties in the Highlands and Islands; and in some, Mar Lodge Estate for example, management of a large part of it is specifically aimed at the retention of moorland. The place of heather moorland in the Scottish landscape, its value for wildlife and its financial value for field sports and tourism is therefore a key consideration in the management of these properties.

Before human intervention, moorland was a natural component of the boreal forests, created by natural events. In the absence of nearby tree seed the vegetation cover that established itself was mainly dwarf shrubs, including heather. Over time that heather aged and died and tree seedlings, initially often of birch, gradually invaded the moorland and re-established a woodland, which itself then aged and died or was destroyed by fire. The circle of such events repeated itself endlessly in various permutations, such that the true relationship between moorland and forest was dynamic, not static. Today, by repeated burning and heavy grazing, it is as if we have stopped the successional clock.

As we will see later, at Ben Lomond and Ben Lawers for example, even dwarf-shrub moorland dominated by heather – which does at least provide some summer grazing for grouse and hares and winter grazing for sheep and deer – is not the end point if grazing pressures are too heavy. Heather and other small shrubs such as blaeberry and willows can be replaced by various unpalatable grasses and rushes, such as mat grass and heath rush, that further impoverish the natural heritage interest and, because of their unpalatability, coincidentally reduce the grazing value of the land.

There are several economic reasons for the retention of carefully managed moorland below the tree-line, and there is also an ornithological one in that the habitat is attractive for a number of waders, such as whimbrel, golden plover, dunlin and greenshank, that otherwise might not occur in this country except in small numbers. However, there is a counter-argument that the restoration of scrub and woodland could support an equally attractive and interesting bird fauna, such as capercaillie and black grouse, redwing and fieldfare, crossbill, redpoll and wryneck. Another argument put forward against allowing moorland to return to native woodland is the landscape one. Moorland has been described by landscape architects as *uniform, expansive, remote, wild and contrasting* against mountain peaks and forest. It actually shares those landscape attributes with the natural dwarf-shrub heath above the tree-line, it is just more accessible. It is in fact a *cultural* landscape that has become, like shortbread, something that everyone associates with Scotland; unfortunately it has also become a relatively limited and limiting vision. During the debate, initiated by the Cairngorms Partnership, about the proposed re-creation of the Caledonian pinewood forests in Speyside and Deeside, fear was expressed from some quarters of the replacement of the open moorland by the forests, as if this would happen overnight. In fact, with natural regeneration, it will take at least two or three generations for there to be any significant effect on the landscape. Each succeeding human generation will grow up along with an almost imperceptible landscape change, and the evolving scene will be absorbed painlessly into a new cultural landscape perspective.

The condition and management aims on each property with moorland are often very different, and on some, as we will see, there are inevitable conflicts between the aims of restoring woodland, or continuing viable agricultural grazing regimes, whilst retaining moorland. There is also the vexed question of how to judge the quality of moorland, as we will see at Mar Lodge Estate; the difficulties in restoring dwarf shrubs where unpalatable grasses and rushes have become established through heavy grazing as at Ben Lomond; the situation where the moorland is virtually above the tree-line as in the Northern Isles; and the question as to whether the wet moorland of Torridon is natural.

Red deer

Red deer is the largest of the remaining native wild mammals of Scotland, and as such holds a very special place in our natural heritage. Anyone who has heard the roar of the rutting stag in late autumn, watched a hind feeding its calf in mid-summer, or through a car windscreen viewed a large hind or stag group feeding near the road in the winter months at any number of places in the Highlands, would not wish to see the demise of this animal. Equally, many do not know just how much more impressive, in terms of size and productivity these animals should be, nor know the damage they cause to their own

Red deer
hind and calf

preferred environment. To understand the place of red deer in the culture of the Scottish Highlands today and the threat it poses to our native forests, such as the pinewoods of Mar Lodge Estate and to our natural heritage in the uplands generally, we need to look at the history of the species and our complex relationship with it from the time people first encountered and hunted it.

First, red deer is a very widespread species, found across Europe, Asia and North America, as well as south of the equator. In Britain it is one of the two indigenous deer, the other being roe. It is adapted to a mixed diet, grazing on open land and browsing in forests. However, in most of its present range in Scotland, due to reduction of forest and exclusion from most plantations, it is now an animal of the open hill. Partly because of this restriction to an exposed habitat and to the poor fertility of most of the Highland soils, the Scottish red deer is a much poorer specimen, in terms of size and productivity, than its European cousins and also relative to those introduced from Scotland to a more benign habitat in New Zealand. Our native Scottish red deer therefore, grand as it may appear, is generally far below its true potential.

In Scotland, in Mesolithic times, there is no doubt that the red deer was a favourite quarry of hunters as it provided both meat and hide, as well as antler and bone from which many tools could be fashioned. Pressure on its population from people however only came with the Neolithic farmers who began the real destruction of the red-deer forest habitat, and its range became progressively restricted from that time onwards. By the beginning of the second millennium AD, at the time of the first stable Scottish Royal lineage of Malcolm III – perhaps in the absence of regular wars for supremacy that previously occupied the Scottish nobility, both local and national – hunting became a privileged sport. Red deer was the largest and therefore most prestigious game quarry left, as the other large game had become extinct around this time. The noble beast, not surprisingly, became reserved for Royalty and their 'mormaers' or 'thanes'. From the record of medieval literature and art it is obvious that hunting became the pre-occupation of the ruling class from that time.

There followed a period therefore of strict control of hunting, well illustrated by the passing of several Acts prescribing penalties for the illegal killing of deer in the sixteenth century. It has been argued that these controls helped red deer to survive in Scotland whereas in England it had become extinct; and that may be so. By the seventeenth century red deer had become restricted to north of the Highland Boundary Fault and by the mid to late eighteenth century had become even more restricted within that area, through further destruction of its habitat and hunting, until there were only a handful of concentrations in nine deer forests (mostly open range with few trees) including Mar. Hunting in that period consisted of large-scale deer drives, often involving hundreds of people.

In many places in the Highlands and Islands the grazing pressure preventing regeneration of the remaining remnants of forest of all kinds in the past, came also from domestic cattle, ponies, goats, sometimes pigs and from the primitive sheep. With the introduction of the Blackface and the Cheviot, widely introduced from the south by the end of the eighteenth century and the clearances that followed, increased grazing pressure and burning to remove the surplus growth of heather and tree regeneration became the norm. However in Mar and in other pine forests, such as Abernethy and Rothiemurchus, red deer, for sporting, took precedence over sheep *and* people, and some of the forests survived, albeit in a condition of stasis due to continued grazing. Others, as we will discuss under Mar Lodge Estate, were felled for timber.

In the nineteenth century the stalking of deer on the open hill rapidly became more popular and the number of deer forests increased to 45 by 1838, with ever-increasing areas of land being set aside exclusively for deer stalking. The Victorians took up the sport with relish, fuelled by the growing interest in Scotland generated by the romantic-historical novels of Walter Scott and the myths of Ossian and aided by Landseer among many others. Later, in the twentieth century, writers like John Buchan and popular books on stalking further fuelled the passion.

By the beginning of the twentieth century there were over 213 deer forests of around 1.5 million hectares, or 8 per cent of rural Scotland, supporting around 150,000 red deer. Today's figure for red deer in Scotland is now double that at around 300,000. Since there has been a great development of commercial plantation forestry since the turn of the century – the FE estate alone is over 1.5 million acres – it is obvious that there must be increasing grazing pressure on the remaining open land and native forest. And if one takes into account the fact that the sheep population has also expanded greatly this century, then one is left in no doubt as to the threat to the natural heritage of our uplands and forests. Scotland may hold a substantial proportion, 28 per cent, of the European red-deer population, but it is too high a number for the land – the area of Scotland is a long, long way from being 28 per cent of that of Europe! Efforts are now being made to reduce the Scottish red-deer population, but with real signs of reduction only in a few specific areas where management aims include the general health of the natural heritage.

On the Trust's property of Mar Lodge Estate, as on most Scottish estates in the twentieth century, the traditional rationale behind red-deer management has been found to be unsustainable, and it has only been through research, such as that carried out in Rum, Glen Feshie and a few other places over many years, that this has been understood. The form of management carried out, exacerbated by the lack of sporting appeal in shooting hinds, has unfortunately kept the deer, and particularly the hind,

Golden eagle and
mountain hare

population much higher than necessary to produce a supply of trophy stags, the goal for most red-deer managers. Restricting the optimum habitat of red deer by keeping numbers up and not allowing sufficient regeneration to provide forest cover, has, as we have noted, resulted in a physically poorer animal. Managers worked on the theory that the more hinds there were in their herd, the more stags would be produced; and if the stags with 'poor' trophy heads were selectively culled, the herd would end up with stags which would inherit 'good' heads. First, there is no evidence to suggest that selective culling has made any difference to the quality of the head of the animal: it is the environment, habitat and climate, that is the major factor here. Second, research has shown that a large hind population is inimical to a large stag population and that the end result of failing to control hind numbers is that fewer and poorer stags are born and survive.

To address the problems of managing red-deer populations across estates boundaries, Deer Management Groups (DMG) were established by the Red Deer Commission (now the Deer Commission for Scotland [DCS]). These cover fairly discrete red-deer areas and are made up of the local estates, including Trust properties, with support from the DCS. Co-ordinated management to control deer numbers, of course, can be difficult if the management aims of neighbouring estates are different. The DCS, however, has powers to cull deer on private land, and to charge the owners for the exercise, if they consider deer numbers are not low enough.

The method of culling, whether by professional stalker or by paying guest, on Trust property is sometimes dictated by conditions attached to benefactors' contributions to acquisition costs. For example, one of the Trust's early benefactors was Percy Unna who stipulated that in his *Principles* (Appendix I): '. . . deer stalking must cease, and no sport of any kind carried on, or sporting rights sold or let; any use of the property for sport being wholly incompatible with the intention that the public should have unrestricted access and use.'

Accordingly, in principle, there can be no sport stalking on Glencoe, Kintail or Ben Lawers: all properties acquired with Unna money. On the other hand, a condition of the Easter Charitable Trust's donation at Mar Lodge Estate is that sport stalking must continue!

Reasons for culling can be a minefield of contradictions, and managers must therefore be very clear in their objectives. Culling for humanitarian reasons may be pure rationalisation, whether one genuinely believes in it or one uses it as a cover for other less attractive reasons. In later chapters, particularly those on Mar Lodge Estate, Torridon and Kintail, we will look

Stalkers and ponies
on path at Kintail

more closely at some of the reasons for and the methods used in deer culling by the Trust on its properties.

Woodland restoration

Through past management, little of our native woodland still survives. For example, in Angus and Perthshire, a region fringing the Highlands, we know from recent detailed surveys (*The Future for Tayside's Native Woodlands*; Tayside Native Woodlands 1995) that, despite the presence of many planted woodlands and commercial forests, native woodlands cover only 2.5 per cent of the land and that these woodlands vary in size from mere scraps at 0.01 hectares (100 × 100 metres) to 119 hectares. The report of that survey summed up the national importance of these native woodlands:

> In many ways the pine, birch and other native trees represent for many Scots the essence of our Scottish countryside. Celebrated in legend, poetry and song these woods still have a value today, not only as a wildlife habitat for plants and animals, but as a place where farmers and land managers still find benefits from the shelter, timber and game that these woods produce in abundance.

These are our last remnants of ancient woodlands and forests that stretch back to the end of the last Ice Age and are irreplaceable treasure chests of diversity. One just needs to compare the monoculture of heather moorland or bracken-infested pasture with the variety of species, the architecture of trunk and limb, the nuances of light and shade within a pine, birch or oak wood from which the former communities were derived, to appreciate their loss. Woodlands also play a pivotal role in creating and maintaining good soils and controlling run-off in wet climates and are vital on the banks of burns and rivers where they may control erosion and where their shade maintains cool and even temperatures for spawning fish, before the leaves fall as nutrients to enrich the waters.

Plans and action for the re-creation of these native woodlands, both through planting and through natural regeneration, have been gathering pace over the last fifty years or so, culminating in the formation of several voluntary bodies promoting native woodland, most recently the Millennium Forest for Scotland with its plans to create large new areas of native woodland by the year 2000. There is much discussion of course, due to the very limited amounts of native woodland in some areas, as to their original composition and as to where these native forests, both did and did not, occur.

One of the most controversial issues facing those who support the restoration of our native woodlands is – just why did they disappear in the first place? There is no doubt that a great deal of our original native forest has been cleared by our own activities, but what part did the deteriorating climate, commencing around 4000 BP, play? Was the onset of wet and cool weather the major factor in the death of forests and the spread of blanket-bog and moorland, and did management activity simply exacerbate these developments? The jury is still out on that one, or rather the defence and prosecution are still finding new evidence to support their cases! The nub of the debate is that if the climate change was predominantly responsible for the loss of trees in a particular area, we are wrong to try to 'restore' trees to that area. Whereas if people were predominantly responsible then there may be a very good case – improving soils or restoring diversity – for restoration. The problem of course is not that simple, for even if the latter is the case, the absence of tree cover over hundreds, if not thousands, of years may have resulted in soils no longer capable of supporting trees.

In some areas, such as the lower ground at Mar Lodge Estate and Ben Lomond for example, it is fairly clear from the existing evidence that tree cover was removed by management and can fairly easily be restored. In other situations, such as at Torridon, it is not clear what has happened, while at upper West Affric the most recent research suggests that the forest was already retreating, possibly for climatic reasons, before people settled there. At Mar Lodge Estate it may well be that tree cover can be restored by natural regeneration; however at Torridon, where there are so few trees surviving, natural regeneration, if it succeeds, could take hundreds of years to re-establish woodland. That then raises the question of whether or not to plant trees that will then provide additional seed for natural regeneration? Unfortunately, if there are very few native remnants, that can raise yet more questions – what species to plant and from where to collect the seed? We will return to the debate on what is 'native' woodland, and when and where it is 'correct' to plant or sow, particularly in the chapters on Torridon, Ben Lawers and Mar Lodge Estate. We must now touch on another controversial topic very much related to native woodland protection and regeneration, deer and sheep management, as well as access – fencing.

The approach to the management of our native woodlands over the last half-century has been dictated by political and financial imperatives, namely the pressures for commercial forestry, the cash return from grazing stock (including sheep and cattle), and the high prices that can be obtained from letting (and selling) deer forests, which has inhibited efforts to reduce grazing and promote natural regeneration. These financial imperatives have resulted in a vast number of relatively small fenced enclosures across the countryside, designed to keep out grazing animals. Although they are expensive to erect and maintain, deer fences can attract grants from both SNH and FA, i.e. taxpayers' money. More recently, fencing activity has been markedly encouraged by the large sums of money available under the Millennium Forest for Scotland (MFS) schemes.

Fencing, as a solution to over-grazing, has a number of drawbacks. First, erecting fences can simply be an easy way of avoiding dealing with the thorny problem of over-grazing. Fencing can simply be an excuse to allow over-grazing to continue outside the enclosure; and the more areas that are fenced for protection, the more difficult it will become to deal with the problem. Second, fences create unnatural blocks and sharp edges that detract from the landscape. Third, the fences form a barrier, both irritating to walkers who usually climb over and damage them and fatal to large woodland and woodland edge birds, such as the capercaillie and the black grouse, that do not see them as they exit the trees until it is too late. Additionally, if high grazing pressure remains around the enclosure, there is no way that the fences can be removed, as the woodland will become a magnet for browsers and simply be destroyed.

In the short term and for very specific situations there is no doubt that fencing will protect remnant areas of native woodland. If on the other hand fences have to remain in place indefinitely, without *any* grazing or trampling, that simply results in the growth of rank ground vegetation which severely inhibits regeneration. Ideally, there has to be a balance between the numbers of grazing animals and tree regeneration, and if fences are being erected for pragmatic reasons in the short term – e.g. the Trust does not have control of the grazing population of sheep or deer outside the fences – the long-term plan must be to reduce the grazing population to the optimum level before the fences are due to come down. In later chapters we will discuss why fences are going up on Ben Lawers but are coming down at Mar Lodge Estate!

Before we leave woodland restoration we need to touch on the rationale behind the Trust's efforts to eradicate *Rhododendron ponticum* from areas of native woodland. Rhododendrons are attractive and popular plants with their large blossoms, and are one of the relatively few exotic shrubs which do well in the wet, cool and humid climate of the west coast, a climate similar to their original Asian and Himalayan temperate mountain home. One just has to visit the Trust's property at Inverewe to see how effective rhododendron can be in a garden landscape. It is therefore rather difficult for visitors to understand why conservationists want to see them removed from the wild – which after all has no other native flower of such size.

Most of the introduced rhododendrons and other exotics that we plant in our gardens are not a problem to control. The species *Rhododendron ponticum* however, thrives on the wet and acidic soils of the west, regenerates freely and spreads inexorably through woodland and onto moorland. Its heavy foliage shades out native ground flora and sapling trees and shrubs, and is of no benefit to native birds or animals. It has the potential

Hill track on the landscape, Beinn a Bhuird

therefore to entirely eliminate native woodland and shrub communities. It originates from the woodland policies around the 'big' house where it was planted along with other exotics last century, and gradually, through lack of management, has spread outside those policies – at Torridon for example. It is such a successful plant in Scotland, lacking any controlling species, that outside policies, it has to be entirely eradicated or remnants will quickly re-establish dominance. There are several techniques used in eradicating *ponticum*, from simply pulling out the roots – which is actually a very hard physical task – to the spraying of a systemic herbicide on the full plant or on the regrowth following cutting back which usually involves several years of herbicide treatment. A great deal of dead rhododendron is not a pretty sight, but within a year or two the stems rot down and become hidden in the new undergrowth and young trees that replace it.

Access

There can be little doubt that the early Mesolithic people exploring the Highlands quickly found those passes well known today such as the Lairig Ghru, the Lairig an Laoigh and Glen Shee in the Cairngorms, or the high passes from Kintail through to West Affric. Later, many of these passes became the 'drove' roads for the black cattle or even today's main

Ben Lawers stream
and walkers

communication routes. Many more are today also increasingly popular
routes for the ever-growing army of walkers who leave the urban centres at
the weekends and on holidays and take to the hills.

Apart from those early communication routes the only other hill tracks,
until relatively recently, were those up to the peripheral settlements, to the
shielings and perhaps temporary tracks for forestry purposes. With the

development of deer stalking as a sporting pursuit in the mid-nineteenth century, many stone footpaths and pony paths were built. The effects on the landscape of these tracks and paths were minimal; even the permanent stone stalking paths as they were usually well constructed and followed the natural line and curve of the slope. This century however, an increasing number of roads for vehicles to carry guests up to the stalking and to grouse shooting, to assist the gamekeeping staff in management and of course to take skiers up Cairngorm, have been carved across hill slopes onto the upper moorlands and plateaux, destroying the natural patterns and lines of the landscape.

Access then, to the areas beyond human settlement and up onto the fragile and hitherto relatively undisturbed high plateaux, has become increasingly easy and the very integrity of these wilderness areas now compromised. The ability to take vehicles higher up the hills has coincided with improved communications on the national road network. What were once remote walking and climbing areas, that took an uncomfortable day's bus ride on narrow winding roads just to reach, are now relatively quickly and painlessly accessible. With a huge increase in hill walkers in this country since the 1940s, now supporting several industries in manufacturing and services, the existing paths and tracks have, in some cases, been overwhelmed. Pressure of numbers and extension of goals – for example to climb all the Munros – has created a huge number of new 'informal' paths: paths that have not been planned or constructed for the purpose and that are

Mullach an Rathain, Torridon

therefore ill-defined, resulting in an ever-widening ribbon-network stretching from public roads and estate tracks up to the highest peaks. In later chapters we will see what the Trust is doing on its most popular walking areas on Ben Lomond, Glencoe and Ben Lawers to address those problems.

Not all these paths of course have been open to the public, and it is only in very recent times that the boot has found the other foot, with landowners and land managers now on the defensive. It used to be almost unquestioned that access to the hills in deer forests was prohibited – and not very long ago too. It could not be said now, as the Director of the Nature Conservancy did in 1976 that '. . . a casual entry to private land may be unwelcome and during the deer-stalking season (approximately mid-August to mid-October) positively foolhardy' (*The National Trust for Scotland Guide*). As this book goes to press there are strong indications that the new Scottish Parliament will legislate for a freedom to roam.

The Trust of course, unique among the conservation bodies, has a policy of 'open access' and did not feel the need to sign a recent concordat agreed by both conservation bodies and landowners. However, it has its own concerns in relation to the provision of footpaths and the signs that often accompany them. As we noted under the section on red deer, one of the Trust's most generous benefactors, Percy Unna, who became President of the Scottish Mountaineering Club (SMC) in 1936 and who helped the Trust purchase Glencoe, Kintail and Ben Lawers, laid down fairly strict conditions attached to his donations. Percy Unna was an engineer of Danish and German extraction, also an experienced European mountaineer, who had a special love for the mountains of Scotland. He had seen the tourist developments in the Alps and their urbanising effects on the wild quality of the mountains, and was particularly concerned that the wilderness element of the Scottish mountains should be protected. In a letter to the Chairman of the Trust Council in 1937, following the purchase of the Dalness section of Glencoe (to which he was the principal anonymous donor), he set out the 'Unna Principles' (see Appendix I) which he intended should be applied to all the properties to whose purchase he contributed, and to all mountain areas in Scotland and ultimately beyond. These principles were set out of course in the 1930s when the number of walkers heading for the hills was substantially less than today, and one has to question whether or not they are now entirely relevant.

*   *   *

In this opening chapter I have aired a number of countryside management issues from which the Trust cannot isolate itself. In fact, as the owner of 1 per cent of rural Scotland – more than any other individual (or Estate Trust) apart from the Duke of Buccleuch, the Trust is obliged to address these issues, knowing that the eyes of Scotland are upon it.

In addition, as a charitable conservation body, owning so much land of high conservation value on behalf of the people of Scotland, the Trust must demonstrate to others how to approach these management issues, and with the utmost rationality; it must set out management aims for each property with the utmost clarity; and it must manage on a sustainable basis.

This is a tall order for a body that has come rather late to recognising its responsibilities to natural heritage management, and in the following chapters we will see just how far the Trust has come.

We now turn to the properties themselves.

Chapter 2

Ben Lawers

Origins

Travelling north from Edinburgh or Glasgow, whether going to the north west via Crianlarich, due north though Atholl and over the watershed to the Spey, or across Strathmore towards Aberdeen and the north east by Glenshee or by the coast, one hardly comes within sight of some of the most botanically rich mountains in Scotland. In the central part of Scotland particularly, because of the long east–west glens in which lie Loch Earn, Loch Tay and Loch Rannoch, the main north–south routes skirt to the west and east of the mountains of Breadalbane, the broad lands of the Scots. It is in these green mountains that lies the most important area in Britain for mountain plants. The reason why this area is the most important is rather complex, and we need to have a closer look at the geology of the country if we are to understand it.

The bulk of the Scottish Highlands, from the granites of Mar Lodge Estate and the Cairngorms to the Torridonian sandstones of the north-west and Torridon itself, are composed of acidic rocks, giving rise to soils low in nutrients and often with poor drainage. As is illustrated in other chapters, dry heather moorlands with occasional remnant pine and birch forest predominate in the central and east Highlands, and wet heaths, grasslands and blanket bog in the west and north. In only a relatively few places do rocks rich in basic minerals occur, which give rise to nutrient-rich soils and very different and more diverse floras. However, stretching from Caenlochan in the east to Ben Lomond in the south west, just north of the Highland Boundary fault, are a range of hills where the original limey shales of the Dalradian were metamorphosed, compressed and folded during the great Caledonian Orogeny 500 million years ago, into calcareous schists. Where these rocks outcrop, in upper Glen Clova and at Caenlochan and high on the Breadalbane range at Ben Lawers, Meall nan Tarmachan and Ben Lui particularly, there is a general absence of the browns of heather and their

Facing page
Tall-herbs enclosure,
Ben Lawers

replacement by the greens of grasslands; the result of fairly intensive grazing by cattle, ponies, the ubiquitous Scottish sheep or red deer over many hundreds of years.

Because of the rich soils, the friability of the schists and the altitude of the outcrops, these sites contain the greatest diversity, and some of the rarest, of arctic-alpine flowering plants, lichens and bryophytes in the British Isles. The very best site is the Trust property of Ben Lawers, including Meall nan Tarmachan. The simple fact is that the severe climate high in these hills prohibits the growth of most lowland plants and only arctic-alpines and montane plants, adapted to the extreme conditions, can grow and survive there. It is a habitat of instability, regular soil freeze and thaw, with rocks splitting and debris constantly spilling downhill. Also, although there are several arctic-alpine plants that can tolerate acidic conditions and that are therefore widespread across the mountains of Scotland, there are relatively very few calcareous habitats at altitude that can support the more demanding and rare species.

The alpine grasslands on these high-level schists would never have been forested and have long been a favoured grazing area for red deer in the summer months. Below 700–800 metres on Ben Lawers however, there is predominantly species-poor grassland and some blaeberry heath, which *would* originally have been forested.

Ben Lawers from across Loch Tay

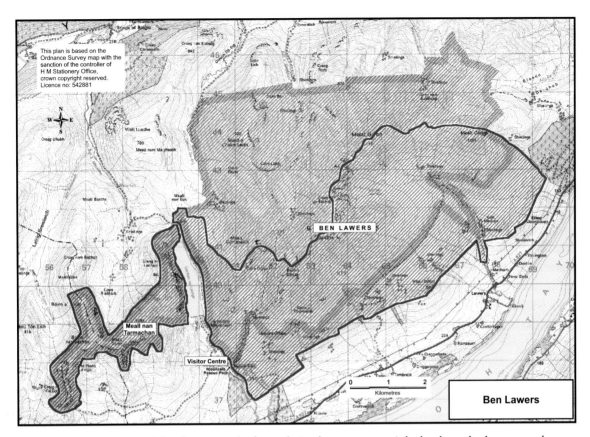

This plan is based on the Ordnance Survey map with the sanction of the controller of H M Stationery Office, crown copyright reserved. Licence no: 542881

BEN LAWERS

Meall nan Tarmachan

Visitor Centre
Mountain Rescue Post

0   1   2
Kilometres

Ben Lawers

Figure 2.1
Map of the
Ben Lawers area
(Legend: see p. xviii)

The first record of people in the area goes right back to the hunter-gatherers of the Mesolithic around 7000 BP. These people may have been partly nomadic and it was not until the Neolithic farmers established themselves, a few thousand years later, that a settled population began to make use of the forest and its soils to create fields and enclosures and, like the red deer, to exploit the summer grazings at high altitude on the Ben Lawers schists. There they would have grazed their cattle and primitive sheep, similar to the Soay sheep of St Kilda. From this period onwards the woodlands of oak, ash, elm, alder on the lower ground and predominantly birch and rowan on the higher, interspersed here and there with communities of tall herbs and montane willow scrub, began to disappear, partly through clearance for arable land and to create pastures and partly through direct exploitation for timber for its many domestic uses. The presence of grazing stock would then have destroyed much of the accessible low-growing scrub and trees and have hindered natural regeneration by eating seedlings. We do not yet know how early it was when stone shelters and stock-proof enclosures were created on the high-level pastures; shelters for people to stay in the summer months and enclosures to protect stock from wolves. The first evidence of the date of these shielings is from fifteenth- or sixteenth-century pottery found at a shieling at the top of the Ben Lawers Nature Trail enclosure. From then on at least, the high altitude pastures became a very important part of the tenant agricultural system that operated there for several hundred years.

The benefits from these grazings, which were highly regulated at that time as far as the number of grazing animals that were allowed, were not of course only from their direct exploitation, mainly by cattle, but also sheep and ponies. They were also derived from the practice of putting the animals beyond the hill dyke, out of the unenclosed arable rigs and meadows during the summer months so that grain crops and hay could be grown and harvested, and so that other rough grazings within the hill dyke could be conserved for the winter. Because of the excellence of the grazings on Ben Lawers some of the shielings are quite large and complex – one group being made up of 48 huts, much larger than the average Highlands shieling.

The change to predominantly sheep grazing came in the late eighteenth century when the Estates annexed the shieling grounds, the hill was divided and Blackface sheep were introduced. As sheep gradually increased in number through the early nineteenth century – as they did in so much of Scotland – they replaced the cattle. In some areas the number of sheep doubled over a period of twenty years, setting grazing levels which have continued to this day.

There are records of ownership of Lawers from the middle of the fourteenth century. James III confiscated the land from the then owners in 1473, for their involvement in the murder of James I, and gave it to Sir Colin Campbell of Glenorchy for his assistance in bringing the perpetrators to justice. From then until this century the lands of Lawers belonged to the

Alpine gentian

Earls of Glenorchy and Breadalbane. It was from the 3rd Earl that the farms of Ben Lawers were let in the late eighteenth century. Incidentally it was a Campbell of Glenlyon in Breadalbane, who played an important part in the massacre at that other Trust property, Glencoe, in 1692.

Flora

We have touched on the very broad divisions of the vegetation, but now we need to look a little more closely at the very special plants and communities if we are to understand present management policies. First there are the high-level communities that occur elsewhere in Scotland, those of the leached grasslands and woolly hair-moss heaths. The former are superficially the most attractive, dominated by mat grass, but peppered with the soft green leaves and yellow flowers of alpine lady's

Alpine forget-me-not

mantle, also the sweet-berried blaeberry, other fine grasses and lichens. The latter usually occurs on the more exposed ridges where winter winds clear any snow and only the hardiest plants can survive. Where there are sheltered hollows and the snow does lie for a period, often there are sharply delineated patches of mat grass.

Another high-level community is termed an alpine 'cushion' grassland, so called for its pincushion-like plants, such as moss campion embroidered with its tiny pink flowers and mossy cyphel with its equally tiny white flowers. This is among the most attractive of all flowering communities in the British Isles, but one almost has to go down on one's hands and knees to appreciate it! It contains some of the Ben Lawers rarities and is therefore a magnet for botanists, but it is also one of the most attractive to sheep for its fine and sweet grasses. In addition to the cushion plants, others flowering in mid-June are the white flowers of alpine mouse-ear, the large purple flowers of the mountain pansy, the blue flowers of heath milkwort, the little red bristles of alpine bistort and the almost invisible yellow flowers of sibbaldia only 3–4 mm across. Then there are the delicate fairy flax, the variable eyebright, the almost insignificant frog-orchid, and many more! This community occurs on the slopes of corries, often within vegetated screes, where there is constant enrichment from the movement of soil downhill. The plant which perhaps epitomises the delicacy and beauty of these arctic-alpines and which occurs particularly on unstable soil, is the tiny, deep-blue alpine gentian, which has its largest British population here.

A fragile habitat related to the cushion grassland, best not to enter or only with great care, and which again is extremely important on Ben Lawers for its rarities, are the scree slopes. Unstable situations such as this are the natural home of pioneer plants such as the arctic-alpines. Where screes are composed of small stones forming gravel slides, flowering species occur such as the fairly common, but no less lovely, yellow saxifrage. Also mossy saxifrage along with the alpine willowherb, and more common mountain species such as mountain sorrel, as well as the very rare mountain sandwort.

A community easily missed and usually ignored by the non-botanist, as there are so few flowers to catch the eye, is that below high-level springs and flushes, and by mountain streams – which is probably just as well as the soils are usually saturated, spongy and easily damaged by trampling. However, this inconspicuous plant community, the type-locality for the British Isles, is probably the most important on Ben Lawers in terms of its rarities. It is rich in mosses, liverworts and sedges, characteristically the russet sedge, but also the bristle sedge that occurs only on Ben Lawers, the scorched alpine sedge that occurs in only a handful of other places in Britain, and the very rare snow pearlwort. Where there are screes composed of large boulders creating plenty of shady and moist habitat occur a number of ferns, including both male and lady fern, holly fern, buckler ferns and the smaller and more delicate oak and beech ferns.

The most spectacular plant communities on Ben Lawers, in terms of the size of the plants and therefore display, are those on calcareous cliff ledges. They are of a large size mainly because these are naturally tall herbs when out of reach of grazing animals, such as red campion, wood cranesbill, melancholy thistle and the graceful globeflower, its tight and large petals curling and overlapping to form a single ball of soft yellow on the top of its slender stem. Then there are several umbellifers, wonderfully structured like giant candelabra, such as the wild angelica and hogweed. In addition are green spleenwort, the alpine saxifrage, alpine fleabane and the very rare alpine forget-me-not, its flowers mere pin-pricks of blue. Grazing favours some species against others, encouraging the growth of those that can grow and spread vegetatively, such as the grasses and sedges, which then crowd out others. The cliff faces and ledges then, often support a wider diversity of plants than the grazed grassland beneath them. This beautiful display of tall herbs is seen to best advantage at the end of July and in August when most are in flower.

In the same situation there is another group of plants susceptible to grazing, several of which require the nutrient-rich substrate perpetually created by the erosion of the cliffs and for which Ben Lawers is the most important site in the British Isles. These are the very rare montane willows such as the downy willow, woolly willow and net-leaved willow. Along with them often occur rowan, birch and greater woodrush, although these

Downy willow and tall herbs on ungrazed ledge

willows tend to grow at higher and more exposed locations than those where trees can grow.

Inadvertently, I might have given the impression that all these plant communities are well defined and juxtaposed on the hill like pieces of a jigsaw puzzle. In reality they overlap and merge and one or more may thrive within another. In addition the labels given to communities perhaps hide the fact that there are often variations within them. Ben Lawers is no exception to this generalisation and therefore, taking management action for one species, by inhibiting or introducing grazing in order to safeguard it, is almost bound to affect another, possibly adversely.

We have touched on just some of the montane and arctic-alpine vascular plants, but it is not possible in this chapter to cover all those that occur on Ben Lawers, nor even all the rarities. Ben Lawers has five species of flowering plants that are afforded full legal protection under the Wildlife and Countryside Act (1981) and another thirteen that are listed within the *Red Data Book* and a further 36 species that are nationally scarce: a very impressive list! It also has a commensurate range of rare bryophytes and lichens, and probably invertebrates – although as yet little systematic work has been done on them. All in all, Ben Lawers is, botanically, the most important mountain in the British Isles and one of our top ten sites of natural heritage value. It is quite clear therefore that the Trust has immense responsibility on Ben Lawers for a very unique remnant of our natural heritage.

Acquisition and visitor management

The first part of Ben Lawers was purchased by the Trust in 1950 and amounted to 3,104 hectares. Since then, through both purchase and donation, the Trust has gradually expanded its area of ownership. The initial sections of the four grazing hills that make up Ben Lawers that were acquired by the Trust came with the associated grazing rights of the eleven farms on the southern margin of the property. These grazing rights had their origin in the last century.

Ben Lawers was the first property acquired by the Trust for its ecological importance, the original reason for its purchase being the conservation of its flora. In the early days, protection of this interest was thought only to require the retaining of the *status quo* as far as management was concerned and the presence of Ranger staff to police the site and to educate the public, particularly walkers and climbers who might inadvertently damage the plant communities. Being the highest mountain in the Breadalbane range at 1,214 metres and within the top ten highest mountains in Britain, it has always attracted walkers. These were the reasons that lay behind the construction of the Visitor Centre at 430 metres in 1972, its purpose being to interpret the flora for visitors and to increase their understanding and therefore awareness and care of the flora.

In Chapter 1 we touched on the subject of the ever-increasing numbers of walkers taking to the hills and the very serious damage that is being caused to footpaths all over Scotland. On Ben Lawers, where automatic people-counters have shown that a minimum of 22,000 walkers use the main footpath annually, serious erosion forced the Trust in 1980 to begin the challenging and expensive task of repair. The problems of footpath repair at Ben Lawers epitomise the general problems facing anyone repairing or reconstructing paths on mountain and moorland. First, the logistics of getting a team of workers and tools daily to the site and, when necessary, materials such as large stones to form the risers and cross drains. Second, it is expensive. Third, the higher one attempts to carry out the work, the greater the problem of keeping lifted vegetation alive during and after repairs, as has been found with vehicle track rehabilitation on Mar Lodge Estate. It is an expensive business: for example the Trust has had a recent grant of £134,000 from the EU to cover just five years' work. The minimum costs for high-level footpath repair is of the order of £100 per metre. However, repairs carried out on a steep section of the path on Meall nan Tarmachan in 1998 which required the use of a helicopter to lift stones, cost nearly £200 per metre! To put these costs in some perspective with other upland management costs, standard sheep fencing may be £3.50 per metre and deer fencing £6.

Footpath repair, even at this price, is necessary, not just because of the landscape impact, but because ever-widening unmanaged paths can directly damage scarce and attractive plant communities, while indirectly they can create numerous new drainage channels multiplying that effect. On Ben Lawers the Trust has secured funding for a further five-year programme of footpath repairs including work at high altitude on both the Ben Lawers and

Tarmachan ranges, which will add up on completion to over twenty years of continuous effort since 1980!

Changing attitudes towards management

The history of the management at Ben Lawers illustrates the evolving attitude of the Trust to countryside properties ostensibly acquired for nature conservation since the 1940s and the general rise of nature conservation concerns in Britain. In fact in many ways Ben Lawers has led the field within the Trust, initiating a real acceptance of responsibility for the natural heritage aspects of all its properties. Since the story of what happened on Ben Lawers has had such an effect on the Trust's attitude, and continues to do so, it is well worth telling.

Although the first part of Ben Lawers was purchased in 1950 the Trust did not employ any seasonal staff until 1963 nor permanent staff until 1972 when the Visitor Centre was opened. In that year the Trust also signed a Nature Reserve Agreement (NRA) with the then Nature Conservancy (NC), part of which released funds from the NC to support 50 per cent of the costs of a Warden. However, a grant, including funds for the Visitor Centre, was also offered from the Countryside Commission for Scotland (CCS), for 75 per cent of the costs of a Ranger, and the Trust, taking the opportunity to have its bread buttered on both sides, took both grants and employed Ben Lawers' first permanent Ranger. The National Nature Reserve (NNR) of Ben Lawers was not declared until 1975. One of the principal aims of management, as part of the NRA, was to maintain a varied and numerous population of flora and fauna, especially certain species and communities that were scarce, or whose survival was threatened. Lest it be thought that Ben Lawers is a simple management unit it should be pointed out that the NNR (and NRA) cover more than just Trust property, so that the Trust in administering and managing the NNR requires to liaise very closely with neighbouring estates and farms in order to co-ordinate management across the whole site.

In the mid-1980s a review was carried out on the role of the Trust staff, in relation to the funding contribution from both bodies. The conclusions of that review indicated that although the Trust had developed the presentational and interpretive aspects of Ben Lawers, as per the Agreement, it had done little if anything in regard to the protection or enhancement of the montane flora: the principal reason for the NNR designation and for purchase of the property in the first place! This was not due to a lack of knowledge on the part of the Trust on the state and future of the montane flora, but to the many additional responsibilities staff on Ben Lawers were having to undertake at that time.

In the late 1980s, by which time the Trust had been responsible for Ben

Lawers for almost forty years, local staff, who had been able to carry out intensive surveys and who had been more closely monitoring the individuals of some plants and the impact of sheep grazing for a number of years, came to the conclusion that during the Trust's period of tenure there had actually been a diminution in some plant populations, maybe even extinctions, and that they could not tell if that included some of the rarest species for which Ben Lawers was famous! This was, potentially, a devastating indictment of the Trust's management, or rather lack of it, and tantamount to suggesting that the Trust had been proudly showing visitors around one of the most important national buildings of historic interest in its care, say Craigievar Castle, while not investing in any maintenance and ignoring the fact that it had been falling apart for years! A programme of action to rectify this situation was prepared by the local staff, supported by an enlightened attitude in the Regional office, that enabled these serious concerns to be addressed by the Trust's Council in 1990.

First, it was recognised that staffing levels required to be increased to enable monitoring of the rarest species. Second, it was officially accepted that much of the loss of, and present threat to, some communities, was due to past and present grazing pressures. For a long time it had been accepted that regeneration of woodland was impossible in the face of so many sheep, but it had not really been accepted that there were other communities, perhaps more important in conservation terms since there were precious few examples left (such as montane willow scrub and tall herbs) that were equally under threat. At the same time it was recognised that some communities, alpine cushion grassland for example, probably actually required grazing (to combat aggressive grasses) for their survival.

The small coterie in Scotland involved in the promotion and re-creation of native woodland, contains within it an even smaller cell devoted to the restoration of native scrub – the community which naturally occurs at and above the natural tree-line. There are literally only one or two places left in Highland Scotland where native woodland extends up to and beyond the natural tree-line, although of course on the coasts and islands of the west and north woodland may be very near it. These enthusiasts are ensuring that this unique element of our native vegetation will not be lost, often comparing the richness and diversity of the woodland and scrub that survives on the west coast of Norway to the impoverished version left in Scotland. The main reason why there is so much diversity left in Norway compared to here, is that Norway has never had the same tradition of sheep grazing on the scale of Scotland. In fact sheep grazing only became more common there after the Second World War, occurs only on the alpine pastures, and the sheep are taken off in the winter. It is through the efforts of this small band and the work at Ben Lawers that several of these precious remnants have been secured in Scotland, providing the stimulus for further and larger-scale restoration projects.

Blackface sheep on the hill

In the far past, willow scrub and tall-herb communities would have been limited but reasonably widespread on Ben Lawers, within and above the tree-line. The acceptance of this within the Trust, at the highest level, led to the inevitable, though politically difficult, conclusion that in the long term, if the Trust was really serious – not just about protecting these communities, but actually enhancing them – it would have to seek to obtain control of the grazings on Ben Lawers. The radicalism of this conclusion by the Trust in 1990 cannot be over-emphasised since it threatened the rights, never mind livelihoods, of the farmers who grazed sheep on the hill. These rights to graze went with the farms and the Trust could only obtain them by the purchase of the farms themselves as they came on the market. Without these rights however, it was doubtful if the farms would remain viable and the Trust therefore found itself in a very sensitive local situation.

Meanwhile, the Trust recognised that there were some species under such immediate threat of extinction, such as the woolly willow, of which there were only two well-separated individuals of the same sex remaining, that other action was required. It should be noted that willows and juniper are dioecious, in other words the sexes occur on different plants and both are therefore needed to ensure regeneration. Many individuals of these plants are hanging onto ledges and it is only a matter of time before erosion carries them away, as has already happened to several since the Trust took over as landowner. At this time little action was being taken anywhere to protect these willow communities, one of the exceptions being the enclosure around montane willows on the NNR at Inchnadamph in the far north west of Scotland. For the Trust to consider erecting fences around such remnants was a tacit admission that the grazing regime was not compatible with the conservation of elements of the flora of Ben Lawers. It was a controversial decision then, to erect the four enclosures in the late 1980s around some of the remaining populations of certain willow species and around potential tall-herb sites below the ledges to which they had become restricted through grazing.

This action by the Trust however, was generously supported by the other landowners and grazing tenants concerned, which was an encouraging indication of the level of their understanding of what the Trust was trying to achieve. Both these plant communities require reasonably nutrient-rich damp soils and it was judged that the areas immediately adjacent to the remnants – below the ledges, or stream sides – were the optimum sites where regeneration might take place. Such trials would also give some indication of just how feasible it might be to increase the area of some of these communities on a much greater scale. The first experimental enclosures, erected in 1987, were two fairly small but electric-fence enclosures, both for tall herbs, but one also for mountain willow. The success of these enclosures, in terms of the growth of the willows and regeneration of the tall-herb vegetation, led to the erection of two more enclosures at and above the tree-line. This initiative at Ben Lawers led to the NCC erecting the very large enclosure around scrub willow and tall-herb ledges at Corrie Fee within the Caenlochan NNR around 1990.

The radical management at Ben Lawers, recognising the need for active intervention and positive management, which in a large part inspired the idea of this book, did not stop at simply enclosing the remnant willows. It was realised that some plants, such as juniper and the woolly willow, would still not survive even if fences were put around them as, in the absence of plants of the opposite sex, there could be no fertilisation. The only option, apart from monitoring the individuals until they died, was to plant another individual of the opposite sex nearby. However, there are so few of these plants and they are so geographically scattered, that other potentially controversial problems arise. First, in the case of juniper, of which there are seven plants on Ben Lawers, there are no local sources of seed, and seed from distant plants may be genetically different. The same problem exists for the two woolly willow plants, their nearest relatives being 10 kilometres and 70 kilometres distant. However, with willows, the problem is compounded by the fact that they hybridise. Not only could these relatives be genetically different, but their seeds could carry hybrids that should not then be crossed with the Ben Lawers material. It is a dilemma that has not yet been solved, but there is not a lot of time left!

If the problems of genetic difference and hybrids are resolved and the populations are saved, in the sense that viable seeds are produced from the two extant willow plants, another controversial challenge presents itself, that of extending or creating new areas of montane willow scrub by planting from these seeds. Expansion by natural regeneration from these two plants will inevitably be very unpredictable. If there is no grazing around them there may be no niche in which the seeds can germinate and grow. On the other hand if there is grazing, the seedlings will probably be browsed and killed. Who knows how long it will take to find the right grazing balance? To circumvent this problem in the short term, seedlings raised in a nursery can be planted out in several non-grazed situations until there are enough large and healthy individuals, making up several small populations, to withstand any damage from grazing introduced to create seed beds. The long-term aim however, must be to establish appropriate grazing levels without fencing. Many ecologists view this action as 'gardening', as creating artificial communities and against the accepted principle of non-intervention.

The fact that nearly all of our present vegetation is anthropogenic (derived from the activity of man), 'artificial' or 'un-natural' was briefly mentioned in Chapter 1. This can be an argument used in defence of planting woodland or scrub where it might have occurred previously, rather than waiting for natural regeneration. It is used to oppose the argument that it is gardening, or that it is not re-creating a natural community, or maybe even that it is trying to establish it where it never was. If the present vegetation is anthropogenic anyway, is it not just as legitimate to create a more diverse and attractive alternative that may be closer to that which existed before?

Another argument in favour of the planting of almost extinct native plant communities such as montane willow scrub, is that not all of us can go to Norway to see something like the original. By planting, one can use the example to draw attention to the almost extinct species and the richness of the communities in a much shorter timescale than by natural regeneration, allow many more people to enjoy them and perhaps encourage others to reduce grazing pressures elsewhere to allow similar communities to expand by natural regeneration. The purpose of restoration or re-creation is to attempt to restore just some of the richness and diversity of such communities to what is now an impoverished landscape. In the end perhaps, restoration is just as much about aesthetics as science!

We have concentrated so far on those communities, mostly on the high ground, which have suffered severely from too much grazing, but we must not forget the alpine cushion grasslands, described earlier, which, on the other hand, probably owe their presence to grazing, although the present level may be too high. This community has several rare species too, which it has been suggested could suffer if grazing were removed and they came under greater pressure from the growth of grasses. In the case of some species, the alpine gentian for example, the reduction or absence of grazing may well result in fewer plants, but those that do occur are likely to be taller, showier and possibly set more seed. There is also the possibility that some species, presently restricted to ungrazed situations, such as the alpine fleabane, could re-invade grassland. Who is to say which is the more favourable situation, or which is the 'natural' situation? This is new ground for conservationists and we need to carry out more experimental management in this area with an open mind.

Devils-bit scabious on ungrazed ground

Meall nan Tarmachan, the SAC, opportunity and an EU LIFE Programme

The second objective of management in the 1998–2003 Ben Lawers Management Plan is:

To maintain the important habitats on the property in favourable condition.

In the years 1991 and 1994 the Trust, acting under the new policy with regard to the need for grazing control, acquired more ground at Ben Lawers. On the first two occasions farms were acquired along with their hill-grazing rights. Part of one was then sold on, to recoup some of the costs, with the Trust retaining the hill-grazing rights. When Meall nan Tarmachan, along with the grazing and sporting rights, was purchased in 1996, with the entire funds being raised from public subscription under one of the Trust's most successful recent public appeals, the total area of property on Ben Lawers belonging to the Trust rose to 4,728 hectares. However, the purchase of Meall nan Tarmachan was not just the acquisition of another very important piece of the natural heritage of Ben Lawers, but a unique opportunity to develop and take forward, on an unprecedented scale, the radical management measures following the 1980s review.

One of the spurs for rationalising the grazing management of Ben Lawers, as it has been at Glencoe, Torridon and many other non-Trust sites in Scotland, came from an unexpected quarter – the European Union. In 1994 the Habitats and Species Directive required all European States to schedule certain rare and endangered plant communities as Special Areas of Conservation (SAC), to protect them from further deterioration and to bring them by management and restoration, if necessary, to 'favourable conservation status'. Although this status has not yet been defined, it is assumed to mean that the communities are large enough and have appropriate management safeguards to assure their sustainability in the long term. Those habitats on Ben Lawers that have been identified by the EU as requiring special attention (Qualifying Habitats), include montane willow scrub, tall herbs, high-altitude flushes, alpine cushion grassland and crevices in lime-rich rock. This legislation has raised difficulties on Ben Lawers and on most other SACs in that bringing one Qualifying Habitat to favourable conservation status may be at the cost of damage to or even the loss of another.

In 1996, the Trust in partnership with SNH, ITE, SWT and MLURI, obtained EU 'LIFE' funding for a study of the effects of grazing on three upland sites: Ben Lawers, Glencoe and Torridon. This study concluded, in early 1998, that on one part of the Ben Lawers grazing rights, owned by the

Trust but still being exercised, grazing should cease, whilst the Trust should continue to take the opportunity to acquire other grazing rights if and when they became available. The study produced a Grazing Plan which attempted to define the grazing level requirements for each Qualifying Habitat.

Because many of these habitats are quite small, in some cases (montane willow scrub) hardly exist and because so little study of the effects of grazing have been carried out on them, it has proved impossible to give definitive grazing levels for any! Sometimes, what little work that has been done, is conflicting or confusing. For example, it was thought that a lack of flowering of some plants could be taken as an indication that the grazing pressure was too high. However, a study of one of the rarities, the alpine gentian, which we have already noted, showed that the absence of grazing, although it might encourage flowering, also resulted in fewer plants!

The Meall nan Tarmachan addition to the property has almost the full range of the Ben Lawers arctic-alpine plants, with remnants of sub-montane herb-rich birch woodland and both the montane willow and the tall-herb communities. The site has

Alpine fleabane

been described by the Trust as having what may be the richest or most diverse tree-line plant communities in the country! The SAC communities which have conflicting management needs, are scattered across the Trust property at Ben Lawers, many in areas where the Trust does not have grazing control. The Grazing Plan therefore recommended that the SAC be divided into two parts to simplify the different Qualifying Habitat management requirements until more control of the grazing could be achieved on the Ben Lawers Range and more research could be done to determine the optimum grazing levels on grassland and flush communities. On the Tarmachan side it is proposed to concentrate on the 'grazing-sensitive' habitats of montane willow scrub and tall-herb communities, and on the Ben Lawers side, where the Trust does not have complete grazing control, to meet the apparent needs of the 'grazing-dependent' habitats of the grasslands. In one stroke this dramatically simplified the management problems in trying to meet the SAC requirements on the Ben Lawers/Meall nan Tarmachan property. However, it must be regarded as a short-term solution only, as the long-term goal for Ben Lawers must be the full and natural integration and overlap of all these communities across the whole property. As the Trust itself recognises in the fourth Objective in the 1998–2003 Management Plan:

To restore the natural communities of plants and animals which have been destroyed or impoverished by man's activities, over most of the NTS hill ground.

Perhaps the situation will change in the future when the Trust gains complete control of the grazing on Ben Lawers. But at the moment, with the acquisition of Meall nan Tarmachan with full grazing control, the Trust has the opportunity to press ahead with the restoration of the natural ungrazed communities at least on that part of the property. The project is entitled the Tarmachan Habitat Restoration & Improvement Project (THRIP) and is one of the most innovative and exciting conservation projects attempted in Scotland in a very long time, aimed not just at a single species, such as the sea eagle and the kite (spectacular and successful reintroduction as they are), but at a whole range of habitats with all their diversity and complexity. The total area, ranging from 350 metres to 800 metres, covers 268 hectares (2.5 square kilometres), or 6 per cent of the Trust's total hill land at Ben Lawers! The cost of such a project is inevitably very high, and funds of £266,000 are now in place from bodies such as the EU, MFS, SNH, FC and of course the Trust itself, for an intensive programme of action from 1998 to 2001.

In the very long term – for this project will take many years to come to fruition – there will have to be light grazing as there would have been in the natural situation. In the meantime it is envisaged that there will be at least fifteen years of planting and perhaps 50 years of monitoring. The end result will not be wall-to-wall woodland, but by a combination of planting, natural regeneration, fencing, deer culling and perhaps shepherding; the open communities of flushes, moorland and grassland being encouraged to form a mosaic along with woodland, scrub and tall herbs. This matrix and some of these communities we have not seen in Scotland at this extent for at least a thousand years!

The Grazing Management Plan also suggested that the present grazing level on the alpine grasslands on the Ben Lawers range might be too high. This had previously been recognised by the Trust and a research project to address this has already commenced. Cattle are to be introduced to graze the low-level mat grass-dominated grassland, just above the head dyke, whose grazing quality they should improve by reducing the amount of mat grass, which should then be partially replaced by the finer grasses preferred by sheep. This, in turn, should attract some of the sheep grazing the higher alpine grassland and relieve the pressure there. Trial monitoring of sheep-grazing patterns using a video camera has been used at the start of this experimental project which is expected to last at least five years. The project covers an area of some 90 hectares on which, with the co-operation of a local farmer, 45 cows graze for thirteen to seventeen weeks in the summer months only.

Research, monitoring and difficulties

The first objective of management in the 1998–2003 Ben Lawers Management Plan is:

> To increase the Trust's understanding of the habitats, species and their ecology on the property and the impact of management on these.

Research into the vegetation history of Ben Lawers has proceeded on several fronts. First, peat cores have been taken in the past and analysed. These have given a general picture of the changes over time. Second and more recently, there have been archival searches to establish the forms and levels of agriculture that have taken place. Lastly, with the appointment of a Trust archaeologist, there has been a more systematic survey and some ground investigation at Ben Lawers as at most other Trust properties. This will culminate in a bid to the Heritage Lottery Fund for a Ben Lawers Historic Landscape Project, which will include a significant amount of new investigation of the environmental and botanical history of the area. Archaeology, in relation to the history of management, as a tool in understanding the present landscape, and as a resource of national importance in its own right, has been a much-neglected feature in the natural environment, so this is a welcome step. Today, any plans for the management of the natural heritage, such as the project on Meall nan Tarmachan, must take archaeological sites into consideration and ensure they are not damaged. As with management effects on non-target communities and species, and the landscape, there of course has to be a weighing up between the relative values of what is being gained and what is being lost.

In relation to the SAC designation there has also had to be detailed vegetation surveys, mapping of the habitats concerned and the up-dating of the monitoring of a number of rare species to provide a baseline on which to judge whether or not management is being successful. From the very first discovery of the importance of the Breadalbane hills as a site for rare arctic-alpine and montane flowers by the Revd J. Stuart, son of the minister of Killin, and the slightly later discovery of the drooping brook saxifrage on Ben Lawers by James Dickson in 1792, records of the Ben Lawers rarities, not always accurate, have been kept. By the time of the first acquisition of the mountain by the Trust in 1950, there was therefore a fair body of anecdotal and some written information, sometimes with map references. Casual monitoring then took place up until 1980/81 when a detailed survey of the rare vascular plants, including the location and population size of fourteen rare species, was carried out. This has provided the baseline for the monitoring of these species ever since.

On Trust property at Ben Lawers there are a number of plants protected under Schedule 8 of the Wildlife and Countryside Act (1981) which the Trust monitors on behalf of SNH. There are also the additional *Red Data Book* (RDB) species and several which are locally rare, or threatened and declining, within the NNR. However, monitoring the health of the population of some of the species is far from a straightforward procedure, not least in finding and identifying some of the tiny arctic-alpines, some of whose flowers may be only millimetres across. For example in the case of the drooping brook saxifrage which occurs, like so many others, on unstable ground, just a little natural erosion can cause several individuals to disappear overnight. On the other hand, through natural propagation, several individuals can almost as easily appear elsewhere. There is no point then in monitoring a small group annually, but a need to monitor a large area over a longer timescale. This also means that monitoring can be a time-consuming procedure and requires to be carried out by a good botanist who knows the ground. Incidentally a method has not been found to monitor the alpine gentian, which, being an annual (unique among the RDB species) is subject to even more rapid changes in distribution within its overall habitat. With so many rare plants requiring monitoring at Ben Lawers, the task is a substantial burden on Trust staff time.

Lest we miss the importance of monitoring, it is salutary to remember that at least one species, alpine bartsia, has probably become extinct on the NNR in the very recent past, others have been reduced to only a few individuals and some have declined to the level of one plant only. In the case of alpine bartsia the only action that could be taken now would be its re-introduction and this would raise again the kind of ecological management principles we have discussed and that apply to all work of this kind.

Then there are other problems, similar to those for woolly willow and juniper, such as those associated with the alpine rivulet saxifrage which is a very rare plant in Scotland as a whole and which has declined to the level of only one plant on Ben Lawers. In 1997 53 seeds were collected from this one plant; however, a new and healthy population, if that is the chosen aim, should preferably not be built upon the seeds of one plant. The problem is from where to obtain other seeds that will be as closely related as possible, as this site must have been genetically isolated for thousands of years. In the event, a genetic study of the Scottish populations of this saxifrage has shown

very little variation and it is thought reasonable therefore to bring in material
from a distance to boost the population. The site chosen was the Trust
property at Glencoe from where seeds (under permit!) were collected in 1998
and the next step is to raise these and introduce the new plants close to the
Ben Lawers survivor. There is a lot of controversy associated with this sort of
action, as we do not know why the population is declining, although it is
suspected that individuals have been uplifted by unscrupulous collectors.
Are there other factors such as climatic change or is it just the final result of
too many years of heavy grazing? Meanwhile attempts are being made to
germinate the seeds from the Ben Lawers plant. The problem is that so little
work of this kind is going on anywhere else that there are few people, apart
from Ben Lawers Trust staff themselves, who feel confident in advising!

Roseroot and herbs
on ungrazed ledge

Summation

Ben Lawers, along with St Kilda because of its internationally important
seabird colonies and Soay sheep, along with Mar Lodge Estate because of its
radical pine forest restoration programme and Glencoe with its woodland
restoration and radical grazing plan, requires more resources for management than most other of the Trust countryside properties. In the case of Fair
Isle, which has a comparable range of interests of international importance,

there are fortunately other bodies carrying out monitoring and survey, which relieves the Trust of some responsibility and finance.

Ben Lawers has set the conservation trend for other Trust properties and it, more than any other, even than Mar Lodge Estate, exemplifies what the Trust can achieve when it fully accepts responsibility for the natural as well as the cultural heritage. Ben Lawers is not only a leader within the Trust, it is setting in motion natural heritage restoration that the government nature conservation agency and all other voluntary conservation bodies are watching with interest, in order to learn the new management techniques from the Trust and hopefully to apply them more widely.

While the management of Ben Lawers, through acquisition of grazing rights, is moving towards making the natural heritage, its conservation, study and enjoyment, the principal use of the property (as arguably at only one other property, St Kilda), most other countryside properties, as we will see in later chapters, are moving in the direction of trying to attain sustainable agriculture in balance with the natural heritage interests. The question must be asked, that in undoubtedly now meeting the main aim of acquisition half a century ago, can, or should, the Trust take a more holistic view of the place of Ben Lawers and its management within the economy of the local area, without compromising that aim?

Peregrines displaying
on Ben Lawers

Chapter 3

Canna

There are arguably very few small Hebridean islands with all the attributes of the island of Canna, particularly the relationships of its natural heritage with the human cultural history of the west of Scotland. Many of the Western Isles have very specific attributes for which they are rightly famous, but none quite combine so many in such an attractive setting and of such human scale. It is as if Canna, and its closely adjacent companion Sanday, were made for human settlement.* The island, whose highest point is just 210 metres, is part of the Small Isles and lies just beyond the north-western shoulder of the rugged and much larger island National Nature Reserve of Rum, whose several peaks rising to over 700 metres, dominate the south-east horizon from the present settlement in Canna.

The main island of Canna is approximately 8 kilometres in length west to east and only 2 kilometres north to south at its widest part. Compared to the other inhabited island in this book, Fair Isle, Canna is slightly larger and more fertile. It is essentially two plateaux of almost equal length separated by an isthmus at Tarbert, with the largest area of low and cultivable ground on the raised beach of its south-east edge. The rocks are predominantly composed of basalt formed along with both its close neighbours Rum and Skye and much of this part of the west coast of Scotland, in the great period of volcanic activity in the Tertiary era 60 million years ago when the new world was splitting from the old. The structure of the eastern end is composed of classic basalt terraces, which in early June are golden brown from last year's bracken fronds, separated by columnar crags rising from the southern shores and culminating at the plateau. The western plateau, lacking such distinct structure, has cliffs on its southern shore, while the eastern plateau culminates in cliff, particularly along the north and east coasts. The cliffs have many stacks and caves and support a variety of seabirds.

Facing page
Buzzard and ravens

* The two islands of Canna and Sanday are commonly, and collectively, called Canna, which is the habit I will continue here. Only when it is necessary to distinguish a feature of one from the other will I use both names.

Pastures on Sanday croft with early purple orchid

The western half of the island and the northern high ground of the eastern half support moorland and some grassland interspersed with blanket-bog and wet heath with purple moor grass and mat grass. There are also attractive areas of species-rich maritime heath, in May blue with spring squill, and rich marshy grassland. The eastern half on the whole has drier heather moorland than the western half. Both plateaux have large areas of long-abandoned lazy beds. The northern cliffs support some tall-herb and grassland communities and there is blown shell sand on the much smaller island of Sanday.

The island of Sanday is at the eastern end of the archipelago forming an open 'jaw' to the 'head' of Canna, thereby enclosing a fine eastward-facing and sheltered basin. Around this basin the volcanic agglomerates and conglomerates have given rise to rich (brown forest) soils and there are also good soils at Tarbert. On the inbye on Sanday there is herb-rich grassland and outside the crofting area there is some herb-rich heath. In early June the former, although the primroses are past, is full of tiny grazed flowers with one or two thick patches of early purple orchid at their glorious best and with several larger areas a haze of bluebells.

It is this combination of good soils and a sheltered harbour, linked to the island's position at the cross-roads between the southern Outer Hebrides and the mainland of Scotland, and between Skye to the north and Iona and the islands of Argyll to the south, that has made Canna such an important

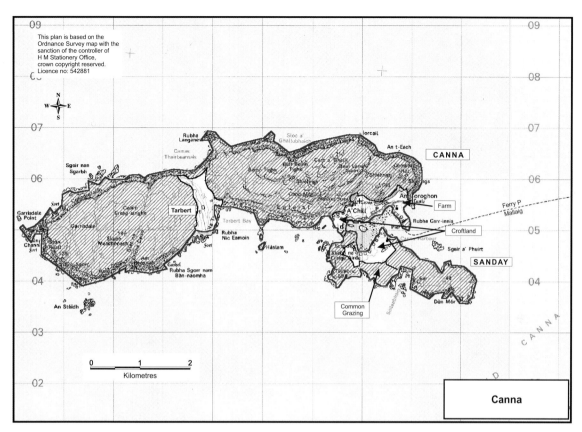

Figure 3.1
Map of the
Canna area
(Legend: see p. xviii)

island in the cultural history of the western islands. The evidence of settlement in Canna points to a long and continuous use of the natural heritage.

History

Canna is very rich in archaeological monuments: a recent survey by the Royal Commission has recorded well over 1,000 archaeological features representing 350 'sites', or over 20 per square kilometre! The earliest signs of occupation so far found go back to the Bronze Age, although pieces of Neolithic pottery have been found and there are also a number of archaeological sites belonging to the Iron Age. It is likely then that such a fertile corner with its sheltered bay and access to fish and shellfish, has supported fishing, arable and pastoral farming for at least 3,000 and possibly 5,000 years. Such a length of time of agricultural management of such a small island has resulted in the removal of all but scraps of the original climax scrub woodland (hazel, birch, rowan, aspen and willow). Agriculture improvement, especially in the nineteenth century, which has led to the destruction of so many monuments and ancient landscapes on the mainland of Scotland, has been limited in Canna, as on many other of the Western and

Northern Isles. There is therefore still a rich and relatively intact heritage of archaeological record awaiting detailed exploration.

The earliest historical records in Canna are linked with St Columba 'Colum Cille' and date to his missionary travels in Scotland between AD 563 and 597, and there are the remains of a monastery and a chapel dedicated to him. Canna's early Christian sculptured stonework is second only to that of Iona. Canna therefore has an extremely important Christian heritage and must have been a key link in the establishment and spread of Christianity in this part of the west of Scotland. The peace of these religious settlements was shattered however, in the ninth century, by the arrival of the Vikings in Scotland who pillaged for over 200 years before settling over a wide area of the Northern and Western Isles and the adjacent mainland, including Torridon to the north.

It was not until Somerled (Somhairle) in 1164, who became the first Lord of the Isles, that the Norse were ousted from control of the Western Isles and coast of the mainland. That Lordship ended in the 1490s, but through his descendants the Clanranald family gained the tenancy of Canna and finally the ownership from the Duke of Argyll in 1805. In 1827 the island was sold to Donald MacNeill under whose ownership 200 inhabitants were cleared. The island was next leased in 1849 by John MacLean who demanded that the whole island be cleared for sheep and a further 36 families were cleared in great poverty, this time to Sanday. It was around this time that the improvements began to the existing farm at Coroghon and that the newly introduced sheep destroyed many of the green fields (lazy beds) which had been so painstakingly won over by generations of farmers, causing them to revert to heather and bracken.

In 1881 Canna was bought by Robert Thom, a Glasgow shipowner, who planted a variety of trees behind Canna House, around the newly built guest house at Tighard, and Corsican pine in the valley of the Haligary burn below Compass Hill. It was Robert Thom who established the pedigree herd of Highland Cattle on the island which still exists today. The last private owner of Canna was Dr John Lorne Campbell who bought the island from the Thoms in 1938. He extended the plantations and continued with improvements to the infrastructure, but will be remembered pre-eminently however, for his Gaelic scholarship and for amassing in Canna one of the most extensive libraries on Celtic languages, history and folklore and a unique collection of folksong and folktale recordings in private hands. In 1981 Dr Campbell and his wife Dr Margaret Fay Shaw Campbell gifted Canna and the library to the Trust and at the same time the National Heritage Memorial Fund gave the Trust a grant of £50,000 for the purchase of the building which houses Dr Campbell's library, and £285,000 towards an endowment fund for the island.

If Canna was not already very special because of its natural beauty,

Sanday

SANDAY AUGUST

wildlife and long cultural, particularly Christian, history, the addition to it of Dr Campbell's library of Celtic studies must make it unique among Hebridean islands. For here also is the written record of the people who have shaped the raw, but sympathetic materials of Canna as their home and who in their turn have been shaped by the island themselves.

I have dwelt a little on the human history of Canna because it is so linked to its present vegetation and because the future of its community is fragile and tied so closely to the future use of its natural heritage. The population of the island, which had risen to 436 in 1821 from around 230 in the mid-eighteenth century, in one generation fell to 127 (1861). Emigration was not all due to clearance for sheep but partly also due to the failure of the kelp industry. By 1900 it had fallen below 100 and has steadily declined to sixteen by 1993. In 1999 there are only eleven adults plus four children.

Natural heritage and designations

Canna is part of the Small Isles National Scenic Area (NSA), all of the island apart from the farm and inbye croft land is an SSSI, and part of the cliffs are a Special Protection Area (SPA). The NSA designation is a recognition of the diversity of contrasting scenery to be found among the four Small Isles of

Rum, Eigg, Canna and Muck 'within the wider coastal setting of the Cuillin of Skye, Morar, Moidart and Ardnamurchan'; and particularly the contrasts between the relatively low-lying, smaller and more fertile satellites and the rugged and almost threatening grandeur of the mountain mass at their centre, that is Rum. In fact the NSA citation dwells on Rum and does not do justice to Canna. Similarly the SSSI citation for Canna, while it recognises that its plant communities are 'characteristic of the Tertiary volcanic areas in the Inner Hebrides', also notes that the communities 'complement the more varied features on the neighbouring island of Rum'. The suggestion of both is that Canna does not quite deserve either designation in its own right. From the preceding descriptions and discussion I hope the reader has been disabused of that impression. Of course neither designation covers Canna's wonderful range of archaeological sites and Christian monuments which none of its neighbours can match. The problem is really not Canna's, it is for official environmental designations which cannot recognise that small is beautiful, epitomised by Canna.

The variety of plant communities and landforms in Canna, because of its small size, are relatively limited in extent, but their very intimacy adds to

North cliffs with feral goats

their attraction: one can almost see them all in a day. In Sanday there is an area of species-rich, shell-sand machair grassland with a number of interesting plants not found elsewhere on the island, including frog orchid and adder's tongue fern. Elsewhere it is the basic nature of the geology of the island that is responsible for the other areas of species-rich grasslands and heaths. Probably the most attractive are the short maritime heaths with least willow, burnet rose and spring squill. Such herb-rich areas support a greater diversity of invertebrates, especially moths and butter-flies, than the species-poor grasslands and heaths which predominate in so much of the west of Scotland, such as at Torridon and on the adjacent island of Rum. In fact Dr Campbell recorded 267 species of butterflies and moths, although very few of them breed on the island.

Unfortunately such good grassland and heath also supports a large population of rabbits which cause a lot of damage. At the present moment the population is quite high, and control, because of erosion problems, is being carried out by the erection of enclosures on the machair in Sanday and by fencing and trapping on the Compass Hill cliffs. However they in turn support a number of breeding buzzards. Goats, long since feral on the northern cliffs, the hedgehog (1939), house mouse, field mouse and brown rat are all also introductions.

The only truly native mammals to Canna are the pygmy shrew, otter and both the grey and harbour seals, of which only the former breeds in small numbers. This limited fauna is typical of islands, particularly small and relatively isolated ones like Canna, which are not easily settled by terrestrial mammals. There are however both palmate and smooth newts and the common lizard, but neither frogs nor toads. Fair Isle, in contrast, has no native terrestrial mammals, amphibians or reptiles.

Because of Canna's relative fertility, its pattern of woodland plantation and its retention of traditional agricultural management, the island supports a varied and attractive terrestrial bird fauna. The most notable birds are perhaps the corncrake that now nests sporadically, other farmland and croftland birds such as the skylark and twite, and the peregrine and golden eagle.

Seabirds

The SPA in Canna, scheduled under the European Wild Birds Directive 1979, is primarily for its seabirds which include common guillemot, black guillemot, razorbill, kittiwake, the common gull and the larger gull species. The most notable however, are the puffin, Manx shearwater and shag, the colony of the last of which is one of the largest in Scotland.

The Inner Hebrides is one of the three main centres for the Manx shearwater in the British Isles, with Rum holding one of the larger populations at around 60,000 pairs. The small population in Canna has declined rather dramatically in recent years and it has been suggested that the brown rat may have been the cause. However, the colony and the rats had been present together on the island for a long time before the colony began its recent decline and therefore the main problem for the shearwater decline may lie elsewhere. This is also suggested by the fact that the Rum population too has apparently declined in the last decade. However, the decline of the Manx shearwater in Canna is such a serious problem, with no definite breeding success in 1998, that the eradication of the brown rat by poisoning is being considered. Such action was successfully carried out a few years ago in Ailsa Craig in the Clyde. First however, steps are being taken by the Trust to ensure that there will be no secondary poisoning of raptors or threat to other protected species such as the pygmy shrew.

Indirect threats to the seabirds, particularly the auks, are from oil pollution and fisheries. The former threat could be partly relieved by the

Golden eagle and fulmar

banning of tanker traffic through the Minch, and the Trust has made representations on this. The latter depends very much on the intensity of fishing effort in fairly local waters, particularly of the small species, such as the sandeel, on which the tern, auks and kittiwake depend during the breeding season. As the seabird colonies in Canna are not large, it suggests therefore that neither is the local food resource and hopefully therefore, not an attraction for commercial fisheries; but it is an area that must be monitored. Canna is one of the four key British seabird monitoring stations covered by the Joint Nature Conservation Committee (JNCC). The others are Skomer (Wales), Fair Isle and St Kilda.

Land birds and land management

There are two bird species closely linked with the management of the land. First the buzzard, feeding mainly on the rabbits. When the rabbit population has been high, so has that of the buzzard, reaching a peak of eleven pairs in 1971. The other bird of Canna and the Western Isles, which has caught the public imagination and become the symbol of the decline of traditional crofting management in the west and north of Scotland, is the corncrake. One hundred years ago the corncrake was ubiquitous across the whole of farming Scotland and its loss is a symbol of a long-term change to more intensive agriculture, particularly the introduction of the mechanised hay-cutter. This has resulted in the loss of tall vegetation, both early and later in the season, which is vital cover for the bird and its young. Unfortunately recent inter-related changes in crofting agriculture such the increasing use of silage and early cutting, agricultural subsidies which have converted so much arable to permanent pasture for sheep, the steady reduction in growing grain crops, plus an increasingly wet climate in the west and north making it increasingly difficult to dry hay, have all contributed to the further loss of habitat for the corncrake. It is not just the loss of cover for the bird, but with increasing use of commercial grass species and heavy grazing, the loss of food – the seeds of native grasses, other native flowering plants and those associated with cropping. Additionally there may be problems for the corncrake in its African wintering ground, although positive management in Scotland does seem to attract birds.

In 1988 a survey of the Inner Hebrides and the Western Isles, which holds 90 per cent of Scottish corncrakes, found 540 calling males, but by 1993 this figure had fallen to 445. In that year some level of management was commenced on 68 per cent of the sites, mainly by the RSPB, and by 1997 the calling male population had risen to 637. Without exception the managed sites showed improvement in numbers whereas those unmanaged showed a drop. By and large the management carried out increased the area of tall spring cover, removed stock from the meadows by late April, delayed cutting of hay or silage until after breeding (August) and increased the area of late cover into September. In most situations this took place within a traditional crofting management regime that included also grain and root crops.

In Canna the number of calling males dropped from three in 1993 to none in 1997. However, in 1997 the Trust commenced management and in 1998 two males were heard calling and might well have bred. In the short term, protection of existing un-managed tall grassland, in wetland and on field margins, has been carried out by fencing and there has also been planting of tall herbs, such as flag, cow parsley and nettle, to give additional early cover. Some of this work has been carried out by the Trust's own Thistle Camp volunteers. In the longer term there will have to be a more radical change in farm and croft management, otherwise only small areas of insufficient size, such as the corners of fields and field margins, will be available to corncrakes.

Agriculture

The clearances, the introduction of large numbers of sheep and the reduction in cattle from the 1850s, saw the gradual reversion of the marginal and hard-won arable and semi-natural grass pasture to heather and to bracken, and to a greatly increased sheep-grazing pressure on the hill. However, the effect of the increased grazing pressure on the well-drained and basic basaltic soils of Canna has not been as devastating as it has been on the poorer Torridonian sandstone hills of other areas of the west of Scotland. The natural relative fertility of the Canna soils has been able to more or less sustain the pressure without great changes and to retain the ability to recover its potential productivity if sheep numbers are reduced and the ratio between them and cattle better balanced.

At present there is one croft in Canna and nine in Sanday; however there are only two part-time crofters. There is no cropping or hay/silage production and all the croftland is down to a herb-rich permanent pasture, grazed mainly by cattle, but with also a few sheep and ponies. This compares with Fair Isle where there is very active traditional cropping; however, the population there is much greater and there is therefore more scope for mutual physical and social support and for sharing the costs and maintenance of small machinery. Grazing land in Sanday that belongs to the Canna home farm, if taken into crofting, might increase the viability of the crofts and might spur initiative. The present Trust Management Plan (1994–99) however, hints that this would not be considered until the crofts

Coroghon from Sanday

became more active, i.e. carry out some cropping/hay management. The crofters do have plans however, under the Crofter Forestry Act (1991), to create woodland on the common grazings in Sanday, which could provide significant shelter for stock in an otherwise treeless island.

Canna's 1,000-hectare farm was managed by the former private owner as a traditional mixed arable farm involving grazing, hay-making and the growing of fodder crops for winter feed. The farm employs several of the islanders, but even with subsidies has run at a loss for a number of years and is unlikely ever to run at a profit, even at the most intensive level. Under the current 1994–99 Management Plan, to encourage wildlife, permanent grassland was to be returned to hay-making, while tall vegetation was to be left at field edges, while the longer-term plan was to bring the farm inbye land into arable. To do this over the whole farm would have required a greatly increased investment by the Trust, and a greater annual financial deficit. It should be pointed out that Canna and the other Small Isles are not part of the Environmentally Sensitive Area (ESA) which covers the islands to the immediate south and therefore has not been able to attract the associated special grants. In recent years the home farm has not been well managed and so a new direction in farm management (1999) proposes reversing the direction of the earlier plan and putting most of the farm back to permanent grassland to try to create a more financially sustainable agricultural regime, while at the same time retaining areas of tall vegetation for corncrakes. This is seen by the Trust as an interim plan to buy time to draw up a long-term solution to meet clearer objectives for the farm. If the Trust does decide to settle for long-term permanent grazing only, then its condition (in the current Management Plan) relating to the release of the home farm grazings in Sanday to the crofters, only if the latter return to a cropping regime, will be rather at odds with its own plans for the home farm.

The thrust of crofting management in Scotland for the last decade and more, has been to try and return to more traditional management, to change what has become permanent grassland for sheep through the mechanism of subsidy and grant, back to hayfield and crop. Such management as we have seen is of benefit to corncrakes, but it also helps to support declining passerines such as twite, skylark and meadow pipit by providing food and cover for them too. A change to larger areas of permanent grassland on the Canna home farm could therefore put these species under pressure. On the benefit side it is intended at the same time to substantially increase the numbers of cattle and lower the numbers of sheep: the latter also to be confined to the hill. Cattle are much less selective grazers than sheep and their manure returns a great deal more nutrient to the soil, so the removal of sheep from inbye and their replacement with cattle will in itself benefit the present inbye grassland, while an increased presence of cattle on the hill will also benefit it.

Highland cattle

In Canna in the 1980s there were 500 North Country Cheviot ewes and 500 Blackface ewes, plus 150 hogs. To reduce grazing pressure the Trust intends to reduce sheep numbers to between 650 and 800 Blackface only. This will help to redress cattle:sheep ratios, which in Scotland generally have been so heavily in favour of sheep for 150 years. The climax potential of the sheltered parts of the hill land, going by existing remnants and similar habitat on Eigg, is birch-hazel scrub or low woodland which is a fairly rare habitat on the Western Islands and very limited in Canna. The Trust has already commenced controlling bracken on the hill by cutting and herbicide treatment, and the presence of more cattle will help prevent its return. The question for the Trust now is whether or not management of the stock on the hill will be predominantly for agricultural purposes, as it will be in the inbye, or also to allow some birch-hazel scrub development which might encourage the expansion of those breeding birds presently in low numbers, such as whinchat, stonechat and whitethroat.

In taking forward this transitional change in management on the home farm the Trust has emphasised that it is taking a flexible approach, and the regime will be changed again if there is evidence of a fall in the important bird populations: only careful monitoring will reveal that. There are also more radical alternatives to the present farm management structure, which could provide social and environmental gains, to which we will return at the end of the chapter. There is no doubt that Canna, with its relatively large area of good soils, climate and shelter is endowed with more potential than any of the other Small Isles – Rum, Eigg and Muck – to be able to strike a balance between economics, population and wildlife conservation.

Shelter-belts

A glance at the map of Canna is enough to indicate that there is a very limited amount of low ground suitable or available for woodland or forestry. On the other hand, when in Canna, it is very apparent that even the small amounts of planted woodland contribute to the landscape, to wildlife, to shelter for the grazing stock and to the domestic garden on a scale quite beyond their actual size. For those who have not lived in a treeless and temperate, maritime landscape, but who have only been temporary visitors, it is often difficult to appreciate just how important woodland can be to those who live there. In the Western and Northern Islands of Scotland wind is an ever-present force and can be physically exhausting and chilling for man and beast, especially in the winter months. With the addition of the salt that the wind carries from the sea, it can burn and kill the early growth of plants. Shelter in this situation, especially natural, is nurture to the body and the soul.

The native woodland that occupied the low ground disappeared from Canna several thousand years ago, cleared by Neolithic and Bronze Age people. The first attempt to reintroduce trees occurred around 100 years ago with plantings by Robert Thom and his son from the 1890s to the 1920s. These were mostly ash, sycamore and some Corsican pine. John Lorne Campbell more than doubled the area of plantation using a great variety of exotic and native species during his time on the island and today there is some 10 hectares composed of up to 51 species. Many of the plantations now require management and not all the species thrive, but the evidence for success is written in the landscape and waiting to be repeated.

Glancing at the map it is also apparent that there are no plantations in Sanday, or west of Tarbert. The former is croft land whose tenants have needed every acre on which to subsist and who have been reluctant to give up the precious ground for trees, although there are now plans to create shelter using the Crofter Forestry grants. Maybe in a hundred years it will be difficult to imagine how different the inbye of Sanday was in 1999 from that of Canna. Perhaps these woodlands will also provide some timber for agricultural and domestic use in the long term. West of Tarbert, on ground very much more exposed than that supporting the present shelter-belts, there may also be opportunities to create more limited areas of shelter, in this case principally for cattle.

The people of Canna

From the foregoing it is clear that for such a small island, Canna has a wealth of diverse interests, any of which singly would make the island a special place, but which together make Canna truly unique. Perhaps the most critical conjunction however, to which all the other interests relate, is that between the people and the natural resource.

In drawing up the overall Aims of Management for Canna (1994–99) the Trust has recognised this:

Turning hay by
traditional means

The Trust should ensure the permanent preservation, for the benefit of the nation, of Canna and Sanday, as an outstanding example of a Hebridean island, with internationally and nationally important landscapes, ecological, archaeological and historical features combined with a small living community which is threatened by its very location and today's economic pressures. The community and cultural aspects of the property are of over-riding importance. The island offers a great potential and should be developed as an educational and research resource.

How are these aims being achieved, where are they not and how might they be?

What if, like St Kilda, Canna was abandoned? It is an expensive place to upkeep, not just with Trust money voluntarily donated, but taxpayers' money also. There are arguments for and against public subsidy for the upkeep of marginal and isolated crofting communities and the alternatives that would face the taxpayer if they were not supported. As far as the three islands included in this book are concerned – Canna, Fair Isle and St Kilda – only the last has been abandoned, but there are many other 'marginal' islands off the western and northern coasts of Scotland. Each has its own scenic and ecological character, but those that are settled have in addition been enriched by a human history and culture. 'Addition' is a totally inadequate word to describe what human settlements bring to a landscape. In Canna and Fair Isle the warp of the land and the weft of human culture are so tightly interwoven that the loss of the latter means the loss of the very fabric that is *place* itself. To stand on the edge of Village Bay in St Kilda today and take in the dereliction of the past, no matter that many buildings have been restored, is to feel that emptiness, that loss of warmth that enfolds one in a human landscape. Looking at these ruins it is not the stimulation of wilderness we feel – where there are no human artefacts and against which we can measure civilisation – but a sense of despair for the many generations of people who invested so much of their lives there in creating and sustaining arable land, apparently for no permanent purpose.

When considering the future management of places like Canna, people are therefore the priority, and that means the whole thing we call community – children, infrastructure, services, productive lives, a sense of belonging, responsibility and local control. Only after all that is resolved is there any point in turning attention and effort towards natural and cultural conservation. That is the reality that faces the National Trust for Scotland, other Trusts, private landlords, local authorities, central government and their quangos, in places like Canna. It is a great responsibility. In the case of Canna and Fair Isle the Trust has recognised this and it is laudable that the Primary Aim of Management for Canna includes the sentence: '*The community and cultural aspects of the property are of over-riding importance.*'

In the 1994–99 Management Plan this has been addressed in several ways. First, a number of improvements will be (and have been) made to the infrastructure, roads, buildings and services, while the Trust's own volunteers have regularly contributed their labour and skills. Second, other sources of income and employment will be explored, such as the possibility of creating new crofts or smallholdings, shell-fish farming and expanding the opportunities for accommodating visitors. The Trust also has a vision for a Centre for Advanced Studies based on the Celtic legacy of Dr J. L. Campbell and for St Edward's Church which could open up a number of direct and indirect employment opportunities. As far as visitors are concerned the Trust will have to be cautious. Visitors and their management could overwhelm the community and character of Canna. Third, and the basis for the success or otherwise of the whole venture, are the funds the Trust can provide through grants and endowments, to underwrite a financial balance sheet which, despite all efforts, may always remain in the red.

Last, and most important, the Trust has stated its intention to give the community a voice in the management of its own affairs. To some it may seem that a private laird who at least lived on the island, was simply swapped in 1981 for an absentee committee. How far such devolution of responsibility goes will be a sign of the Trust's courage and its faith in the community.

Summation

Part of the sense of identity of the community in Canna lies in its sense of fellowship with its neighbours. The Trust intends to try to have the sea links restored with Barra and the Uists which were lost in 1964. There is also a need to strengthen considerably the links within the Small Isles themselves, to co-ordinate efforts as never before. This will be an exciting challenge as Rum is an NNR owned by SNH, Eigg is a now a 'community' Trust, while Muck remains in private and benign ownership. One way might be through better co-ordination of management. For example, there is no doubt that parts of Canna, particularly the western end, with careful management could sustain more cattle, while next door, staff resources of the Rum NNR have to be invested in the raising and care of their Highland Cattle, which are used as mowing machines in the conservation management of the grasslands on the west side of that island.

There may be an opportunity here for co-operation between the two islands, with Canna perhaps annually supplying the cattle as needed. In the other direction, Canna could benefit from a local supply of native tree seedlings for its shelter belts, which could be supplied from the native tree nursery on Rum. Even if Rum takes the radical step of placing its own cultural heritage and community alongside natural heritage conservation as a principal aim of its management, there must still be a number of other such co-operative possibilities that could benefit Canna and the other islands of the Small Isles.

In Canna there is an urgent need for the Trust to look at *all* the opportunities to support and expand the community and to be prepared to be as radical as necessary, because if additional means of securing its viability cannot be found, its future must be in doubt. Ideally, newcomers must have an income directly derived from the resources of Canna itself, although Fair Isle has shown that incomers bringing new skills and initiative can make a substantial contribution to the local community. As far as the Trust is concerned, as the landowner, it cannot indefinitely invest large sums of money in Canna and must therefore look for other sources of financial support to try and help balance the books. The Trust does not need to look further than its own property at Balmacara to see what steps could be taken, both to bring in more people to Canna and to tap other support. If the home farm in Canna were to be broken up into crofts, the Trust and the islanders could benefit from both additional families and the crofting grants. With changes in crofting legislation proposed for the new Scottish Parliament, making it possible to create new crofts, it may not be very long until this option can be seriously considered. Alternatively, some form of share ownership in the farm could be formed by the Trust with the islanders, however this would not bring more people to Canna as would the creation of crofts.

And perhaps there are other ways of raising finance. The more remote, smaller and poorer (in terms of the agricultural resource) island of Fair Isle, with a larger population and infrastructure, runs at less of a loss than Canna. One of the keys may well be the larger size of population of Fair Isle, though

Coroghon and farm fields, looking towards Rum

it has to be said that there are also several part-time jobs in local services and a boat to be crewed there. Because of its status the Trust cannot access certain grant support. However, it could if it set up Partnership Trusts with the community, as on Fair Isle. This could also create a greater sense of 'ownership' for the islanders. As in Fair Isle, it would also be essential in Canna to involve the islanders in the selection of new permanent inhabitants, particularly if they were to occupy new crofts. A larger and empowered community in Canna, like Fair Isle, could create new energy and initiative that, with the Trust's support, would be to the benefit of Canna's natural heritage.

I emphasise again, unapologetically, the thesis that the survival of the communities in Canna, Fair Isle or at Torridon is essential for the care of the natural heritage. Here might be a good place to remind ourselves that the phrase '*for the benefit of the nation*', by definition *includes* the local community. They are as much the nation as anybody else. It is very important that the Trust succeeds in retaining the relatively isolated community in such an important and beautiful island as Canna, for if a national body with such sympathetic aims, resources, experience and single-mindedness cannot, there is little hope for many others. In Canna, care and management of the natural heritage must be part of a greater plan for securing the future for the community.

Chapter 4

Torridon

Introduction

Torridon: the very word suggests a rugged remoteness, a place of struggle and challenge. Approaching from the south on a clear day via Shieldaig, the mountains of Beinn Alligin, Beinn Dearg and the 8-kilometre ridge of Liathach, stand out as an immense, 1,000-metre rocky barrier across the north side of Upper Loch Torridon. Most days however, the mountains are enveloped in low cloud, or rain on the wind, sweeping in from the west, obscuring all but the far shore of the Loch and the crofts hugging the low ground just above the sea. Comparing these mountains with the relatively lush Ben Lawers far to the south, or even Kintail and Affric, less than 50 kilometres distant, the contrasts are striking. Whereas the Five Sisters of Kintail, rising to almost exactly the same height, appear to have almost total vegetation cover, so green in the summer, the upper half of the Torridon mountains appear on first sight almost devoid of vegetation. The layered sandstone peaks and ridges of the latter seem like the bare, worn shoulders and torsos of ancient figures sculpted out of the brown rock, which long ago have lost their heads to the erosive forces of rain, ice and wind. Their flanks, typical of the north west, are shallow in soil and poor in raiment, supporting only a uniform vegetation of straggling heather, cotton grass, deer sedge and purple moor grass. On the valley floors and lower slopes, from which they arise, however, is a deeper covering of blanket-bog with the sweetly smelling and golden-flowered bog asphodel and the aromatic bog myrtle. In the early summer the ground can be dry, sometimes in the winter frozen, but most of the time water runs off the peaks, fills the burns and turns the soils to the consistency of a soaked sponge. Lea MacNally, the Trust's Ranger at Torridon for 21 years, said of the climate: 'If you cannot tolerate heavy rain, salt spray and high winds, then do not live in Torridon.' If anywhere typifies the 'wet desert' of Fraser Darling, it is the slopes and glens of Torridon. The question is though – which was the more important factor in the creation of this apparent desert: people or climate?

Facing page
Torridon Hills

And yet . . . it was not always this way as demonstrated by the tree roots in the peat, the birch and oak fragments in ravines and screes and the Scots pine and broadleaf woodlands on the south shore of Upper Loch Torridon. And yet . . . hidden and protected on ledges of apparently bare cliffs are tall-herb communities, and among the higher naked rocks and screes are a number of rare arctic-alpine plants and a rich bryophyte community. And yet . . . there are golden eagles and ptarmigan, the mountain hare and the red deer; and if one has patience, pine marten, wild cat and otter. And yet . . . the outlooks from the summits of these mountains, over the sea to Skye, over wilderness to Gairloch, Loch Maree, Beinn Eighe and over mountain upon mountain, are breathtaking. In the wrong mood Torridon is heavy with depression, in the right mood wide open to exhilaration. Today, after thousands of years of use by hundreds of generations of people, there are projects to re-create some of the lost forest habitat with its forest soils and all its wildlife, which, given time, could also provide a much-needed additional resource for crofters and their stock.

The beginnings of the history of human occupation of this area of north-west Scotland are unclear, but are known to stretch back at least 3,000 years. Much later it is known that the Scots settled among the Picts in the seventh century AD, but it is only when the Vikings arrived in the late eighth century that the human record becomes a little clearer. After ownership by the Earls of Ross and the Lords of the Isles, Torridon was administered and owned by MacKenzies from the sixteenth century until it was sold to a Colonel MacBarnet in 1838. It was he who was responsible for the clearances of three villages east of Fasag, below Liathach, the area of Torridon village itself. The next owner, Duncan Darroch, was a great deal more benevolent, cleared the sheep, allowed the crofters to graze their cattle once again and saw the establishment of a deer forest and the present village of Torridon. The Estate of Torridon then passed through a number of hands until it was purchased by the Earl of Lovelace in 1960, and it was on the death of the 4th Earl in 1967, that the Estate passed into the hands of the Trust after it had been accepted by the Commissioners of Inland Revenue as part-satisfaction of Estate Duty. The adjoining Estate of Alligin Shuas was gifted to the Trust in 1968 by the sons of the Blair-Gordons who owned it. Together the Estates make up an area of some 6,515 hectares which is managed locally by the Ranger.

It is difficult from our present perspective to see the landscape as it was, the way of life and living conditions prior to the clearances. The geology of the area is dominated by the 800-million-year-old Torridonian sandstones which are hard and acidic; the soils of the Torridon area are therefore poor. Torridon has around 1,847 mm of rain per year (compare with 786 mm at Braemar near Mar Lodge Estate!), so crop production must always have been a difficult pursuit. Fishing was important, but cattle were the principal

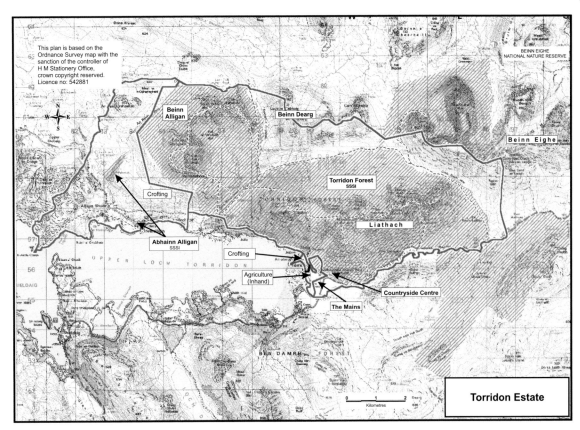

This plan is based on the Ordnance Survey map with the sanction of the controller of H M Stationery Office, crown copyright reserved. Licence no: 542881

Beinn Alligan

Beinn Dearg

BEINN EIGHE NATIONAL NATURE RESERVE

Beinn Eighe

Torridon Forest SSSI

Crofting

Liathach

Abhainn Alligan SSSI

Crofting

UPPER LOCH TORRIDON

Agriculture (Inhand)

Countryside Centre

The Mains

BEN DAMPH FOREST

Torridon Estate

Figure 4.1
Map of the
Torridon area
(Legend: see p. xviii)

economy: in 1794 as many as 3,000 were reported in the area. Following the clearances life continued to be very hard, although Duncan Darroch seems to have done all he could to improve the crofters' lot and allowed them access to local resources of timber and fish, unlike most other Scottish lairds of his day. Today the condition of the land is just as poor and it is just as difficult for the present crofters to make any living from it.

However, records of the past, from tree stumps in the peat, to pollen cores, the names given to landscape features and the profusion of growth that occurs anywhere outside the reach of sheep and red deer, suggest a landscape perhaps not as barren as today: a landscape with scattered woodlands, with fish in the rivers and the sea, pasture and arable land fertilised with the manure of many cattle. The question for the Trust, as for other land managers in the area, including SNH responsible for Beinn Eighe NNR adjacent to Torridon is – just how much and in what specific locations were these woodlands? The situation is not like Mar Lodge Estate where, although the soils are leached they are by and large well aerated and dry and where trees can be planted almost anywhere below the tree-line and will grow. In Torridon the soils are generally also acidic, but they are either thin or blanket-bog and mostly waterlogged. Trees can no longer grow in many situations with or without ground preparation, if they ever did! Should attempts be made then to create/re-create the forest habitat? We will return

to this a little later in the chapter, after we have looked a little more closely at the present situation.

Walkers on
Liathach Ridge

The Trust acquired Torridon principally for its wonderful landscape. In 1961, W. H. Murray carried out a survey of the Highland landscape for the Trust and considered the scenery of Glen Torridon and its surrounding mountains superior to any other district in Scotland, *including* Skye! So it was almost inevitable that the Trust should have taken the opportunity to acquire the estate of Torridon in 1967. Later, in 1981, Torridon was designated as part of the Wester Ross NSA and in 1990 the CCS *Mountain Areas of Scotland* report once again included Torridon in one of only four recommended outstanding mountain areas in Scotland requiring special management. That report described the area thus: 'the outstanding mountain masses of An Teallach in the north and the Torridonian hills to the south, both recognised as among the boldest and most distinctive of Scotland's mountains'.

Such attributes have attracted walkers and mountaineers to the area for a very long time. Today around 20,000 walkers use both the Coire Mhic Nobuill and Coire Dubh paths every year. The Trust's Countryside Centre at Torridon records around 9,000 people through the summer months, while the adjacent SYHA hostel report around 10,000 bed nights annually, and there is a camp site, a number of B&Bs and other forms of accommodation available. The Highland Tourist Board also estimates that around 60,000 per annum pass through the area. For a remote area then, Torridon is a surprisingly popular place. People come for the lowland trek around the north side of Liathach, for the peaks and the seven tops of the Liathach ridge and for rock climbing; and not only in the summer, but in the winter too. Most of the paths that the walkers follow into the mountains, as at Kintail and in many other parts of Highland Scotland, are stalkers' paths which were constructed with great care and skill over 100 years ago, probably by the estate staff of Duncan Darroch when he established the deer forest. Over time the ravages of the climate, exacerbated in recent years by the increasing number of boots bestriding them and the lack of manpower to maintain them, have resulted in damage to the structure of these paths and erosion often far beyond their margins. At Torridon the fairly level path from the Coire Mhic Nòbuil car park was first repaired by the Trust's own Conservation Volunteers, then later upgraded by a professional team, while the path up Coire Dubh and on into the spectacular Coire Mhic Fhearchair has been repaired entirely by professionals, with the help of grants from SNH, Scottish Mountaineering Council (SMC) and EU Objective 1 funds. As money from the Trust's Mountainous Country Fund, first established by donations from Percy Unna, is used in the management of Torridon, his Principles have been taken into account in regard to repair to mountain paths and to signing.

Hinds seeking shelter in remnant native woodland

Flora and fauna

The original purpose of many of these paths was to provide a safe passage for the ponies and guests, up into the hills to stalk the red deer, carry the venison back to the larder and the heads of the stags to adorn the walls of the big house. Today many of these paths still serve deer management as well as providing easy access for walkers. Red deer have played an important role, both in the economy of the old estate and as an attraction for visitors at Torridon. Their economic role, which thrived from the Victorian period, is now virtually over at Torridon, but the appeal of red deer to the public and the latter's admiration for the patience, and skill required by the stalker in their management, especially in Torridon, was due in large part to Lea MacNally and his writings. Lea MacNally was the Trust Ranger at Torridon for 21 years from the acquisition of the property and had a gift for describing his days on the hill among the red deer, the many other forms of wildlife and the elements. He was the epitome of the traditional and caring stalker who believed that, in the absence of natural predators, the death in the winter of a single deer, due to age or malnutrition, was an admission of his own poor management. On more than one occasion he risked his life in terrible winter conditions to stalk and humanely kill an animal he knew would not survive until the spring.

At the last deer count in 1996 there were 285 red deer resident on the Estate, mostly on the north side of Liathach and the north-west side of Beinn Alligin, the hinds outnumbering the stags 2.5:1. This is a reduction on 1991 when the figure was 359.The management of red deer, as we have noted, requires large management units involving several estates and Torridon belongs to the Gairloch Conservation Unit, the very first Deer Management Groups to be set up. In the 1993–98 Management Plan for Torridon the Trust states that as far as red deer management is concerned it '*has concentrated on maintaining a level population of healthy animals*', which in practice has meant culling weak animals and stags with poor head. This has been the mantra of traditional red-deer management in Scotland for a hundred years and more and no one, until Fraser Darling relatively recently, questioned whether the '*level population*' was the right one for the environment on which the deer (and all other wildlife) subsisted, or what exactly was meant by '*healthy animals*'. We know now that the numbers of red deer in Scotland are far, far too high to allow the natural regeneration of native trees and shrubs, that the body size of red deer generally is well below its optimum because it has so few forests in which to shelter and browse, and that deer carcasses are important sources of winter food for birds such as the golden and sea eagles. This last point raises the question of the validity of the principle that it is the deer that are in poor condition – that are considered unlikely to survive the winter – that should be culled. These are the very animals that are going to both provide winter food for predators and return some nutrient to the soils, they are not the animals which are going to ensure the population stays high. Stalking input would be a great deal more efficient therefore in controlling deer numbers if it was concentrated on culling animals across the age-range of the local population and not just the 'poor' beasts. An objective in the Management Plan that states that the Trust should '*ensure a sustainable balance between deer and woodland management*'. If the aim on Torridon is to ensure the survival and expansion of the native woodland, then the aim must be to reduce deer numbers to the level which achieves that aim. If numbers *are* reduced to that level, there would not be the problem of many malnourished deer dying in the winter nor the need for stalkers to risk their lives in culling them!

Arctic mouse-ear

In early June on the slopes of Alligin, in the pre-summer cold and wet weather, the few common flowers of the heath, such as the pink flowers of lousewort, the blue milkwort and the heath spotted orchid, bloom weakly. At this time of year the purple moor-grass looks fresh and lush, but in a short time it will be coarse and unpalatable and will remain largely ungrazed until it withers to brown in the autumn, falls like leaves and chokes the burns and ditches. Occasionally, where there is shading by rocks or bracken, are the pale flowers of wood anemone, an indication of past woodland cover, now limited at higher levels to the occasional rowan protected within the clefts of the boulders in the many areas of scree. Along higher stream-sides and flushes one of the early, dainty and widespread saxifrages, starry saxifrage, is in flower. This early in the year most of the tall herbs on the cliff ledges have yet to flower, but the yellow flowers of the fleshy roseroot are out. On the drier slopes there are scattered club mosses and patches of blaeberry. Higher still among the good grazing on the alpine grasslands the only flower out, though sensibly not totally opened as it is being blasted by wind and hail near the summit of Alligin, is the nationally scarce arctic mouse-ear chickweed, a sub-species of which occurs adjacent to the new Trust property in Unst. Also wind-blasted, but almost invisible against the grey rock and stony soils of the summit, crouch ptarmigan; and overhead,

Ptarmigan

Remnants of woodland in the Abhainn Alligin

swinging away to the south, a golden eagle, perhaps on the lookout for a mountain hare. Despite its barren appearance there are a number of other interesting and rare mountain plants to find on the Torridon mountains, such as the northern rock-cress, alpine hawkweed, alpine hair-grass and curved woodrush, especially if you have the Ranger to help you!

One of the outstanding botanical interests of Torridon, but one that probably appeals to few, is its very rich community of oceanic bryophytes, a division of the lower plants that includes mosses and liverworts. Both groups thrive in moist conditions, and the cool and humid atmosphere of the Torridon mountains and the great exposures of naked bed-rock appear to be ideal for many northern and oceanic species, particularly on the north slopes of Liathach. Planted broadleaf and plantations of mainly pines and spruce occur on the low ground close to the road and there is an occasional patch of native woodland, mostly birch but with oak and hazel also. Although Scots pines appear in these plantations, their origin is not known. Otherwise, looking up to the mountains there is only a scattering of individual trees with scraps of wood to be seen, in boulder fields and on cliff faces. Centuries of exploitation, burning and grazing have all but destroyed the original native forest, sparse and scattered though it may have been. However, hidden from easy view, unless one leaves the road and paths, is the rather special woodland in the gorge of the Abhainn Alligin, both above and below the road.

Apart from the capping of pale quartzites on the Liathach peaks, the only other non-sandstone rock formation of Torridon is the area of ancient Lewisian gneiss at the western end, in which is the bed of the Abhainn Alligin. In contrast to the nutrient-poor soils of the sandstones, the soils derived from the gneiss are relatively base-rich and as a result the flora, including the woodland, of the gorge, is one of the most diverse in Wester Ross. The section below the road consists of a narrow band of oak-ash-wych elm woodland while the upper section is more open with a scattered wood of birch, rowan and hazel. Both sections also have a remnant woodland ground flora including such plants as wood sedge and our largest and most magnificent native fern, the royal fern. At the upper end, where the ravine terminates in a herb-rich heath, are ledges with tall herbs such as globe flower. Apart from the vertical faces all this area is grazed by sheep and deer and therefore there is little if any regeneration of the woodland.

Crofting and agriculture

The population of the Torridon area, along with the rest of the west coast of Scotland, has been falling steadily since its peak in the early part of the last century. Basically, the land cannot support the numbers of the past at the standard of living we expect today. It is likely also that the climate and the soils are not what they were. In addition there are few other local job prospects nowadays that are necessary to boost the income of crofters and to hold the young. Finally, the agricultural subsidies, as noted elsewhere, are not specifically geared to supporting communities.

There are three crofting townships, totalling 44 crofts, on the Torridon Estate. Fasag has no grazings, but Inveralligin and Wester Alligin share grazings on the western end of the property, including the western and lower slopes of Beinn Alligin. The rest of the Estate is in hand and carries no sheep. There is virtually no crofting at Fasag and only quite limited active management of the small areas of inbye at the other two townships; however Inveralligin has plans to develop an area of the grazings for Crofter Forestry. There is only one crofter on the Estate with sheep, amounting to about 350 animals. The grazings boundary fence is no longer sheep-proof, so around fifty sheep graze on Beinn Alligin. The grazings also include the gorge of the Abhainn Alligin and its diverse woodland remnant. The only other agricultural unit is the Mains Farm belonging to the Trust. There is no arable activity on the farm and it is under-utilised; however, attempts to lease it have proved to be economically unsound. At present it is in-hand and part is given over to a resident herd of deer as an attraction for the public, while Highland Cattle are being used in the other fields to contain the grass. Later in the chapter we will see that the Trust has further plans for the farm.

Management

The principal statutory designations on Torridon, that identify the specific areas of interest and importance and that dictate the form and level of management, are the NSA, the SSSIs and the cSAC. Apart from a small area on the Abhainn Alligin scheduled as an SSSI for its woodland, the greater part of Torridon is designated as a separate SSSI for its geological and biological interests. Part of the Trust property is also within the Beinn Eighe NNR, being considered an extension of the range of the Beinn Eighe red deer, as well as being considered by SNH as appropriate ground for restoration of woodland and scrub. The Wester Ross NSA, whose citation frequently alludes to wildness, ruggedness and remoteness, totally encompasses the property. Presumably the authors, while accepting the presence of occasional blocks of policy and commercial woodland, saw the bareness of the lower parts of the mountains as part of the scenic appeal, emphasising the naked wildness of the landscape. The Trust too, have recognised that this element of the natural heritage of Torridon is the most important, highlighting the landscape in the overall aim of management in the 1993–98 Management Plan:

> *The Trust should ensure the permanent preservation, for the benefit of the nation, of the Torridon Estate, as one of the most scenically attractive areas of Scotland, one of the finest examples of Torridonian geology, and a nationally important biological site which still remains relatively unspoilt by development and recreational pressures which are very important. The landscape value of the area is of over-riding importance at this property as one of the most scenically attractive areas of Scotland with a fine core of 'wild country'.*

A further objective of management states:

> *The Trust should ensure the survival of existing native woodland and restore the woodland and scrub in defined areas. . . .*

This last aim has recently become achievable at Torridon, as we have seen on many other properties, through the beneficence of the MFS. The opportunity, or as some might say, temptation, however, is to massively increase the scale of woodland restoration. Will this conflict with the principal aim at Torridon?

Chapter 1 raised the issue of our cultural view of landscape and suggested that our present attitude, which includes those of the authors of the NSA citation, is very much shaped by the existing landscape and what we regard

'Wet desert' at Torridon

as natural. I would suggest that whatever native woodland *can* be restored on Torridon will be just as natural as that which we have at present. However, any suggestion of restoring native woodland of pine and broadleaves to this area has to demonstrate the legitimacy of woodland in the north west, even before consideration of its effect on the landscape or the species to be used. Of all the vegetation communities in Scotland on which native woodland is now being planted as part of the present movement for restoration of our native forests, the wet heaths with their thin, waterlogged and nutrient-deficient soils, that dominate so much of the Torridonian sandstones of the north west, pose the questions as to whether they *ever* supported trees; and if trees *were* to be planted, would they survive without artificial help?

To return to the questions raised in the first section of this chapter – what is the origin of the '*wet desert*'? If it is purely the geology and climate then the present limited range of plants clinging to it is probably very near the climatic climax community and there is nothing we can, or should, do in the name of restoration. If it is entirely anthropogenic in origin on the other hand, then there may be a legitimacy in restoration. The cause of course could have been a combination of geology, climate *and* people, and possibly other factors. Whatever the origin however, that does not mean it is *possible* to restore woodland: the geology, present soils and present climate may preclude it. If global warming is a reality and means an even wetter climate

Pine marten

in the west and north of Scotland, then the chances of establishing (or re-establishing) trees on these poor soils are even less. We are left then with very limited areas where we can be very sure that woodland would have existed, and still could exist; and on these sites seed trees could be planted. If the Trust limits its woodland management to the removal of grazing and encouraging natural regeneration only, then natural expansion will be very, very slow. On the other hand one can be sure that where seeds fall on suitable soils trees will grow, but where they are not meant to grow they will not, *whatever* the reason for their lack of presence now.

Notwithstanding, the evidence for the legitimacy of native forests at Torridon has been accepted by the Trust and by other grant-giving bodies, including SNH and FA, the former continuing to carry out planting commenced many years ago on the neighbouring Beinn Eighe NNR. Even the Qualifying Habitats for the cSAC include Caledonian Scots pinewood, which is given priority over the open habitats of dry heath, alpine and sub-alpine heaths. With very little suggestion that the 'landscape' label will hold it back, a bold plan has been prepared by the Trust for the restoration of more than 250 hectares (2.5 square kilometres) of native woodland over a nine-year period. This will include, first, five deer-fenced enclosures amounting to 109 hectares, around existing fragments where the creation of new woodland will be principally by regeneration, with some limited planting, such as at Coire Dubh and Coire Mhic Nobuil. Second, bringing 70 hectares of native woodland between Fasag and Coire Mhic Nobuil into management. Third, the planting of 78 hectares above these remnants. Most of the funds necessary for this will come under a WGS of the FA and the balance from the MFS. In addition, 9 hectares of commercial forest will be thinned to encourage their replacement by native species. The total cost of this element of the project will be around £400,000. The seeds for the native trees will come from the local area, and in the case of Scots pine from Shieldaig, which has been shown by the FA to be the most closely related provenance. Each of the areas has been very carefully selected and it is intended that the fences will be sited to be as unobtrusive on the landscape as possible, while new plantings will reflect both the ability of the soils to support trees and a combination of the native species most likely to have existed there. This means that the greater part of the area to be managed for woodland will be achieved by natural regeneration and will be sparse on the areas of wet heath.

The plan for woodland restoration at Torridon, however, is part of a much larger habitat restoration project accessing MFS funds, linking both to the local crofting community at Inveralligin and to the needs of the cSAC. Those latter management needs are being identified through an EU 'LIFE' upland grazing project, such as has been carried out at Glencoe and Ben Lawers. Other very important parts of the project include education through the direct involvement of local schools. There will also be interpretation that will take visitors through the enclosures, explaining the purpose behind them and the re-opening of the old footpath between Fasag and Inveralligin. Before the project gets under way, however, there are two very important tasks to be accomplished. First, a survey of all archaeological remains, now well under way, so that they can be avoided when planting, as such sites, apart from their inherent value, may well hold important information on past management and vegetation cover. Second, commencing the very difficult task of eliminating all the *Rhododendron ponticum*, that pernicious rhododendron species which has so devastated the oak woodlands of so much of the west coast. Eradication is a very necessary but expensive

NTS Thistle camp, rhododendron clearance

exercise, and at Torridon alone will cost around £45,000 to complete.

The forest restoration project will link at its western extremity with the Inveralligin Crofter Forestry (CF) scheme, which will replace some of their hill grazings with woodland and may therefore seem quite a radical step for the crofters to take. However, there are fewer and fewer financial returns for keeping sheep on the hill, and on the common grazings at Torridon sheep numbers are less than a quarter of the original souming. Management of sheep is not what it used to be, in fact the present fences on the Inveralligin and Wester Alligin grazings are defunct and will be re-erected as part of the overall restoration plan. This will prevent sheep and other stock from damaging the new woodland and from straying, as they do at present, onto Beinn Alligin itself where the needs of the cSAC communities require grazing reduction and control. The immediate benefits of the CF scheme are very limited and may only provide some short-term local employment in the construction of fences and planting. In the longer term there will only be need for maintenance, but in the more distant future, the succeeding generation of crofters will benefit from both improved shelter and improved grazings within and adjacent to woodlands and possibly from the timber itself.

Not all of the woodland restoration project is focused on the hill. An important component is planned for the low ground in Glen Torridon itself east of the Mains Farm and Visitor Centre. Here existing blocks of planted woodland are to be incorporated into a much larger fenced area which will include an area of hill for natural regeneration and an area of previous pasture attached to the Mains Farm for planting. This latter area, and at Glen Cottage, will provide an opportunity for the planting of alder and willows by the River Torridon, on a scale not available on the western end of the project. The new fences also present an opportunity to improve the landscape quality of the area by the removal of the present roadside fences and the setting of the new well back and almost hidden from the main road. The final link in the project is to improve the habitats within the Mains Farm itself by, for example, the creation of shelter-belts and hedgerows, the creation of species-rich grassland and the management of the riparian zones along the watercourses and ditches. All this will create a greater diversity of habitat which will enhance the variety of birds, perhaps including corncrake, and other wildlife using the Farm grounds. This part of the project will be achieved by using funds from a private donation made specifically to Torridon. As with Ben Lawers, such a scale of management will require careful monitoring over many years to ensure that the intended results will be achieved, particularly as regards natural regeneration.

Outside the area of both the Trust and Crofter Forestry woodland restoration, on the common grazings, lies the Abhainn Alligin gorge with its nationally important remnant woodland, tall herbs and species-rich heath.

Ring ouzel

This site is a wonderful example of the effect of geology on vegetation. The junction of the two rocks – Lewisian gneiss and Torridonian sandstone – is the upper limit of the gorge and the actual course of the Abhainn Alligin itself. The former rocks are on the west and the latter on the east and above the limit of the ravine. The contrasts between the remnant woodland of either side of the burn, with mainly birch and only limited amounts of hazel and oak on the acidic sandstones of the east side, and more plentiful oak and hazel plus aspen and holly on the basic gneiss of the west side; and the contrasts between the species-rich heath at the upper, basic part of the gorge and the species-poor heath outside the gorge, are both very striking.

The present level of grazing, which is well below previous levels, is judged not to be damaging to the site, but it is preventing regeneration of what is now only scattered trees in the upper part of the ravine. The rich woodland is there because of the good soils derived from the basic gneiss, and the good soils support good grazings; so the site, surrounded otherwise by poor grazing on the Torridonian sandstone, is peculiarly attractive to both the sheep and, particularly in the winter months, to red deer. Just like Ben Lawers and many other hill properties then, Trust managers are faced at Abhainn Alligin with the almost universal problem of how to reconcile the needs of a nationally important woodland that has to have reduced grazing if it is to survive, an adjacent species-rich heath that requires grazing, a crofter who is trying to make a living from his sheep, and the native red deer who are looking for shelter and sweet herbs.

The numbers of red deer on Torridon are relatively small, around four per 100 hectares. Unfortunately however, even small numbers attracted to very limited areas of woodland and good grazing, can prevent regeneration. In addition, the areas of woodland and heath to be enclosed as part of the large project will reduce the area normally available to wintering beasts coming down from the mountains and from over the north side of the property. It is inevitable then, at least in the short term, that deer numbers will have to be reduced to even lower levels to see if regeneration can take place, as stated in the present Management Plan. If that action is not successful then sheep may need to be excluded from the ravine also. As this is on common grazings, such a change in management will have to have the agreement of the crofters and may involve compensation. At this point no decisions have been made to change the *status quo*. If, in this comparatively limited area, there has to be a choice between the survival of the woodland or the species-rich heath, the former will take precedence as the more important habitat on a national and European scale.

Summation

In case the fact that I have dwelt rather long in this chapter on some of the issues of woodland restoration and the MFS woodland plan for Torridon has given the reader the impression that an enormous amount of woodland is to be created, it is worth noting that the area proposed to be fenced for woodland represents less than 4 per cent of the property! The conclusion regarding the effect the woodland restoration project will have on the landscape, even though it may be extended to neighbouring estates, is that it is so relatively small on the scale of the wildness that is Torridon that it will not detract from it. On the other hand, even this limited amount of woodland cover will bring a new diversity and richness to the environment of the lower hill and shore and, because of its close juxtaposition with the Torridon mountains, may even enhance their rugged and barren appearance!

Projects such as this, and others illustrated in this book, that include elements of co-operation with the local crofting community to whom it will also bring benefits, are hopefully just the beginnings of the new culture of investment in the natural resources of the Highlands and Islands. Of the crofting communities looked at in this book, that at Torridon is probably the most fragile because of the poorness of the local natural heritage and because of the lack of local employment. The activities of the Trust at Torridon will undoubtedly improve the local natural resource, but much of that

Sundew on
blanket bog

improvement, apart from the crofters' own Forestry scheme, lies outside the involvement, or control, of the local community. Unlike the other properties that have crofting communities, Canna, Fair Isle and Balmacara, but similarly to Kintail, there is nothing in the management aims for Torridon that recognises the needs of the crofting community or their place in holistic management. As we will see in the Fair Isle chapter, partnership with the community can release a great deal of goodwill and energy that ultimately is of great benefit to the natural heritage. For the first time in many generations something is being returned to the natural heritage of Torridon: can the Trust go even further? Could there be a better management link with Beinn Eighe NNR and a greater role in management for the local community?

Falls of Glomach in spate July 98

Chapter 5

Kintail and West Affric

Introduction

This property is made up of what were relatively recently the three separate estates of Kintail, Falls of Glomach and West Affric. To avoid confusion, I will use each name separately when discussing that particular Estate; and to avoid having to use all three names when I am referring to the whole property, including the Falls of Glomach, I will either use the Trust term 'property' or use the title of the property, Kintail and West Affric.

There was a brief allusion in the last chapter to the contrasts in the mountain landscape of Torridon with Kintail. Where the mountains of Torridon appear superficially barren with a fairly uniform vegetation of heather, deer grass, cotton grass and some purple moor grass, Kintail has a lush and superficial green-ness about it, which is predominantly the result of a complete vegetation cover dominated by grassland. Both are in the region of 6,000 hectares in extent and the pronounced contrasts in their vegetation and its grazing quality is further illustrated by the fact that, whereas Torridon carries around 350 sheep and also 350 resident red deer, the Estate of Kintail carries 1,590 sheep and between 800 and 1,200 red deer, depending on the time of year. There are also feral goats on Kintail which are the most destructive grazers as they can reach sites inaccessible to sheep and deer, and wreak great damage through browsing on shrubs and trees. The reasons for the great contrast in vegetation cover between the two estates, although they share a very similar west-coast climate, stems from the underlying geology and to an extent from the history of land use. The rocks of Kintail (and West Affric) are sedimentary in origin, just as at Torridon, but they are sandstones, shales and mudstones, laid down in shallow waters some 1,000 million years ago, 200 million years before those of Torridon. Unlike them, they have undergone profound metamorphic alteration to become granulites and schists which have given rise to slightly better soils than those at Torridon. Kintail then, as far as human history is concerned,

The Five Sisters of Kintail from Loch Duich

has been a much more productive and probably a more exploited resource than Torridon. It is probable in fact, just like Ben Lawers which has even better soils as we saw in an earlier chapter, that the predominantly grassland vegetation of Kintail has been to a large extent created by fairly heavy and continuous grazing pressures over a very long period of time, which in turn has meant a heavy loss of the original tree and shrub cover. The loss of tree and shrub cover in turn means that the rain runs straight off the hill, causing rapid fluctuations in the burn and river levels leading to erosion on the steep slopes and large outwash fans on the glen floors.

Between the Kintail and West Affric sections of the property there is a major geological break. On the east side the rocks are of slightly different composition to those on the west; this and the differences in dip, plus the fact that to the east, in West Affric, the rocks are highly folded, has resulted in different landscapes. In Kintail the glens are steep and narrow, leading westward, while West Affric has a more open landscape with wider glens, less steep slopes and deep peats which in the distant past have smothered woodland and farmland. Climatically too, there are differences between the two major parts of the area. To the west in Kintail, the climate is more maritime – windier, wetter and milder, but to the east in West Affric, winters are colder with considerably more snow lying for longer periods into the spring.

Across the whole property there are a wide variety of glacial and

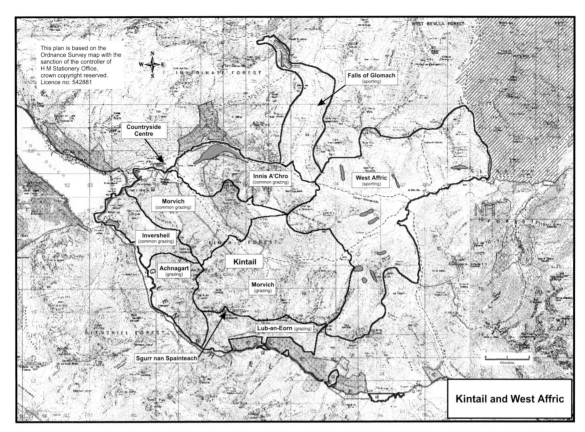

Figure 5.1
Map of the
Kintail and
West Affric area
(Legend: see p. xviii)

peri-glacial features, the finest being the great rock slides of late-glacial times on the south side of Beinn Fhada resulting in deep fissures on the side of the mountain, considered to be the best examples of their kind in Britain. There is some terracing that has resulted from the freezing and thawing of high-level slope soils on Beinn Fhada and there are, of course, the Falls of Glomach, among the highest falls in Britain, that plunge down from the hanging valley of Gleann Gaorsaic into the deeply excavated Glen Elchaig. There are also many fine coires, while the glens of Kintail themselves are classically and spectacularly steepened by glaciation.

Not surprisingly, the magnificent scenery of Kintail and West Affric was highlighted by W. H. Murray in his Highland Landscape assessment for the Trust in 1962, and the whole area lies within two NSAs. The Kintail NSA states that

> Three long mountain ranges terminate around the head of Loch Duich: Beinn Fhada, the Five Sisters of Kintail, and the Cluanie Forest which culminates in the Saddle. These glens which radiate from Loch Duich between these mountains, which form the watershed of mainland Scotland within a few miles of the western sea, are short, steepsided and deep . . . it is the grandeur of the mountains that makes the scenery here so magnificent.

West Affric is at the western end of the Glen Affric NSA, whose main features are the Caledonian pine forests, the lochs and the river of the Glen itself, set between high conical mountains. The Glen Affric NSA states: 'From the rich woodland at the dam to the stark mountains of the upper glen, where all is moor and heather, it displays a fine variety of glen scenery.' As it suggests, the magnificent native Scots pine and birch woods are actually in East Glen Affric, and West Affric itself has little of this woodland remaining, if it was *ever* covered by woodland to the same degree. This is also reflected in the fact that the Affric-Cannich Hills SSSI terminates just within the eastern boundary of West Affric.

Kintail and West Affric then, on either side of the watershed that runs south from Sgurr Gaorsaic to Beinn Fhada and Sgurr a Bhealaich Dheirg, complement each other in their landscapes and to a certain extent in their vegetation, with remnant birch woods on heathery hills and blanket-bog on the east, and with remnant oak-birch-hazel-ash woods on grasslands to the west. The approaches to the two parts of the property from the east are equally complementary. To Kintail, coming west by Loch Cluanie, the landscape is wide open, almost treeless and barren, and then suddenly there is the long plunge down Glen Shiel with the steep green hills gradually closing in on either side. The approach to West Affric is up narrower and heavily wooded and planted glens from Cannich until the road ends at the eastern end of Loch Affric with still another 7 kilometres up the Loch and into the more open and heathery Glen before the boundary of the property is crossed. There are no crofts on Glen Affric and no sheep, but there are three crofting townships on Kintail. These major differences in character between the two estates is reflected in some differences in their management – as we will see.

Human history

The major human link between the estates is very old. The original drovers' road, that brought the black cattle from this part of the west coast to the markets, ran from Morvich and the shores of Loch Duich via Dorusduain, Gleann Choinneachain, to the Bealach an Sgairne at around 530 metres (1,600 feet), before descending to Loch a Bhealaich, on to Upper Glen Affric and so to Beauly and Strathglass. There was also a later, less steep and somewhat lower route up Glen Lichd via the waterfall on the Allt Grannda to Camban, joining up with the first in Upper Glen Affric. These passes would have been in regular use, however, long before then.

The lands of Kintail are steeped in stories and myth going back at least 1,000 years and would no doubt have been occupied by the Picts before they were absorbed into the culture of the Scots. In the thirteenth century,

Snow bunting

following King Haakon's defeat at Largs, the lands were given to the progenitors of the MacKenzies of Kintail, later to become the Earls of Seaforth, in reward for their help by a grateful Alexander III of Scotland. Following the defeat of the Jacobites in the eighteenth century the Seaforths became impoverished and eventually sold out, as so many Highland chiefs did in the early part of the nineteenth century, to the new sheep proprietors.

Not very far down the River Shiel from the site of the battle of Glen Shiel in 1719, is Achadh nan Seileach, just one of the many Highland settlements cleared for sheep, whose sad story, repeated all over the Highlands and Islands, was so evocatively portrayed by James Hunter in his book *The Other Side of Sorrow* (1995). Describing this particular clearance he says:

> So total and far-reaching were the clearances now set in train that, by the time evictions ceased, no more than fourteen of Glen Shiel's thousands and thousands of acres remained in the occupancy of descendants of the people living here at the point when Samuel Johnson and James Boswell had put in their brief appearance.

(Johnson and Boswell passed by this site on their Highland journey in 1773.) Later in the nineteenth century, when wool prices slumped, the Estate of Kintail turned, again as happened in many other parts of the Highlands at this time, to a sporting income from red deer. It was in the early part of the twentieth century, not so long after the 1886 Crofters Holdings Act, that the present common grazings were created.

Glen Affric was also a private sporting estate until its acquisition by the Trust in 1993. Part of the condition of the sale to the Trust was the retention of sporting rights by the owner until February 1999. Likewise the sporting rights on the Falls of Glomach, acquired in 1943, are held by another tenant, SMECH properties, until the same date and we will return to the Trust's plans for deer management in those areas later in the chapter. Kintail was acquired in 1944 by Percy Unna and given to the Trust anonymously. Acquisition of West Affric was made possible by money donated by the Myles Morrison Bequest and the Chris Brasher Trust. These donations and the condition of sale of West Affric have also had a strong influence on the management of the property. This was the largest property owned by the Trust in 1993 and almost double the size of the next largest (Torridon). Shortly after however, even the scale of this property was dwarfed by the acquisition of Mar Lodge Estate in 1995!

Flora and fauna

On the low ground at Kintail, within the croftland, are fine saltmarshes, the largest at Croe Bridge, Morvich. There are also one or two traditional hayfields, but otherwise there is not a great deal of active crofting. On a midsummer day the flowers of the irises are open, giving splashes of yellow in the fields and in the early morning the cloud is down to about 500 metres, hiding all the tops. Before climbing the stalkers' path through Gleann Choinneachain to Beinn Fhada one passes through patches of bog myrtle on the wet glen floor, then bracken and then mountain fern and purple moor grass sprinkled with the same few heath flowers as seen at Torridon: tormentil, milkwort, bedstraw, heath spotted orchid and bird's-foot trefoil. Gradually deer grass and mat grass begin to dominate and as the cloud thins and the sun breaks through, crags and peaks appear and disappear. On the plateau of Beinn Fhada at just under 1,000 metres are important snow-bed communities and a high-level heath with blaeberry, crowberry, lady's mantle and cloudberry, whose large and distinctly rose-like flowers have yet to open. Here the walking is a little easier after the stiff climb.

Descending to Gleann Lichd and walking back down the glen to Morvich it is very apparent that over-grazing, and probably muirburn, has resulted in the extensive loss of heather and other dwarf shrubs and continues to threaten the widespread remnants of woodland which cling to crag and steep burn sides. Although only a very small part of the property has an SSSI designation, the summit heaths of Kintail are at least of local value and there are several rare mountain plants on West Affric including alpine saw-wort,

Riparian woodland

globe flower, russet sedge and the delicate alpine lady fern. In addition to the flora the property supports a wide range of our wonderful mountain birds, though not all regularly breeding, including golden eagle, black-throated diver, greenshank, dotterel, snow bunting and ptarmigan.

Perhaps, though, the most interesting feature of the property's natural history is the diversity of woodland relics. For example, on Kintail there is alder by the River Croe and by the River Shiel at Achnagart; hawthorn-hazel wood at Shiel Bridge; ash-hazel along the Abhainn Chonaig at Dorusduain with a species-rich woodland on the slopes and crags above. There is another species-rich woodland on the crags below the Falls of Glomach and mixed broadleaves at several places in Gleann Lichd. In West Affric, reflecting the peat cover, there are also many small remnants of birch woodland, with rowan, goat willow, eared willow and aspen. There is also a solitary Scots pine.

Recognising the great potential for the restoration of a wide variety of woodland types, the Trust and SNH entered into a Management Agreement over West Affric in 1994 which provided the Trust with a one-off endowment payment of £50,000 and the promise of additional assistance, under certain condition, perhaps the most relevant of which is:

> *Where the environment is suitable, the ideal objective is to attain the situation where red and roe deer are free-ranging in and around woodland which is self-sustaining through natural regeneration . . . this will require the area covered by native woodland to be extended and the impact of red deer reduced to a level which allows natural regeneration to take place.*

It is suggested in the Agreement that such management should be applicable throughout the property, i.e. over Kintail and the Falls of Glomach also. However, there are greater hurdles to be overcome due to the grazing and, on the latter, due to sporting tenure.

Black-throated divers

Visitors

Many people come to this particular area of Scotland to walk during the summer months, even for day visits from Glasgow and Edinburgh. Several thousand stay at the various Youth Hostels and probably more than 20,000 come to the Caravan Club at Morvich, in addition to those who come to the hotels and B&Bs. The major attraction of the property is of course the mountains. There are ten Munros wholly or partly on Trust property, in addition to Sgurr na Moraich and Sgurr nan Saighead which are part of the Five Sisters and not far below 3,000 feet. Then there are another twenty Munros in the area. The attraction on the property is for hill-walking rather than mountaineering, the most popular route being the ridge of the Five Sisters – a strenuous day's walking equivalent to a climb of 10,000 feet! The other very popular path is to the Falls of Glomach from Dorusduain over the Bealach na Sroine, a round trip of 12 kilometres. There are two Rangers at Kintail and guided hill-walks by arrangement. The Trust, as with all its properties, operates a policy of open access on the property, even during the stalking season, and therefore it is very popular for walkers all year round. The success of the open access policy during stalking, as at Mar Lodge Estate and at the Creag Meagaidh NNR for example, where stalking continues to be carried out with minimum disturbance, has played a large part in changing the attitudes of many private estates to access during stalking, leading to the recent concordat on access by all interested parties under the umbrella of the Access Forum led by SNH.

There are a number of major footpaths on the property, of which two routes are public rights of way. Footpath restoration and repair has centred on the main Rights of Way, the original drovers' roads, which lead from Morvich through to Glen Affric via Gleann Lichd or Gleann Choinneachain. Approximately 16 kilometres of these paths have been restored by volunteer work groups, contractors and ranger staff at a cost of around £150,000 over the last ten years. As it was Percy Unna who purchased Kintail for the Trust, his Principles apply; there is open access and, apart from repair to existing footpaths, there are no new paths to make physical access to the hills any easier. Also in accordance with them the interpretive facilities at Kintail are at the Countryside Centre down at Morvich.

Grazing

The Trust should ensure the permanent conservation, for the benefit of the nation, of Kintail, the Falls of Glomach and West Affric as examples of outstanding and nationally important landscapes and remote and relatively unspoilt areas of significant recreational and nature conservation value.

Tucked in between Inverinate Forest to the north, Glenshiel Forest to the south, the Forest of Kintail to the east and the salt water of Loch Duich, are the three small crofting townships of Morvich, Innis à Chro and Invershiel. Together they consist of the 21 crofts on Kintail, their inbye amounting to only 21 hectares. Most of the active inbye croftland is within the first two townships and each township has common grazings on the hill. However there is only one crofter at Innis à Chro who runs 260 sheep on that common grazings, while the Morvich crofters operate a sheep stock club and run 650 sheep over much of the western half of Kintail, including the Morvich common grazing. There is also an area in Glen Shiel (including Invershiel grazings), Achnagart with 680 sheep, that is leased and another area there in hand.

One of the central planks of management at Kintail and West Affric – as at other large Trust properties such as Torridon, Glencoe, Ben Lomond and Ben Lawers, on NNRs with Management Agreements and on private estates – has been the *laissez-faire* principle of letting the hill look after itself. This reflects the importance of sheep in the economics of upland agriculture and the misplaced reverence for the traditional management of red deer: reflecting also the lack of the overwhelming and objective body of evidence now available, that indicates just how much traditional management has impoverished our natural vegetation cover. The Trust, like other bodies responsible for nature conservation, has gradually become aware of this and in 1992 set up a Grazing Working Party (GWP) which recognised that 'The management of grazing is perhaps the most complex issue facing the Trust in the management of its countryside estate'. In 1993 the GWP produced a report that recognised that several of its countryside properties, including Kintail, were suffering ecological impoverishment and continuing deterioration of nature conservation values as a result of over-grazing. The following year, in 1994, the Trust commissioned a study of the grazing effects on Kintail.

The study used the Macaulay Land Use Research Institute (MLURI) Grazing Management Model which is designed to assess the potential year-round stock carrying capacity of heather moorland and was carried out over two areas of the property, the Beinn Fhada plateau and southern slopes and the lower slopes of Gleann Lichd. On the latter the utilisation of young heather shoots was 53 per cent (at Ben Lomond it is intended to reduce utilisation of heather to between 20–30 per cent) while on the former it was 70 per cent! These levels of grazing remove too much of the annual growth, there is little flowering and eventually the heather plant dies. At higher altitudes the heather is being replaced by mat grass (as at lower levels, Ben Lawers) and on the lower and wetter slopes by purple moor grass. In areas of better soils the heather moorland can be replaced by fine grasses such as bents and fescues, but continued heavy grazing, particularly sheep, can also result in the replacement of this grassland by mat grass. Both mat grass and purple moor grass are not palatable to sheep and have spread to dominate ground that was once heather moorland. Such transformation of the vegetation is also damaging to the nature conservation value of the land, for heather moorland supports a much greater range of plants, and animals such as ptarmigan, grouse and mountain hare for example, which in turn support resident golden eagle, than the acid grassland that has replaced it.

The report concluded that, although there has been little muirburn in the past five years the present condition of the vegetation is due to past burning as well as to past and present levels of grazing. The high grazing pressures on the lower ground were due to a combination of cattle, sheep and deer, while on the higher ground the main culprit was probably red deer as there were higher numbers of those than sheep. In both cases there is not sufficient heather available in the winter months to support the present grazing stock. To prevent further deterioration, never mind recovery of heather cover, the report recommended a reduction of overall grazing pressure, although if this was accompanied by an increase in cattle numbers on the lower ground, both purple moor grass and mat grass would be reduced in extent while bracken would be held at bay.

The theme of recent management at Kintail has therefore become restoration, but with crofters and tenants having their own grazing rights on the hill and with certain conditions laid down by those who assisted the Trust in their acquisition of the property, this means some accommodation and compromise, and increasingly, partnership, if the Trust is to achieve its goals. This the Trust is doing by encouraging use of the Countryside Premium Scheme (CPS) which on the Morvich grazing has resulted in the removal of 235 sheep there. This is in addition to a further 300 which have been removed from various of the grazings over the last six years as crofters have gradually reduced their input into sheep farming. Lower down the hill, problems of overgrazing on the saltmarsh and erosion caused by cattle and sheep grazing on the river banks are being met by fencing. Steps have been taken then to address reducing the sheep grazing pressure, but what is the situation regarding red deer number?

Red deer and woodland management

In conjunction with neighbouring landowners, the Trust should aim to achieve and sustain a resident deer population which will enable woodland to naturally regenerate and exist in a state of equilibrium. The management of deer should be kept in hand and no extension of leased stalking rights should be considered.

It is all in the first phrase!

The Kintail property is surrounded by private sporting estates and there is a great deal of movement of deer across the march, which can double the numbers at certain times. Agreement will have to be reached to reduce the numbers of deer that move between the estates, and that must mean a reduction in the neighbouring population. Deer management over this area is co-ordinated through a Deer Management Sub-Group, with the assistance of the Deer Commission for Scotland (DCS). It is through this avenue, as well as direct discussions with neighbours, that the Trust will have to influence its neighbours. At the present moment this Kintail and Affric Sub-Group is developing a Deer Management Plan to meet the different needs of the various estates. What is the Trust to do however, if neighbouring estates will not reduce their deer populations? Who should then do the fencing? Should not the neighbour whose high deer numbers are damaging Trust ground put up a march fence?

In the meantime efforts have been made by the Trust on Kintail to bring down deer numbers over the past 25 years. Are there signs of this in the Kintail counts over recent years?

Unfortunately not. The population of red deer on the Kintail property is roughly what it was 25 years ago, allowing for the fact that there is a great deal of movement across the march. There has been a consistently higher cull since 1995/96, but it has not been enough to reduce the population in the same period. The problem is that the level of cull is too low, for example the 1996/97 cull was only 18 per cent of the 1996 population and the 1997/98 Cull was only 14 per cent of the 1997/98 population, whereas a cull greater than 20 per cent is required to reduce a population. The ultimate aim of deer

Stalkers and the stag cull

Table 5.1 Red deer numbers and cull figures for Kintail

	Stags	Hinds	Calves	Total
1973	427	387	160	974
1984	490	615	160	1,265
1993	263	480	127	870
1994	267	567	41	875
1995	381	627	199	1,207
1996	209	441	208	858
1997	402	567	234	1,203

Total Kintail cull figure for the same period:

1972/73	119	1990/91	111	1994/95	122
1983/84	100	1991/92	105	1995/96	161
1988/89	141	1992/93	147	1996/97	154
1989/90	143	1993/94	108	1997/98	171

management on Kintail is to bring deer numbers down to the level of five per 100 hectares (four per 100 hectares at Torridon), so there is a need for substantial additional efforts and resources to accomplish this, never mind the assistance of colder winters to bring the hinds within easier reach! As well as benefiting the dwarf shrubs such as heather, this is the level of grazing at which it is thought there can be successful regeneration of the woodland relicts.

Meanwhile there are still many sheep and some cattle on the hill, which altogether means that there will be very little natural regeneration of the remnants of the once diverse and widespread native woodland. This is being addressed, under an MFS umbrella, by erecting a series of enclosures around some of the best remnants at both West Affric and Kintail. At the latter, two enclosures, of around 38 hectares in total, have been erected in Glen Shiel and a third of 26.3 hectares, also around a mixed broadleaf remnant, near the head of Gleann Lichd on the banks of the Allt Grannda and between it and the path up to the Five Sisters. Another scheme in Kintail involves supporting Crofters Forestry Schemes at half-a-dozen scattered locations amounting to around 180 hectares, under which 50 per cent of fencing costs are met by the FA and the remainder paid over a period of five years if the regeneration targets are met. As at Torridon, these schemes probably would not have gone ahead if there was very active croft sheep management and as at Torridon, the fences will have to be deer-proof.

Luid en Eorna enclosure on the steep green slopes

The total area that is being enclosed on Kintail will be nearly 250 hectares. In the more open landscape of West Affric four enclosures amounting to 50 hectares have already been erected and there are plans for more over the next few years, but for three reasons fencing will not be on the scale as on Kintail. First, such structures in the more open landscape of West Affric would detract from its wild land quality. Second, apart from immigrant wintering stags, the Trust has full control of the grazing: and thirdly, there is strong evidence that this western end of Glen Affric was already a fairly open landscape with relatively few trees prior to the first human settlements. Instead there will be more effort on West Affric, where deer numbers are a half to a third of those on Kintail, to reduce their numbers rather than fence. Most of these areas to be fenced on Kintail and West Affric are planned to protect the existing resource and to encourage regeneration.

Pine stump, West Affric – a remnant or a pioneer?

The Trust's general policy in relation to the restoration of native woodland in the West Affric part of the property is then quite different from that on Kintail. The evidence that the woodland in upper West Affric was disappearing, possibly due to climatic reasons rather than due to the activities of people, was uncovered by a broad ecological and palaeo-ecological study by Stirling University. The results of this study suggest that the single Scots pine in the Trust's property in West Affric is not a relic of a former forest removed by people, but an outlier of the main pine forest in Glen Affric, struggling to survive! Further results of the study suggest that the original woodlands of West Affric were broadleaves made up mainly of birch, hazel and rowan. If this is the case then it would be wrong to artificially encourage the spread of Scots pine in West Affric.

The Trust is not working on its own at West Affric; just as it makes use of the expertise of other voluntary organisations on other sites, here the Trust is co-operating with Trees for Life (TFL). TFL, based at Findhorn, is a voluntary body promoting the restoration of native Caledonian pine woodland. For some time it has been working with FE in the main part of

Glen Affric restoring native Scots pine woodland and has carried out a great deal of preliminary survey work there aimed at restoring its native woodland cover. The Trust's West Affric Management Committee (WAMC), set up after its acquisition, therefore has sought the assistance of TFL in administering, implementing and monitoring the woodland restoration work on West Affric. TFL will collect seed and cuttings of local provenance and raise them in its own nursery for planting, if required. Any planting however, will await the final results of the investigations of Stirling University, which are intended to provide more information on the history of the forests and the reasons for their loss and therefore guide future woodland restoration and management. However, such detailed and intense investigation need not postpone the reduction of grazing pressure and the concomitant natural regeneration of native woodland fragments.

Summation

Kintail was purchased for the Trust by Percy Unna and, according to one of his Principles (Appendix I), there should be no sport stalking of deer, hence the stalking has been kept in hand. However, this is now interpreted as a concern relating to access rather than a condemnation of blood sports. Disturbance to stalking from open access has been shown, not least on West

Hinds

Affric and the Falls of Glomach, to be an over-stated problem. Therefore, as far as the Unna Principles are concerned, there is no reason not to let the stalking on Kintail.

West Affric was acquired, in part, by a donation from the Chris Brasher Trust (CBT), one of whose conditions was also that there should be no commercial stalking, except during the period of the current stalking lease, which has now ended. However, as experience has shown that this poses no threat to open access, the CBT has now accepted a Trust proposal to re-let the stalking, but this time with strict conditions on both the numbers to be culled, the methods to be used in extraction from the hill, and of course with open access. The Trust is now in a position to reduce deer numbers in West Affric to a level which will not damage regeneration of the woodland fragments, as well as making a profit out of the cull! There are surely lessons here for other Trust properties, never mind the other parts of this property. The Trust is also now in a position at West Affric, as at Mar Lodge Estate, to reduce the size of the deer population fairly rapidly, removing the need for any further expensive and intrusive fencing around the woodland remnants.

Open access, which is one of the first principles of management at all Trust properties, perhaps has more of a potential for creating problems of disturbance to wildlife and deer management at this mountain property and at Mar Lodge Estate, than at any other. Torridon is fairly remote, has relatively fewer visitors, has a very small deer population and a fairly restricted mountain bird population. Ben Lawers has a small red deer population, a very important flora vulnerable in some places to trampling, few mountain birds and a large numbers of visitors, who, by and large, stick to the footpaths. Ben Lomond has stock farming, a limited range of vulnerable flora and fauna, and a very large number of visitors who again mainly stick to the footpaths. At Kintail and West Affric, and at Mar Lodge Estate, where there are large red-deer populations requiring relatively intense stalking periods, there are also diverse and important populations of mountain birds vulnerable to disturbance and there are relatively large numbers of visitors who not only walk the paths, but very often have the mountain summits as their main goal. Visitors in these circumstances require a great deal more information in the form of leaflets and staff on the ground than at other mountain properties if they are to understand and support the aims and methods of management. Mar Lodge Estate, through its large endowment, is capable of meeting this need, but at Kintail and West Affric there may be problems in finding funds to support this.

There remains one other grazer on the property, the feral goat, which will have to be dealt with, for they will be the first to find a way through or over fences. Feral goats might be compared by some to sycamore and beech, naturalised and attractive species that are now part of our natural heritage. Unfortunately, a better comparison is with *Rhododendron ponticum*. In their

Feral goats – an endearing addition to our fauna, or a pest?

domestic place they are very attractive and useful, but in the wild they are destructive to our native shrubs and trees, and should be eliminated

Kintail, like Canna, Balmacara, Torridon and Fair Isle, has crofting communities within the property and there is therefore an onus on the Trust to work with them and to help them achieve the best level of management. As at Torridon, the innovative long-term restoration management of the natural resource can only be of benefit to the community, in terms of amenity, landscape and opportunities for at least short-term employment in fence construction, maintenance and deer culling. There may also be employment, both in the future in thinning and extraction, at least on the Crofter Forestry elements and on other conservation projects the Trust is encouraging. Perhaps there is also an opportunity to create local employment (accompanied by training), at least seasonally, by increasing the Ranger presence on the hill to provide information for visitors.

The long-term woodland restoration project will link with and extend the FE work in Glen Affric and TFL's work in the wider West Highlands, while creating new areas of native woodland in Glen Shiel and around the crofting areas at Morvich. Overall, this vision, with its generous investment of effort by a number of government agencies, the Trust and several other voluntary bodies and charities, will result, as at Torridon, in a hugely enhanced landscape and enriched natural environment and perhaps a new optimism in the local communities. It will also mean that the area will become even more attractive to visitors, who will bring more income to the area, but who will need to be sensitively managed.

Chapter 6

Balmacara

Introduction

In this chapter we return to a gentler terrain, but in many ways to a more complex management situation. The natural heritage interests at Balmacara are so diverse and physically intertwined that at first it is, quite literally, difficult to see the wood for the trees. The heart of Balmacara Estate is 15 kilometres or so to the west of Kintail. It is then only another few kilometres until one reaches the Atlantic coast of Scotland, where the landscape and the light can lift the spirits after being so overshadowed by the mountains and clouds of Kintail. At Balmacara there are gardens and woodland policies, ancient woodlands, crofting townships, runrig fields and common grazings, the planned village of Plockton, forestry plantations, an SSSI and a Marine Consultation Area (MCA), and Balmacara Square and Farm, among a number of other interests. Here we are mostly interested in the native woodland, crofting and in the plans for Balmacara Farm itself, but first we need to put them in the context of the whole Estate, its geography and history.

Previous to the nineteenth century, the history of the Estate is poorly documented. Kyle Akin must always have been an important coastal route on this part of the west of Scotland, the alternative route being on the exposed coast to the west of the island of Skye. It was here that King Haakon sheltered his fleet on the way to defeat at Largs in 1263. From then until 1807, Balmacara, like Kintail, was part of the wider estates of the MacKenzies of Seaforth, the last of whom was responsible for the establishment of the village of Plockton (then simply Ploc) in 1794. Like the other west-coast Trust properties, Balmacara was affected by the clearances, and there are still visible remains of old settlements in several places. Thereafter the Estate passed through several hands before it was left to the Trust in 1946 by the Hamilton family, Lochalsh House coming separately to the Trust.

Because much of the Estate is under crofting tenure most of the Trust's management at Balmacara to date has been within the Lochalsh House

Facing page
Crofting landscape, Drumbuie

woodland gardens, apart from one or two footpaths, much of this work being carried out by the Trust's volunteers and those on the Trust's Thistle Camps. The woodland garden covers some 5.26 hectares and has mature trees of Scots pine, larch and beech planted last century. Since the Trust took over there has been considerable development of the gardens including the planting of bamboos, fuchsias, hardy ferns, hydrangeas and Maddenia rhododendrons. There is now a car park, footpaths and an interpretive display in the Coach House, which attract around 5,000 visitors annually.

There was one famous, or infamous development, that very nearly took place at Balmacara, or at Drumbuie to be specific. In the early 1970s, during the North Sea oil boom when there was an ever-increasing demand for oil rigs and oil production platforms, major construction companies raced to find suitable sites to fabricate these huge structures and to reap the huge financial profits. The sites had to be on the Scottish coast, as near to the oil developments as possible, adjacent to deep water, in sheltered situations and backed by a large area of flat land. One such company lit on Drumbuie, which was also served by a railway line, and lodged a planning application to develop a fabrication yard. There was a great deal of discussion locally, and a group of crofters at Drumbuie, concerned for the impact such a huge development would have, formed themselves into an organisation and with widespread support vigorously opposed the development. The Trust supported their stance, fearing the impact of such a large-scale and short-term

Haymaking
on the croft

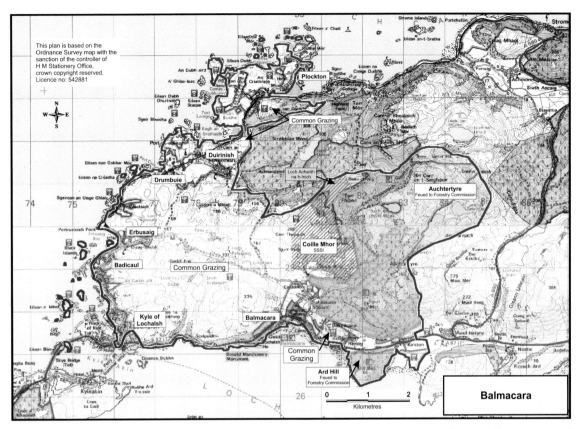

Figure 6.1
Map of the
Kintail and
Balmacara area
(Legend: see p. xviii)

development on such a small community, and was backed by Ross and Cromarty County Council. This was also the first time that the Trust had been put in a position in which it had to defend its inalienable land against major development and, because of this challenge to the Trust's fundamental principles, its case was supported also by the (English) National Trust. The planning application was called in by the Secretary of State for Scotland, the ensuing public inquiry lasted for 46 days and finally found in favour of the Trust. The Trust's share of the cost was £30,000. A fabrication yard was subsequently constructed a short distance away at Kishorn, outside Trust land. That yard had a relatively short life and the extent of the impact that it might have had at Drumbuie can still be seen there quite plainly today.

The Estate of Balmacara runs to 2,272 hectares, which may put it at the lower end of the Trust's countryside properties in scale, but certainly not in complexity. The property includes a small part of the villages of Balmacara and Plockton, the Kyle of Lochalsh, eight crofting townships and large areas of common grazings on which patches of native woodland are scattered. The Trust therefore has a very large number of superiorities and leases, the majority of the latter relating to crofts. One of the principal feus relates to the disposition of 640 hectares to the FC in 1970, to the west of Auchtertyre Hill. Here native oak woodland in the care of the Trust was subsequently ring-barked and underplanted with conifers. With Land Reform proposed under a new Scottish Parliament and particularly the abolition of the feudal elements of Scottish land law, there will have to be a wholesale review by the Trust of the implications for this property in particular. The land feued to FC, if it was ever bought back or sympathetically restructured by the FC, has the potential to make a substantial contribution to the Estate.

The natural heritage

The Kyle peninsula lies on the band of Torridonian sandstones and grits overlying ancient gneiss, that stretches and tapers down Scotland's west coast from Cape Wrath to Islay. Like Torridon itself, the soils of Balmacara are mainly peaty and acid, supporting species-poor moorland and grassland communities. However, there is an area of neutral soils at Coille Mhór and there are other pockets of better soils derived from fluvial and glacial sands and gravels, in addition to those on the raised beach in the main crofting area on the eastern and north-western shores. This latter area, because of its long and continuing history of low-intensity croft management, has a diversity of habitats, including hayfields and grasslands which have attracted corncrakes for many years.

Because of the hummocky nature of the land there are several areas of peat bog and numerous small lochs which drain by burns the short distance to the sea. The lochs are important wildlife sites in their own right, those on open moorland supporting one of the most elegant of our native and northern waterfowl, the red-throated diver. While it prefers small lochs and lochans, its near relative, the black-throated diver, breeding on neighbouring Kintail, prefers larger bodies of water. The latter has its British stronghold in Scotland's north-west mainland, while the red-throated diver is more widespread, breeding also on the western islands and particularly the northern islands, including the lochans on the blanket-bog of the Trust's new property in Unst, Shetland.

The coastal waters and shores of the property, in addition to one or two fine saltmarshes, for example at Kirkton, are also very important for wildlife. The coast from the Plock (lump) of Kyle to Plockton is within the Loch Carron MCA, described as having 'extensive sediment shores which support eel grass beds, rich and diverse bivalve populations in the sand and living maerl . . . exceptionally well represented here'. The bivalves, particularly the mussels, support a large resident eider duck population which, like the large numbers of breeding migrant terns, use the safety of the numerous small islands on which to breed. One particular island also supports a major local heronry. Another island important for its wildlife, and part of the Trust's Balmacara property, although now partly feued to the Scottish Office, is Eilean Dubh, over which passes the Skye bridge. This island is just one of the

Eider duck

many refuges for otters that inhabit these sheltered and shallow coastal waters.

Compared to all the other mainland countryside properties discussed in this book, the landscape of Balmacara is relatively low and rocky, rising to 452 metres (1,483 feet) at Auchtertyre on land feud to FC, but only 266 metres (870 feet) at its second-highest point at Carn Thollaidh. The bulk of the centre of the Estate, on the common grazings, is treeless and wet, undulating acid moorland and grassland. The main areas of semi-natural woodland are along the southern fringe, to the east of the common grazings where the main agricultural holding is situated, and there are corridors of woodland from Erbusaig to Balmacara and at Duirinish and south of Plockton. The crofting townships and inbye are mainly on the west and north-west coast. The Estate is not covered by any landscape designation and does not have the grandeur of the other mountain properties; nevertheless the variety of landforms and vegetation, its position adjacent to the sea and the blend of coastal crofting and rocky moorland create a diverse and attractive landscape. There are also wonderful views to Applecross, Skye, Loch Duich and Kintail.

The main natural heritage feature of nature conservation value on the property is Coille Mhór or 'the big wood' of which 240 hectares is designated as an SSSI. This is an ancient and semi-natural broadleaved woodland of mainly oak (four hectares), ash/hazel (four hectares) and birch, with also hawthorn, rowan and willows, which, as the name suggests, must have always been the largest area of native forest locally, even before areas were felled, or under-planted, between the two World Wars and replanted with conifers. There is a rich diversity of woodland flowers, including woodruff

Coille Mhór and
Auchtertyre Hill

and enchanter's nightshade, and a nationally important woodland lichen flora. The woodland is fairly open in structure, particularly at higher levels where oak gives way to birch as the main species. Here is much wet heath and the open water habitat of Loch Achaidh na h-Inich which has tall fen and floating macrophytes supporting good populations of dragonflies. The loch is also an important frog-spawning area and supports breeding common gull and sandpiper, as well as a variety of visiting summer and winter water-fowl. There are a number of breeding woodland birds including long-tailed tit and great spotted woodpecker, and badgers and pine marten are resident. All these features of native woodland have survived since the end of the last ice age, and, apart from a poor performance from oak, the woodland is showing healthy signs of regeneration due to very low grazing pressure on the common grazings. There is also a significant area of mixed hazel/oak/birch/ash native woodland at Port Ban along the Allt Duirinish and a number of other pockets of native woodland on the Balmacara Estate which are all also naturally regenerating. This is a fairly unique situation among the west-coast ancient oak and ash/hazel woodlands, which here are reaching their north-west limits, demonstrating the potential for their expansion over areas which they used to cover, but which now are either down to common grazing or plantation forestry. There are also problems of bracken growth and *Rhododendron ponticum* infestation in places which are inhibiting regeneration and, in the latter's case, destroying native ground flora also.

Native woodland management

The Trust should encourage sound woodland and habitat management by those who hold the stewardship of the land on the Estate. Liaison with SNH and the FA should focus on the regeneration and maintenance of existing woodland, particularly in and around Coille Mhór.

This is just one of the many aims of the Trust in the 1993–98 Balmacara Management Plan. At the moment several opportunities for further encouragement of native woodland regeneration are being looked into at Coille Mhór such as the erection of fenced enclosures, while there are also opportunities for *Rhododendron ponticum* clearance and the expansion of other areas of native woodland within the croftland and the common grazings through Crofter Forestry. The first active management of any of the native woodland by the Trust, however, is occurring on the fringe along the coast between Balmacara and Kyle of Lochalsh, on land that is in hand. About 106 hectares of woodland here is being fenced off from the common grazings over the next two years under a WGS to allow natural regeneration. There are to be access improvements in this area too, reinstating the original path from Kyle to Balmacara by connecting existing fragments with newly constructed stretches.

In 1998, the last year of the current Plan, through MFS, the opportunity has arisen to give proper recognition to the place of the native woodland as a key natural heritage feature of the Estate. At the time of writing, a proposal is being put together to establish a community woodland extending to 427 hectares, with the support of MFS. This would cover the majority of the existing remnants of native woodland, including Coille Mhór, areas of planted mixed conifer broadleaved woodland at Kyle Hill, old policy woodland and rhododendron-infested Creag nan Garadh at Plockton, and at the same time co-ordinate the variety of separate schemes mentioned above. At all these sites management will only be to encourage natural regeneration of native trees, in some places by thinning or felling exotics, in others by fencing or rhododendron clearance, and in all cases there will be paths and public access. Where there are only small numbers of cattle on the common grazings there may not even be the need for fencing. Although there is a great potential for regenerating and expanding the existing patches of woodland on the common grazings, it is likely that large areas, particularly on the wettest and poorest soils, were never and never will be covered by woodland. However it will be of great interest to those involved in restoring other similar areas on the west coast of Scotland to see, given the opportunity, just how widely natural expansion might occur. If neighbouring estates, including FE, participate and extend the project it could cover almost the whole of the Kyle peninsula west of a line between Kirkton and Plockton. The end result of this proposed project could be an enormous contribution both to the natural heritage and to the economy of the area.

Crofting management

The Trust should encourage local crofters to employ the best current practice in their management of the inbye croftland within the estate, and should take an open view of all Crofter Forestry proposals which meet the criteria stated in the Trust's own Woodland Policy.

The Trust should attempt to reduce the level of absenteeism and encourage new entrants to crofting who intend to manage their crofts more actively.

Crofting represents by far the largest form of land use at Balmacara, there being eight townships, namely: Badicaul, Balmacara, Drumbuie, Duirinish, Erbusaig, Plockton, Port an Eorna and Kirkton, composed of 75 crofts with 123.5 hectares of inbye and 1,059.4 hectares of common grazings. Of all the properties with crofting tenure, discussed in this book, only Fair Isle with 157.8 hectares, has a larger area of inbye (Iona, not discussed in this book, has 224.8 hectares of inbye). A large area of inbye on its own, of course, does not necessarily mean there will be active and successful crofting units: soils, climate and other factors, as we will see in a moment, are just as important.

At Plockton, a relatively large township and planned village, there are

Corncrake

absentee tenants and only a handful of active crofters. There is very limited arable management, but cattle are run on the common grazings, which includes the village and the streets! The bulk of the croftland here was lost when a previous owner, Sir Alexander Mathieson, who was otherwise a good landlord, took it away in the mid-eighteenth century to build his 'castle' at Duncraig. At Badicaul there are four crofters, the common grazing is very poor and there is little active crofting. At Port an Eorna, on the other hand, the Trust has supported the establishment of five new-entrant crofters. At Erbusaig, which was once a fishing village until it was cut off from the sea by the railway line in 1897, there are six crofts. At Balmacara itself, ten crofts were created in the early 1920s under Lloyd George's Land Settlement Act (1918) which was enacted to give land to the returning soldiers from the First World War. Later, five of the crofts were taken into the Balmacara Farm, when they fell into disuse and one was feued. Under Balmacara Square we shall discuss the radical steps being taken by the Trust to revitalise this area.

The most active crofting townships on the Estate are at Drumbuie and Duirinish, which, along with Fair Isle on Trust properties, disprove the myth that cropping on croftland is dead. The two townships share the same flat area; but it is the former, with its majority of active crofters, who have proved to be among the most successful in Scotland. Twice, the Drumbuie crofters have been runner-up for the Crofting Township of the Year, presented annually by SNH in conjunction with the Scottish Crofters Union, and in 1996, a year after Fair Isle, they won the award. At Drumbuie the inbye is managed in the traditional manner under runrig, that is with each croft having scattered individual strips of the unfenced and contiguous small-scale fields. The fields are run under a five-year rotational cropping regime that includes oats, potatoes, turnips and grass or silage. In the summer all domestic stock are kept out of the inbye, from 1st April to 1st November, after which they are let loose within the township.

The only fenced areas are where cattle may be kept in late or where early grass growth, from February, is being encouraged, either for an early bite or for cover for corncrakes. Several crofters at Balmacara, covering 3.5 acres of the inbye, have joined the Corncrake Habitat Scheme and taken up the Trust's own Early Cover Scheme which involves protection of small areas from early grazing and in some cases the planting of iris and cow parsley.

The result of traditional management on the property is an agriculturally productive area of very high natural heritage value, with semi-natural, species-rich grasslands, crops and tall-herb meadows that are the breeding and feeding areas for a great deal of wildlife, including a number of otherwise declining bird species such as the skylark and the twite. Walking through the rigs of Drumbuie in midsummer one is surrounded by a riot of colourful and scented flowers, a buzz of insects and a flutter of small birds, all set within a patchwork of different textures spreading out from the small

Haymeadow, Plockton

collection of houses. Without fences it is like having the freedom of some-one's garden: in flower are eyebrights, sorrel, clovers, buttercups, orchids such as the white and slim lesser-butterfly and the brilliant northern marsh, both red and yellow rattle, bitter vetch and grasses, such as Yorkshire fog, timothy and sweet vernal grass, to name but very few. Standing in the township of Drumbuie overlooking the well-managed and attractive scene it is sobering to reflect that if this was a single farm, run by a single family, it would probably not be economically viable.

Why is it that the crofting township of Drumbuie works where many others do not? The reason is probably the result of a collection of factors, simple, complex and fortuitous. The first and basic condition is that there is a relatively good soil and climate: this corner of Kyle, lying on low ground and by the sea, may benefit from being in the rain shadow of Skye. Second, as on Fair Isle, there are other job opportunities that hold the young, that offer flexible hours, but not so well-paid and attractive that the young no longer want the crofting lifestyle. Third, there is an indefinable community spirit which means that the majority in the township are active, and finally there are one or two leaders in the community. Community spirit creates a self-support system that means one crofter can agree with another, often of the same family, to maximise their skills and interests, whereby one may look after the crops on both crofts while the other looks after the stock; or as on Fair Isle where the cost of maintaining machinery is shared. At Drumbuie it may help that all the houses are grouped together and not scattered and adjacent to their own fields. It may also be that the battle against the oil rig construction proposals helped to unite the township and reminded people of the quality of life they already had. There is also a kind of feedback which kicks in at a certain level of active management, giving a sense of self-confidence to the township partnership, that makes people want to play an active part, and also makes it difficult for individuals to absent themselves from management. There is no doubt that the traditional structure of management at Drumbuie is helped by the fact that the houses do not take up any good ground, but are situated on the grazings. The runrig system, with its absence of fences, also means that all in the township must co-operate in management, particularly in the timing of the introduction and withdrawal of grazing stock, and that it is not straightforward for anyone to turn to permanent grassland and introduce sheep without the additional cost of fencing. Drumbuie and Duirinish are, however, exceptions to the rule and it has to be said that there are many inactive crofts and absentee crofters on the Balmacara property.

Balmacara Square

Almost from the moment it purchased Fair Isle in 1954 the Trust has been active in supporting the crofting community there. The Trust's attitude to crofting generally, however, has regularly been that of the traditional

Twite

Balmacara Square,
looking towards Skye

landlord, often acting as a quasi-planning authority, and it had the
unfortunate reputation for raising niggling objections to building improvements and setting awkward conditions to developments. Support and
encouragement to crofters on Trust land has been variable, but relatively
recently it has become more widespread and proactive, for example through
encouraging conservation management for corncrakes. The Trust's attitude
to community support continues to evolve and this can most recently be seen
in its active involvement with crofters in encouraging Countryside Premium
Schemes and Crofter Forestry, such as at Kintail. The most novel developments, each in their own way, however, are at Fair Isle where the Trust is
working in partnership in some areas, and at Balmacara Square where, for
the first time on Trust land, new crofts are being created. In both cases a
number of other public bodies are involved, whose finance and experience
are essential to the success of such projects. At Balmacara they include Skye
and Lochalsh Enterprise, Highland Council, Crofters Commission (CC),
SNH, Scottish Homes and funds from Leader II, all contributing to a project
that will cost in the region of £1 million!

The home farm at Balmacara Square extends to 149 hectares of which
37.8 hectares (93.4 acres) is arable. Up until 1992 the whole farm was leased
as one unit and from then until now it has been leased as three grazing units.
It has to be said that, while some of the crofting areas such as Drumbuie and
Duirinish were being well managed, the home farm fell into some neglect, or
at least was not managed to its potential. The neglect was not just of the land

itself, but of the early nineteenth-century B-listed farm buildings used by the crofters until 1992. Over the last few years, however, the Trust has been developing plans to revitalise the buildings and the land: plans that will create new opportunities for the local community which amounts to no less than resettlement! In the final chapter I will return to the revitalisation of the Highlands and Islands; suffice it here that this step by the Trust is extraordinarily radical, setting it irrevocably on a new course, which will have repercussions across its many activities and properties in the future. And it is not just *what* the Trust is doing here, but *how* it is doing it, that is of interest.

The centre of the plan is to restore the steadings and convert them to use as five long-let houses, plus four craft units, Ranger base and as an interpretive focus. With other upgrading of the immediate environs, such as the mill pond, public parking and a possible partnership arrangement between the Trust, the community and FE over neighbouring forest land, the whole area will be improved and more attractive both to live in and visit. The heart of the plan however, is the creation of eight new crofts on the original home farm, the tenants of which will become the new managers of the countryside and, through management agreements with the Trust, the custodians of the natural heritage.

Under the Crofters (Scotland) Act 1993, it is not possible to create new croft land, so the Trust is having to use a little imaginative, but quite legal, sleight of hand, to carry through its aims. Luckily at Balmacara there were still four out of the ten original crofts created under the 1918 Act. It is quite legal, with the agreement of the landlord and the Secretary of State, to extend these grazings and then apportion them to existing crofts. These will then be subdivided to create new crofts. So at Balmacara the grazings will be extended over the original home farm and then the inbye broken into eight parts, each to be of between two and seven hectares.

At the same time the Trust has held public meetings and established a locally and democratically elected community liaison group to work on the project during both the planning stage and subsequent management of the area. Effectively, a new partnership model is being explored between the community and the Trust as landowner, with both represented on a management committee, who will select the tenants. A condition of tenure for the new tenants will be a management agreement covering conservation and that removes the crofter's right to buy. This latter point may have to have the approval of the Land Court.

Summation

The principal aim of Trust management at Balmacara states:

> *The Trust should ensure the permanent preservation, for the benefit of the nation, of the Balmacara Estate with its crofting-based community and unusually wide range of interests including countryside/nature conservation, coastline, architecture, gardens and probably archaeology. The conservation of virtually all these aspects should be carried out by a co-ordinated approach with the local community.*

Perhaps the key points here for the natural heritage are the recognition of the importance of the human community and the importance of the need to manage the Estate '*with* the local community'.

The new model of a landlord/tenant relationship at Balmacara Square, involving democratic representation of the tenants on a management committee, which taps both the energy and experience of the local community and the support – financial and political – of the landlord, is one that is going to be watched with some interest by many other communities and landowners throughout Scotland. To the natural heritage of both the inbye and common grazings it brings active, integrated and sustainable management under the mutual agreement of landlord, tenant and the community. Of course, this is not a complete partnership in the full sense of the term as the Trust's land is held inalienably. However, it is a courageous and generous step by the Trust and surely must offer the opportunity, on the basis of goodwill at the very least, to enter into a closer and more co-operative relationship with the existing crofting townships on the Estate, perhaps resulting in more of the inbye land being brought back into good management. Perhaps also crofters will make more use of the Trust as landlord, in relation to absenteeism.

The benefits of such co-operation, which could be multiplied several times with the support of MFS, to one of the most important elements of the natural heritage at Balmacara – the native woodland – could be inestimable. If such co-operation could include agreement on grazing levels and the outlawing of muirburn there could be lasting benefits to the common grazings. This, as we have seen, would allow the woodland resource to expand dramatically and become of as much value to the community as it is to the natural heritage. Perhaps here too, as at Ben Lawers and recently suggested by the Woodland Trust at Glen Finglas, consideration might be given to supporting the shepherding of grazing stock on the common grazings, to the further benefit of woodland regeneration and employment.

The Trust should carry out an acquisition appraisal of the Forest Enterprise (FE) land which was once part of the Balmacara Estate and encourage FE to sell those areas identified as most suitable on sound conservation grounds back to the Trust.

This management objective is presently fifteenth in the Management Plan, which is an indication of its priority as far as the Trust is concerned. However, as a clause in the feu charter obliges the FE to discuss the future management of the forest in regard to conservation amenity and recreation with the Trust anyway, there is perhaps little reason to try to resume ownership. Either way the integration of management of the FE land with that of the Trust offers some exciting opportunities. First, there are the areas of the feued land still containing elements of native woodland adjacent to the Coille Mhór woodland SSSI, which could be restored if properly managed. Second, would be the opportunity to restructure the plantation to make it both contribute more positively to the landscape and improve its amenity value to locals and visitors. At the present moment, through the Balmacara Project Liaison Group, there is in fact discussion with FE about the possibility of tripartite partnership covering the management of the forest. However, if the feued plantation were to be re-purchased in its entirety it could play a key part in making the whole Estate financially viable.

At Balmacara the Trust has the opportunity, more than on any other property, to demonstrate how a large and diverse estate can be managed in partnership with the local community and others, to the benefit of the natural heritage and to the community. The property also demonstrates the concomitant need for the Trust *and* communities, to be able to bring together the bewildering number of funding bodies and to be able to produce integrated plans. Having already taken the first radical steps at Balmacara Square, the Trust should push on and further extend the boundaries of true holistic management.

Chapter 7

Mar Lodge Estate

Introduction

The Cairngorm Mountains, including Mar Lodge Estate, right in the physical heart of Scotland, have the most severe climate of all the properties discussed. This is an area dominated by hard and unrelenting granite rock that rises to a peak of 1,309 metres at Ben Macdui, the second highest in Britain. From its cairn one can walk 5 kilometres north over the high plateau to Cairn Gorm itself (1,245 m) and on and down to Glenmore beyond. Immediately, in all other directions however, the ground drops dramatically. To the west the slope plunges 700 metres over forbidding screes to the Lairig Ghru, that deep, narrow, long and rugged pass that links Rothiemurchus and the Spey to Mar Lodge Estate and the headwaters of the Dee, and on the south, links to another path through Glen Tilt to Atholl. On its high, northern rim, Mar Lodge Estate holds the largest alpine zone in Britain with all its very specialised plants and birds, and on its lower slopes some of the largest remnants of the Caledonian pine forest, that once dominated the northern uplands of Scotland. The word Caledonia, incidentally, comes from the *Caledones*, a Pictish tribe who occupied the Central Highlands for several centuries more than 1,500 years ago.

Around 500 million years ago, in the area which is now the Highlands of Scotland, a great thickness of sediment was laid down on the floor of an ancient ocean. Subsequently these sediments were uplifted and metamorphosed into schists, such as at Kintail and Ben Lawers for example, during the great Caledonian Orogeny, creating mountains of alpine proportion. During this time vast quantities of magma formed below these sediments and gradually rose through the earth's crust. At some places they spilled through the upper layers, as at Glencoe. At other places, notably the Cairngorms, they rose only to within a few kilometres of the surface where they condensed into granite. Millions of years of erosion followed removing some of the schists and revealing the granite core which is now the Cairngorms.

More recently, only 2.5 million years ago, following hundreds of millions of years of erosion, there was a major cooling of the climate and glaciers formed over the mountains. It was these series of glaciers that carved out the present outlines of the mountains of Scotland and the shape of the Cairngorms and that of Mar Lodge Estate that we see today, deepening and shaving the sides of existing glens, carving through original watersheds and creating the multitude of corries, such as at Braeriach and Beinn à Bhuird, around the edge of the plateaux. Rock and gravel debris from the retreating glacier, from 10–15,000 years ago, left moraines on the valley sides and floors: meltwater sometimes cutting through bedrock to form channels, which are now dry, and redistributing morainic sands and gravels in the lower glens. At the end of the Ice Age, while temperatures rose fairly rapidly on the low ground, they remained low in the mountains, causing frost action to shatter rocks, producing extensive blockfields on the plateaux and screes on steep slopes. Freezing and thawing of the water in the thin soils still continues to this day, producing stone-striping, terracing and lobes of debris at the higher altitudes.

All these immense and varied geological and geomorphological activities in the Cairngorms have created a unique mountain landscape of international importance, where the whole story is laid out for our interpretation in the rounded summits, the deep glens and corries, the moraines and screes: an ancient and worn face that may be the future for the, as yet, young and chiselled features of the Alps, the Rockies and the Himalayas.

The development of the vegetation and early human settlement

The soils that formed from these acidic granite and schistose rocks and their morainic debris, when fresh, were relatively richer than they are today. Through aeons of rainfall they have become leached, now lack important minerals and cannot support the diversity of plants that can be found on the calcareous rocks of Ben Lawers or Glencoe. On the summits and ridges this acid soil is thin and well drained, supporting a sparse vegetation characterised by three-leaved rush and woolly hair-moss, and in the slightly drier eastern part by lichens. Only on the occasional lime-rich flush on the higher slopes, as at Dalvorar, is there any quantity of minerals such as calcium, that can support the more demanding plants species, such as the yellow saxifrage and the Scottish asphodel. In 'snow-beds' where snow-lie may persist well into the spring and early summer, the plant cover is mat grass and lichens with prostrate alpine lady's mantle and the tiny sibbaldia with its beautiful, blueish-green leaves. This is the realm of the dotterel, the snow bunting and the ptarmigan, arctic species that, like many of their plant companions, are species on the edge of their range in the British Isles and that may come under threat from climatic change.

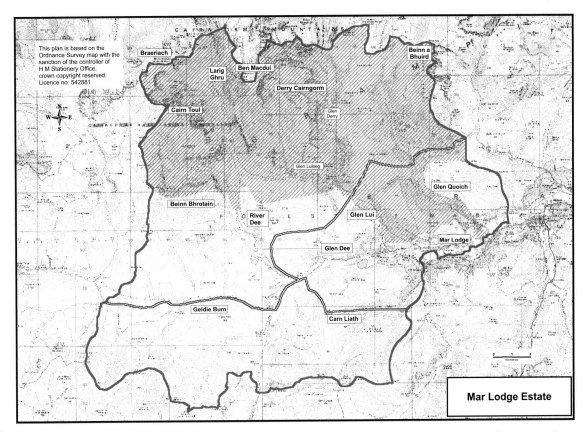

This plan is based on the Ordnance Survey map with the sanction of the controller of H M Stationery Office, crown copyright reserved. Licence no: 542881

Braeriach

Larig Ghru

Ben Macdui

Beinn a Bhuird

Derry Cairngorm

Cairn Toul

Glen Derry

Glen Luibeg

Glen Quoich

Beinn Bhrotain

River Dee

Glen Lui

Mar Lodge

Glen Dee

Geldie Burn

Carn Liath

Mar Lodge Estate

Figure 7.1
Map of the
Mar Lodge Estate area
(Legend: see p. xviii)

Below the level of the highest plateaux, but at the level of many other ridges and summits, between 900–1,000 metres, the dwarf-shrub heath is dominated by wind-pruned heather, with mountain azalea also common. It is also rich in the berries that are important for birds (and quite tasty for humans!), such as the slightly bitter black berries of crowberry, the red of bearberry and the mauve of blaeberry.

Peat now covers large areas of Mar Lodge Estate below about 900 metres, supporting open heather moorland, with deer grass and purple moor-grass. Under the pines, although still acid, occurs a less peaty soil, and under birch, peat is virtually absent and there is a brown and more fertile soil. Birch of course is a soil 'improver', unlike pine and heather which are acidifiers. Below about 600 metres Scots pine, for which the poor granite soils of the Cairngorms and its cold winter climate are ideal, has come to dominate the forests that developed around the periphery of the mountains. Subsidiary species to pine and birch are rowan and aspen, and the main shrub is juniper. Tree species that require better soils, such as oak and elm, and shrubs such as hazel and the montane willows, are mostly absent, although alder and other willows would have been common along the lower reaches of watercourses.

The first human visitors to the area would have found that the broadleaved trees of the lower Dee gradually gave way to a mixed forest of birch and pine with juniper as they made their way up the river. Below the

tree-line therefore there would have been a mosaic of habitats alternating between forest and moorland. Above, they would have found the pine and birch gradually becoming less vigorous and more stunted. Then they would have passed through the area of sub-alpine scrub until the last remnants of the forest and scrub gave way to an open moorland of dwarf shrubs and then finally the fellfield terrain of sparse vegetation, gravel and bare unvegetated boulder. Today that scene, above the scrub-line, is almost unchanged; but below, over the course of some 8,000 years, there has been substantial alteration to the original resource.

The impact of Mesolithic people with their primitive tools on the area of Mar Lodge Estate would have been minimal. The Neolithic farmers and their antecedents that followed over the next thousand years however, had much more impact by grazing, burning and cultivation. The Cairngorm soils, as we have noted, are inherently poor and from the earliest days making a living must have been hard. The periphery of the mountains have always been only marginal areas for farming, and the agricultural description – 'less favoured' – is a kind term for such land. It is clear that in some areas pine and birch woodland survived within the Mar Lodge Estate and right down the Dee at least as far as the present Muir of Dinnet (where birch is making a come-back today) well into historical times.

The area called Mar, which originally stretched from the Dee to the Don and as far westwards into the Cairngorms as Mar Lodge Estate today, was one of the seven original earldoms of the new Alba established by the unification of the Scots and the Picts almost a thousand years ago, and it probably existed as one of the Pictish fiefdoms well before that! In late medieval times, the earldom fell into the hands of the Royal House of

Stewart and the forests of the estate became a favourite hunting ground. In 1565 Mary Queen of Scots granted the lands of Mar to Lord Erskine (of Mar). During this period control was maintained by the owners on tree felling so as not to interfere with hunting. Ironically, considering the threat that red deer pose to much of our remaining native woodland today, it was possibly the very fact that the Forest of Mar was a hunting forest, that saved the trees from complete destruction.

Later history, the forest and red deer

Following a thousand years of slow decline of the forests and the sub-alpine scrub, it was the political and religious clashes from the seventeenth century that were the catalysts for the next great environmental changes in the vicinity of Mar Lodge Estate, as they were for other large areas of Highland Scotland. After the failed Jacobite rising of 1715 the Earl of Mar lost his lands to Lord Grange and Lord Dun. These new owners began to exploit the forests in a way their predecessors had not and dramatic changes occurred to the forested landscape of Mar Lodge Estate over the next 100 years. In 1735 Mar was then purchased by Lord Braco of Kilbryde in Ireland. He was elevated in 1750 to Earl of Fife and Viscount MacDuff, and for another 200 years the estates remained in the hands of his descendants.

What then happened to the remnants of the Caledonian pine forest on Mar Lodge Estate during this period? Saw mills had already been established in Glen Lui and Glen Quoich by the end of the seventeenth century. Through the early part of the eighteenth century the commercial extraction of pine appears to have co-existed with farming and hunting. The remains of 22 townships along with their small patches of cultivated fields have been recorded on the estate (not necessarily all occupied at the same time), mostly on the lower ground. Their occupants once grazed their animals in certain parts of the forest and of course took their domestic cattle and primitive sheep stock higher up the glens to the summer grazings at the shieling. The remains of 300 of these shielings have been found on Mar Lodge Estate and this gives an indication of both the human population and the grazing pressures which must have existed at that time. In 1726, however, when the then landowner, Lord Grange, perceived conflict between his timber and his tenants in Glen Lui and had the latter cleared. Following extraction of the timber, resettlement was allowed and this pattern was apparently repeated in the upper glens throughout the eighteenth century. Even though this occurred only a couple of hundred years ago it is difficult for us with our relative security of tenure and employment, or at least state support, to imagine being uprooted lock, stock and barrel, and thrown out of our homes with all our worldly goods with no means of support for ourselves and our children. The attitude shown at this time by the landowners towards the tenants was also reflected in the clearance of the townships on the haughlands around the newly named house of Mar Lodge itself. As on many Scottish estates at this time the environs of the 'house' were landscaped by the establishment of parkland and woodland policies of tree species recently arrived from the New World.

The exploitation of the native forest however continued and by 1776 Glen Lui was said to consist of only thousands of tree stumps, and 50 years later in 1826 there was no woodland at all left in the upper part of that glen. Although clearances of settlements for sheep took place on many estates in Scotland from the late eighteenth and through the nineteenth centuries, as occurred at Kintail, Ben Lawers and Glencoe for example, the poor heather hills and the bitterly cold winters on the Cairngorms made them unsuitable for large-scale sheep farming and there were no clearances for those reasons on Mar Lodge. Sheep farming on Mar Lodge Estate was in fact abandoned by the mid-nineteenth century. From then on red deer and sport became the *raison d'être* of the estate management, and in Glen Ey, then part of the Mar Lodge Estate, in 1840, a whole settlement of nine clachans was cleared to provide pasture for these animals, such had become their importance in the eyes of the owner.

The results of this exploitation of the Forest of Mar, combined with an increasing grazing pressure, was a total loss of pinewood from the upper

Glen Lui, Scots pine remnants

Red deer

glens Luibeg, Derry and Quoich; and its gradual fragmentation in the lower parts of these glens and in Glen Lui, and the loss of pinewood on the southern facing slopes of Creag Bhalg above the present Lodge linking the latter with Glen Quoich. But not only were the very trees removed: by the end of the eighteenth century the grazing pressure from red deer had reached a level such that there was to be no regeneration for the next 200 years. The forest, although not barren, had become moribund.

In the Victorian era plantations of conifers were established in several places such as the Linn of Dee, Linn of Quoich and at Derry Lodge, possibly regarded as some atonement for the loss of native woodland. During and after the two World Wars there was further exploitation of Scots pine for timber and therefore further loss of the native pinewood, notably the felling on Creag Bhalg by the Canadian foresters in World War II. Later in the 1970s further plantations were established primarily for deer management purposes, but also for timber. As with earlier plantations some Scots pine was planted. After the Cairngorms became a National Nature Reserve efforts were made by the Nature Conservancy to encourage the owners to protect the pinewood and several small experimental enclosures were erected in the 1950s, with some planting of trees of local origin in Derry Wood, Upper Glen Derry and Luibeg. In the 1980s further small enclosures were erected at Luibeg and Glen Derry, totalling around 50 hectares.

In the second half of the nineteenth century, with the giving over of much of the Estate to stalking, red-deer numbers rose. To manage this deer forest three substantial lodges – Bynack, Geldie and Derry – were then constructed for gamekeepers and shooting parties. The effect was a deer population out of balance with the natural resource on which it depended and quite inimical to forest regeneration, hence the moribund state of the woodlands and pine forests. There are few figures for past red-deer numbers on the estate. A Red Deer Commission survey in 1983 counted a total of 3,634; Scottish Natural Heritage estimated 5,568 in 1991 and 4,489 in 1993. The lower figure for 1993 has been ascribed to a heavier than usual cull over the winter of 1992/93. This was a period of mild winters when a high survival rate meant a rising population throughout Scotland, unless culls also rose, as they did at Mar Lodge Estate under the ownership of John Kluge from 1989 to 1995. When NTS acquired the estate in 1995 the total number of red deer was 3,353.

Surveying the history of land use of Mar Lodge Estate it is apparent that there was a gradual and long-term increase in the number of people using the land from a very early period. The rate of increase rose sharply in the seveenth century to a peak in the early eighteenth century, with expansion of subsistence agriculture. Thereafter, following clearances for forestry and red deer in the eighteenth and nineteenth centuries, the number of people living and working on the Estate fell dramatically. In recent years the inhabitants have been restricted to a core staff involved with the principal aims of management – sporting, with some agricultural and forestry employment, and staff to run, often seasonally, the 'big house' and the lodges. Basically such a staff consisted of stalkers, gamekeeper, seasonal ghillies, an estate foreman and support, and housekeepers. Around 10–12 permanent staff and their families are housed in estate cottages.

Access to and through the land, prior to sporting management last century, was freely available. There were the old drove roads through the Lairig Ghru, Lairig an Laoigh and over to Glen Tilt which were also footpaths for the locals. With the development of deer stalking, the clearance of settlements, and the construction of lodges, came the pony paths and, latterly, roads for the conveyance of staff and guests high up into the moorlands. As the 'tradition' of sporting management, including that for grouse shooting and salmon fishing, developed and its financial return to the Estate increased, access for non-staff was increasingly inhibited. Where there were once small agricultural communities well up the glens with livestock driven higher to the shieling in the summer months, then Victorian lodges for gamekeeper and guests, there are now only ruins. Where subsistence-agriculture families lived and worked and were replaced by gamekeepers and their families, there are now only footpaths and a few bulldozed roads. The owner, the stalker, the gamekeeper and the sportsmen do not want their livelihood and their sport threatened or disturbed. The early Rights of Way campaigners, however, won limited access to certain traditional paths.

Since the 1940s the number of walkers using the Cairngorms has increased more than twenty-fold, and estates such as Mar Lodge have been unable to stem the flow; rather they have tried to learn to live with it, albeit discouraging access to certain areas and seasons to minimise disturbance to the stalk or the shoot. Apart from the problems associated with disturbance – the occasional loss of a good stag to a client, or half a day's hind culling – estates have been faced with the enormous and growing problem of damage to footpaths by the growing numbers of walkers who are perceived as using estate land but contributing nothing to its finances.

The natural heritage and designations

So we have briefly scanned the history of 10,000 years on Mar Lodge Estate. Today the scene, above the scrub-line, is almost unchanged; but below, over the course of some 8,000 years, there has been substantial change to the original resource. In the case of the Forest of Mar it has been the destruction of virtually all of the sub-alpine scrub zone and most of the Caledonian pine forest with its diverse communities of plants and animals, and the creation of a very much enlarged and impoverished moorland below the tree-line. These moorlands today support grouse and waders, mountain hare and, in winter, the occasional deer carcass, all of which help support golden eagles. There are also merlin on the moorland and peregrine on some of the crags of the estate.

The pinewood in Mar Lodge Estate today only occupies approximately 6.5 per cent of the land up to the estimated tree-line, which is an indication of how little is left. Within those remaining pinewoods, whose peripheral trees are so sparse they more or less inhabit moorland, there is a limited 'woodland' ground vegetation with a few specifically pine or birch woodland plants such as twin flower. There are, however, a number of woodland animals, such as wood ants, a few capercaillie, black grouse, red squirrel, roe and red deer, and notably the Scottish crossbill. There are also otter occasionally. Most importantly however, these pinewoods, limited as they are, actually constitute 5 per cent of the remaining native pinewood in Scotland.

From the mountains and from the few corrie lochs the burns cascade rapidly to their confluence with the Dee, often over unstable shingle and polished bedrock. Their clear and acidic water holds few nutrients and supports little aquatic vegetation or invertebrates; neither are there many shrubs and trees to cool the shallow water in the summer months; nevertheless, these are still the spawning grounds for the Dee salmon. Below the Linn of Dee, as the river enters its flood plain, it widens and its bed becomes more stable. From here it winds its way, sometimes in broad loops, in front of Mar Lodge itself and on past Braemar. On the flats at Allana-quoich (where the Quoich joins the Dee) there has been much drainage and river-bank building in the past, to control flooding and to improve grazing. The area, however, still supports a number of wetland bird species such as oystercatcher, curlew, lapwing, redshank, sandpiper and snipe. The Trust has now blocked some of the drainage to re-create a rich wetland area which will complement the other natural features of the property.

Red squirrel

Standing on Carn Liath today, with its incredible view north-west into the heart of the Cairngorms, west over unremitting moorland and north to the only visible remnants of the pinewood in Glen Lui and Glen Derry, it is hard to imagine that once there was a rich forest of pine and birch, ringing with the sounds of capercaillie and blackcock and alive with the shadows of red deer and the brown bear, stretching from the alluvial floor of the Dee, perhaps to within a kilometre of one's feet and threading its way up all the tributaries in the distance: the Geldie; the Dee itself, perhaps as far as the Lairig Ghru (as the adjacent Glen Geusachan means 'Glen of the Little Pine Wood'); the upper parts of Glen Luibeg, Glen Derry and Glen Quoich. Standing on Carn Liath perhaps just a few thousand years ago, one may have been hidden by a scrub of stunted birch, pine and juniper, instead of standing only ankle-deep in a sea of heather.

Notwithstanding past human management of this part of the Cairngorms, Mar Lodge Estate has a wealth of wildlife and landscape designations both national and European, with only the area south of a line through the bed of the Geldie Burn, Carn Liath to Carn Bhithir in the east, without any designation. There are two NSAs and two SSSIs; the Cairngorms SSSI was notified in recognition of the international importance of the Cairngorm

Massif, its geology and its extensive arctic character, and the Eastern Cairngorms notified for the finest and most extensive high plateau and snow-bed habitat in Britain. In 1954 the former became a National Nature Reserve (NNR).

Part of Mar Lodge Estate qualifies as an SPA on account of its internationally important populations of the Scottish crossbill and nationally important populations of golden eagle, peregrine, merlin, osprey, capercaillie and dotterel. Mar Lodge Estate's habitat qualifications as an SAC are a little more esoteric but no less important than the bird and animal species which inhabit them. They range from species-rich mat grass grassland to a variety of heathlands, from alpine and sub-alpine to dry and wet; from high-level spring communities, and scree and rock crevice vegetation, to bog woodland and Caledonian forest. The only other sites designated for their wildlife (or lack of it!) on Mar Lodge Estate, are the *Ramsar* sites of Loch Etchachan and Loch Uaine. These are high-level, arctic-alpine, corrie lochs with few nutrients typically supporting very simple floras and faunas.

As far back as 1945 the Cairngorms, along with Glencoe and Ben Lomond, was recommended as a National Park by the Scottish National Parks Survey or 'Ramsay' Committee and later by the CCS in their 1990 report *The Mountain Areas of Scotland*. In 1992 the Cairngorms were included within the Cairngorms Partnership area established by the Secretary of State, which has meant that there is now a greater effort to co-ordinate all aspects of management of the whole area, from Tomintoul to Atholl and Laggan to Aboyne, including Mar Lodge Estate. Most recently, in 1998, the Cairngorms were recommended by SNH to the Secretary of State; once again, as a National Park. This time the recommendation has been accepted and the Government intends to bring forward legislation to the Scottish Parliament to enable a Cairngorms National Park to be operational from April 2002. The Cairngorms are also on the list of United Kingdom candidate sites in the 'natural' category for nomination under the World Heritage Convention, but as yet there has been no submission. The only extant World Heritage Site in Scotland in the 'natural' category at the moment, is of course the Trust property of St Kilda.

Acquisition by NTS

From the moment it came on the market Mar Lodge Estate was seen by the Scottish public as not just another Scottish sporting estate that would probably be sold to the highest bidder, but as an exceptional part of Scotland's natural heritage and history, a part of the ancient Forest of Mar and, with the recent establishment of the Cairngorms Partnership, an opportunity to extend sustainable management over another key part of the Cairngorm Mountains. Conservationists and naturalists were particularly excited as, within the Cairngorms, of which a large chunk is an NNR, the Estate of Abernethy is in the hands of the RSPB, Rothiemurchus has a management agreement with SNH, the FC own Glenmore Forest Park, HIE own the northern (ski) slopes of Cairn Gorm, while SNH own Inshriach. In addition Glen Feshie (part of the NNR) was at that time up for sale also and a consortium of conservation bodies with the backing of SNH were seeking to purchase it. The acquisition of Mar Lodge Estate by another conservation body would then virtually complete the Cairngorms jigsaw and bring into being by far the largest area in Scotland managed primarily for its natural heritage.

When NNRs were first established not long after the end of World War II, they were legal, but gentlemanly, agreements between the government agency, the then Nature Conservancy (subsequently SNH) and the owners, but these agreements did little more than support the management *status quo*. In retrospect we can see that on the whole these agreements sadly achieved very much less than the original objectives. In some cases, as in the Glenfeshie part of the Cairngorms NNR for example, they were powerless to prevent further degradation of the natural environment through the continuation of high red-deer numbers and suppression of natural regeneration of the pine forest, further establishment of commercial plantations and the extension of hill tracks for sporting purposes.

With the possible purchase of Mar Lodge Estate by the Trust, it was seen by conservationists that there was an opportunity, for the first time, to rationalize red-deer management across several estate boundaries in the Cairngorms and to take in hand the protection and extension of the four key pinewood remnants on the west, north and east; respectively Glen Feshie, Rothiemurchus and Glenmore, Abernethy and Mar Lodge Estate.

In 1994, the adjacent Glen Feshie Estate was purchased by the Wills Woodland Trust, an English conservation charity, despite attempted purchase by a consortium of Scottish voluntary bodies. A great deal of secret discussion therefore took place among the Scottish conservation charities behind closed doors, also involving SNH to ensure that ownership of Mar Lodge Estate did not slip away. The problem, as always, was not just the raising of the purchase price for the estate (likely to be of the order of £5 million), but the need to raise an even larger sum to act as an endowment to provide the finance for long-term management.

Why should such large sums be needed to purchase and manage such unproductive land, whose natural resources had been so abused for so long? There are several reasons. First the 'tradition' associated with hunting the 'royal' stag, the romantic myths attached to the Highlands of Scotland, and the fact that many estates are in the ownership of the Scottish 'establishment', membership of which may be bought with the purchase of an estate. Second, Scotland, alas, is still one of the few countries where anyone, from anywhere, as long as they have the cash, can purchase a large tract of land as a private playground. There is therefore great competition for ownership which has pushed up the price away above the true value of the land. Additionally, the price of an estate is often dependent on the capitalisation of the price per head of stags – the more stags the higher the price – which is one of the reasons so many estates have large deer numbers. Even so, because of the condition of the land, there is usually no profit to be made from such properties: investment in buildings, services and staff will always exceed income from red deer, grouse, forestry or agriculture. This means that one needs to be a person, company or Trust of substantial financial standing to be able to own such property. In the case of management for conservation or rehabilitation of the land, without an endowment, the cost is prohibitive.

The NTS, like other voluntary conservation bodies, was interested in Mar Lodge Estate, but had no funds of its own available to consider taking on such a responsibility. Then, out of the blue, an anonymous trust – the Easter Charitable Trust (ECT), which apparently was keen to see the estate purchased by a Scottish conservation charity – offered the Trust a substantial part of the purchase cost, if the Trust could find the remainder of the asking price and the sum needed as an endowment. Over the following year negotiations were held between the Trust and the owner (Kluge), and between the Trust and various possible funding bodies. The result was that in 1995 the Trust was able to purchase the estate for £5.572 million. £4 million of this came from the ECT and £1.5 million from the National Heritage Memorial Fund (NHMF). The Trustees of the NHMF also provided £8.015 million from the Heritage Lottery Fund for an endowment and a further £732,000 towards capital works to the Lodge and other areas in the surrounding policies. Finally, the Trust entered into a 25-year management agreement with SNH under which the latter agreed to provide £126,000 annually for an agreed management programme for a period of five years.

None of these funds came without conditions of course! By and large, they were close to the Trust's own principal aims and only two of those required by the ECT were in any way unusual for a conservation charity. These aims and conditions of management were subsequently agreed in discussion with SNH, whose approval was a condition of NHMF finance. The principal aim of the Trust at Mar Lodge Estate is:

to manage the Estate in a sustainable manner for the benefit of the nation, ensuring the continuing conservation and restoration of its internationally important geology, flora, fauna, wild land quality and archaeological value

Pines on Mar

The three unusual conditions of the Easter Charitable Trust are:

1. The Trust shall manage the Estate so as to conserve its valuable ecological and landscape features *in harmony with its maintenance as a Highland Sporting Estate for so long as field sports remain legal.*
2. *Declaring that it is intended to demonstrate that the practice of field sports can be reconciled with the Trust's statutory obligation to promote public access.*
3. That part of the Estate lying to the south and west of the River Dee and comprising heather moorland shall be sensitively managed to promote its proper conservation in terms of *grouse habitat*, nature conservation and landscape. (my emphasis)

The ECT is also concerned that mountain bikes should be discouraged on Mar Lodge Estate and the Trust has agreed that the use of bicycles undermines the philosophy of the long walk-in and that efforts will be taken to dissuade the use of any mechanical or wheeled vehicle around the Lodge policies.

The question that we all ask is – who is/are the Easter Charitable Trust and what is his/her/their motive(s) in providing the funding? It is fairly plain that the funding for the ECT has very likely come from the Scottish landowning and sporting establishment. There are two possible reasons for the involvement of ECT that come to mind. First, following the sale of Glen

Feshie to Wills Woodland Trust and the possibility of a radical change in management there away from sporting, those behind the ECT feared that the sale of Mar Lodge Estate to a Scottish conservation charity would lead to the loss of traditional sporting management on yet another very large and influential estate. The only way of preventing this was to buy in and thereby influence the direction of management so that sporting use be retained. The ECT perhaps also recognised the present unsustainable management of many Scottish sporting estates and felt that there were better odds on a conservation charity managing an estate for sporting purposes compatible with nature conservation and public access than a private owner! Perhaps ECT think that Mar Lodge Estate will prove an example to other traditionally managed estates, and management for sport will get a better name if the Trust succeeds. Alas we will not know for certain until, or if, the ECT reveals its identity!

The challenge facing the National Trust for Scotland

In midsummer 1995 the NTS finally took possession of Mar Lodge Estate following over a year of careful appraisal and negotiation with several interested parties and particularly Scottish Natural Heritage in relation to the Management Plan. The climate of expectation was high – conservationists expected radical management, walkers and climbers expected free and open access, the existing staff just hoped their jobs would be secure, while no doubt some others expected increased job opportunities and commercial spin-offs. On the other hand, the ECT wished to see the Estate run for sporting purposes (albeit still at sustainable levels), a wish very much supported by adjacent sporting estates and others throughout the Highlands. Even within the Trust itself and its members these divergent views were represented, from those who wished to retain the *status quo* in favour of red-deer stalking, to those who wished deer numbers substantially reduced throughout the Estate.

From the preceding descriptive sections on the natural and cultural heritage of Mar Lodge Estate and the principal aim of management, it is clear that its primary value to the nation is its natural heritage, its wild land and its archaeology. The last area of interest is not the subject of this book and we will return to the subject of wild land under a later section. As far as the natural heritage designation citations are concerned it is specifically the landscape, geology and geomorphology, the fauna and flora of the plateaux, the variety of dwarf-shrub heath (moorlands), blanket-bog and the remnants of the native Caledonian forest, that are recognised as the most important. The feature that is in the most fragile state is the Caledonian pinewood,

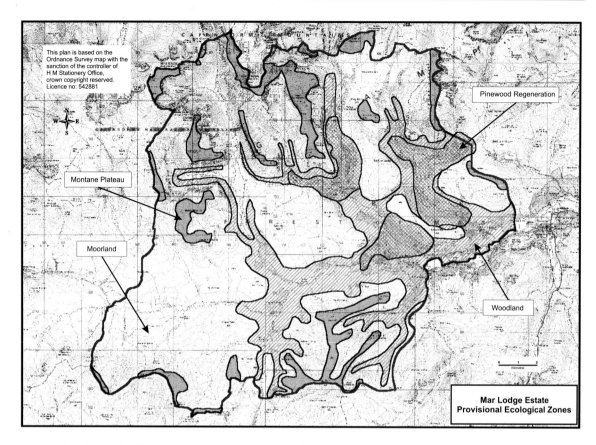

This plan is based on the Ordnance Survey map with the sanction of the controller of H M Stationery Office, crown copyright reserved. Licence no: 542881

Pinewood Regeneration

Montane Plateau

Moorland

Woodland

Mar Lodge Estate
Provisional Ecological Zones

which has been declining for a very long time with no significant regeneration of pine trees since the eighteenth century. The specific threat to the woodland at Mar Lodge Estate is now predominantly from the large red-deer population.

The first step by the Trust, in attempting to marry the competing pressures for 'traditional' management and 'conservation' or sustainable management, was to step up the cull substantially and at the same time to draw up a map of the main ecological zones (Figure 7.2). The purpose of the latter was to identify the existing area of Caledonian pinewood, the areas close by into which the woodland could expand relatively quickly under a very light red-deer grazing regime, and the areas of open moorland where trees are unlikely to establish naturally for a very long time and where traditional deer stalking and grouse shooting could continue. The map also clearly shows the more extensive potential limit of the pinewood up to 600 metres, both the areas of high altitude blanket-bog where trees are unlikely to establish naturally, and the present open moorland above 600 metres but below about 800 metres which would have been the area of sub-alpine scrub, now completely gone from Mar Lodge Estate. Above that are the plateaux.

Figure 7.2
Map of Mar Lodge Estate provisional Ecological Zones

The Caledonian Forest and the deer: Trust management

At Mar Lodge Estate it is clearly not sensible to try to separate deer management from woodland management, for they are inextricably linked, more at this Trust property than at any other. This is principally because of large deer numbers and the decision by the Trust that the expansion of the native pinewood and associated broadleaves should be ideally by natural regeneration without fencing or planting, at least in the early stages, to allow the development of as near natural a forest as possible. Planting usually requires the addition of fertiliser, as the young trees are being transplanted from a relatively rich nursery soil to a poor hill soil. Red deer, however, know which of their salads have been garnished with health-giving minerals and, without fencing, any planted trees will be preferentially selected and rapidly destroyed. As we have seen elsewhere, the principal consequence of the decision not to plant or fence is that the grazing pressure has to be very substantially reduced.

Natural regeneration of a pine or birch forest takes place around its periphery, particularly downwind. At Mar Lodge Estate, owing to the extreme age of many of the pine trees, there is some concern as to whether the seed will be viable and therefore there is a long-term monitoring project of seed production and viability covering selected trees. Under controlled conditions trials so far have shown that the seed is viable, but that of course does not mean that regeneration will happen. The enclosures erected by the NC and NCC in the 1970s and 1980s did demonstrate that in the absence of grazing, natural regeneration of the pinewood would occur, but not in all the plant communities. This is possibly because the ground conditions of vegetation and soil have changed over the centuries since the native forest was present and in many cases there may no longer be an optimum substrate around the trees. Outside enclosures, even if the substrate is ideal, unless the deer population is around two to four individuals per square kilometre, any seedlings that get away will be destroyed by grazing and browsing. Having looked at the distribution of native pinewood and its potential, as against the distribution of open moorland, it became fairly obvious that deer numbers would have to be reduced to around this level in the north and east, where the remnant woodland occurs. On the other hand, the moorland to the south (Dalvorar) and west (North and South Geldie), where there are very few trees, would continue to be managed as deer forest and grouse moor, providing the habitat for other open ground bird species such as waders and merlin.

The next step for the Trust was to establish red-deer numbers over the whole Estate and, more importantly, their distribution. Hinds, for example, have a home range of between one and five square kilometres within which they remain all year round, but stags range more widely and often have different areas for wintering and rutting, in addition to the area they take up for the rest of the year. It was important to know then the numbers of each sex in each area where there were to be different management aims, for only then could the Trust make calculations on the size of the required annual culls. The experience of those who have been managing the deer on the Estate for a number of years has been invaluable in this work. It is known, for example, that about one-third of the stags that traditionally winter on the north side among the pine trees and plantations rut on the south side. The problem for management is that culling too many of these stags, to promote regeneration on the north side, will reduce the number of stags available for guest stalking on the south side. On the other hand, culling too few will hinder tree regeneration. In the short term, part of the answer has been to provide improved grazing or additional feeding for the stags in winter, to concentrate them on small areas away from natural regeneration, but this is being phased out. The opening up, by removal of fences, of several of the plantations may also provide new and alternative shelter for deer and help take the pressure off more sensitive woodlands. Other solutions may be to regularly disturb the stags and move them on, or, as a very last resort, maybe there will have to be *some* fencing, but that would be seen by many conservationists as an admission of defeat. Such problems cannot be answered overnight and the Trust has therefore called in the expertise of the Institute of Terrestrial Ecology (ITE) at Banchory and others to help. Nine of these stags were fitted with radio-collars in 1998 to try to establish their movements in more detail.

A large herd of hinds crossing the Dee – where is the riparian woodland?

The red-deer population of Mar Lodge Estate in 1995 was 3,354, with a sex ratio of 2:1 hinds to stags. By 1998 with a much increased culling rate, particularly of hinds, the total population had been brought down to 2,646: a substantial decrease which is already resulting in an improvement of heather growth in some areas. Using data from recent research on deer and their impact on woodland, a target population of 1,650 red deer, comprising 950 hinds and 700 stags, has been set for the year 2000, the fifth year of management by the Trust. Whereas there will only be around 350 red deer in the Quoich and the Derry, the remaining 1,300 will be in the Geldie and Dalvorar area. This target population, the bulk of which is being retained for sporting purposes, is approximately half of the number when the Trust took over in 1995 and a third of the 1991 population. Such a dramatic reduction, to bring the deer population at Mar Lodge Estate into balance with its natural environment, is an indication of just how far the overall Scottish deer numbers need to be reduced: a principle which has been widely accepted for a number of years, but as yet, has hardly been put into action.

The bulk of the cull at Mar Lodge Estate is to be of hinds and it will be concentrated in the north and east half of the estate around the pinewood remnants. In the first year of operation the Estate staff, with some paying guests, culled 700 hinds and 280 stags which brought in £39,000, not including the venison. This is a healthy contribution to other management costs, although it may be more of a paper gain when all the time and effort of the stalkers in supporting guest stalking is taken into account. It would be interesting to compare the economics of this approach to deer culling with that carried out by the Trust's own staff and with the approach being taken forward at Glen Affric.

Monitoring deer by annual counts is a vital tool in their management, but it is only an indirect way at best, of measuring the success if the aim is habitat improvement. To judge whether or not the level of the deer population is allowing regeneration of forest, or healthy growth of heather and other shrubs, the only way is to monitor the habitat – count the number of tree seedlings or measure annual growth. At Mar Lodge Estate such monitoring, which originated in 1981 with the NCC, now includes kilometre-long permanently marked transects, some end to end, covering lengths of up to five kilometres. Recorders walk the transects measuring any tree growth – date, number, age, size – within a metre of either side of the line. If it is found that regeneration is still failing because grazing levels are still too high, the deer cull will be increased to further reduce the population. Likewise on the moorland there have been fears that grazing levels may be too high for some of the shrub species such as the dwarf birch, and monitoring there too will dictate deer levels in the future.

Such management of the deer should allow regeneration around the immediate environs of the pine trees up to a distance of about 50 metres.

However where there are fragments of other elements of the Caledonian Forest, such as birch, aspen or rowan still clinging onto crags or ravine sides, it is likely, even with a small deer population, that any seedlings or suckers attempting to grow outside these refuges will be selectively grazed. If these sites fail to expand it may well be necessary to further reduce deer numbers or to fence and exclude deer. However, as we have noted elsewhere, fencing is a wasted effort unless deer numbers are further reduced before fences are removed. Most of the proposed forest expansion area has no trees, and planting may be considered in selected sites to provide the germ for further expansion. However, even with very few deer this would require fencing, with all its attendant problems.

One of the general policies of the Trust as far as environmental management is concerned, is the principle of minimum intervention; hence natural regeneration as against planting. As with all principles though, the closer they are examined the less clear becomes the line between keeping to them and breaking them. For example, having reduced deer numbers to a level that should allow natural regeneration around a patch of woodland, or around a plantation of local provenance Scots pine, should anything further be done to encourage natural regeneration, or would that be breaking the principle of minimum intervention? After 200 years of lack of tree cover and fairly heavy deer grazing it is likely that the vegetation adjacent to the trees is not suitable for seed germination or seedling establishment. In the natural situation it may well often have been fire that removed some of that vegetation to present a seedbed and nutrients for regeneration. Why not initially burn the vegetation around the remnant woodland then; that is, as long as there are no signs of regeneration? For the moment the Trust's line lies on this side of burning, planting and fencing; but if no regeneration takes place, the line may have to shift!

A genuine concern of stalking-staff throughout the Highlands of Scotland is that the recent shift of the focus of management from the deer to their habitat, which will result in reduced deer numbers, in turn will lead to a reduction in stalking-staff. At Mar Lodge Estate, with the introduction of Trust staff, there are in fact more people employed now than when it was in private hands, and with a return to more pony use for extraction, more seasonal ghillies are required. Other similar estates, at Abernethy (RSPB) and Creag Meagaidh (SNH) for example, are also indicative of the future increased requirements of staff when managing deer on a sustainable basis. Keeping deer numbers low, particularly when the cover of scrub and woodland has developed, will actually require more stalking effort in the very long term, both because of the cover and therefore difficulty in locating animals, and because the improved habitat will result in a more productive population with higher winter survival rates. Such cover, providing an improved habitat, particularly shelter in the winter months, will also result in larger animals with more spectacular 'trophy' heads if that is what is wanted! Such improvement in quality should also be obvious in the shorter term due to the substantial reduction in overall deer numbers.

It is sobering to realise that the Trust estimate that, under natural regeneration, it could take more than 200 years for the pinewood to return to its natural limits on Mar Lodge Estate. That includes reaching its altitudinal limits in the form of stunted trees way up beyond the 600-metre contour. At Inchriach, within the Cairngorms NNR, reduction of deer numbers in 1974 certainly demonstrated the benefits for Scots pine in this situation. Many people are watching very closely to see what happens to the pinewood on Mar Lodge Estate, and at places like Abernethy, Strathfarrar and Glen Affric, where similar radical deer management is being carried out in order to save and expand the remnants of the Caledonian pinewood (at Creag Meagaidh it is for birch woodland mainly). Nobody knows, for all its good intentions, just how successful or not this management will be. The trick will be to balance patience and action and to untangle and identify the specific factors that are encouraging or hindering regeneration.

Moorland management

The large moorland element in the southern part of the Estate has presented the Trust with something of a dilemma. Although the Trust is carrying out quite radical management in its substantial reduction of red deer in the areas of pinewood remnants and is content to allow the transformation of moorland in that area into woodland in the long term, it does not see, at least at present, a similar evolution for the moorland in the southern part, albeit deer numbers will be reduced to a lesser extent there too. Because of the terms of the financial support from the Easter Charitable Trust, it is obliged to retain a sporting element on the Estate. There are several reasons why, if this has to be, it should be in the southern part, a consequence of which will be to hold this area in check while the rest of the land may gradually return to some of its original diversity. First, this was traditionally the main grouse moor. Second, the low watershed around this area effectively means that the local deer population overlaps significantly with the surrounding traditional 'sporting' estates of Mar, Fealar, Atholl and Glen Feshie, and any radical reduction in deer numbers here might affect these estates and would cause them a great deal of concern! Third, deer numbers will have to be low in the northern parts for tree regeneration purposes. Fourth, most visitors – apart from those following the footpaths up from Atholl and either down to Braemar or on to the Lairig Ghru and Glenmore – are concentrated in the northern half where stalking may often be disrupted. Fifth and finally, much of the southern part of the Estate is at a relatively high altitude, at the margins for woodland and some distance from the existing native remnants, so it will not naturally regenerate for a very long time anyway.

It has been argued elsewhere (Chapter 1) that the case for retaining the moorland monoculture by management for its characteristic birds, including grouse, as opposed to allowing or encouraging it to evolve into woodland, scrub *and* pockets of moorland, is rather a weak one. In this particular situation at Mar Lodge Estate a pragmatic decision has had to be taken as a result of the conditions of the ECT financial support. The *quid pro quo* for sporting is that there will be none of the traditional access prohibitions in the southern area either, while the Management Plan states that any muirburn in this area will be carried out very carefully, avoiding areas of dwarf birch, thin and wet soils. So, although the moorland will be retained, the option for radical management here too – development of scrub and woodland – still remains for the future.

The moorland is the habitat with the most unclear aims of management on Mar Lodge Estate. Objective (8) of the Management Plan states:

> *To conserve the moorland ecosystem (particularly that to the south and west of the Dee) for its varied habitats, communities and species, including the wet heathland communities, remnant scrub and native trees, invertebrates and breeding birds.*

The question is – what is a moorland ecosystem? And what is a good 'quality' moorland ecosystem? The answer, of course, begs another question – what is the purpose of the moorland? Presuming that it is below the tree-line, if it is to be one suitable for grouse and for red-deer stalking, it cannot be one that also has regenerating scrub and native trees. The first is basically an ecosystem held in arrested evolution by fire: a monoculture. The second is an ecosystem evolving naturally towards its climax: a state of diversity. It is very difficult to see how it will be possible to select the areas to be burned for 'traditional' sporting use without continuing to suppress the development of varied habitats, etc. There is also the question of what such an arrested ecosystem, below the tree-line, contributes to the landscape? Would not a naturally diverse moorland, woodland and scrub contribute more than the traditional monoculture?

Landscape management

The effects of the substantial reduction in the red-deer population and the concomitant expansion of the Caledonian Forest will have, in the long term, a significant effect on the landscape: one day the forest will be the foreground to the mountains. In the shorter term the obvious intrusions in the landscape are the coniferous plantations and the hill tracks. Intrusive as the plantations are, one must bear in mind that there is more than enough work for the Trust to cope with on the Estate and there has to be some prioritising and programming of work over a number of years. One must bear in mind also that where plantations have been established recently under FA Woodland Grants, fences may be retained in the short term to avoid having to repay these grants. To return the wild land qualities to the landscape the fenced plantations will be managed in various ways, depending on various factors including their origin, age and location. For example, whether or not fences are retained, heavy thinning has been carried out on the periphery of a number of plantations to soften their abrupt edges. Within some fenced areas, such as at Creag Bhalg, there is a healthy regeneration of trees and the fence is therefore helping those trees to get away. In other cases, of fairly young lodgepole plantations, it may seem curious that the trees have been felled and left on the ground. The brash from the fellings however, is returning some nutrients to the soil and also serving to protect seedlings of native species. In cases where there is not perceived to be a landscape problem, after some peripheral thinning, lodgepole plantations may be left to mature before eventually being felled and sold, so securing some additional income. Since there are both capercaillie and black grouse at Mar Lodge Estate the Trust will have to put up broad and colourful tapes on any fences retained to reduce casualties.

While the plantations of exotic tree species are unnatural blots on the face of the landscape which cosmetic surgery and felling will eventually remove altogether, other scars on Mar Lodge Estate are more than skin deep. Where planted trees have changed only the surface vegetation, roads and tracks have actually gouged wounds into the soil. Incredibly these roads, supposedly to assist with management, were simply bulldozed and driven to heights well over 1,000 metres (3,200 feet), in other words into an arctic-alpine climate and through fragile and skeletal soils. If the hill tracks are to be removed, by restoration to the natural vegetation cover (sparse as it is at high levels), it will take much longer for the wounds to heal, if they ever do.

The track up onto the Beinn á Bhuird plateau was established in the 1960s for sporting and possible skiing developments. The Trust is now pressing ahead with efforts to restore this track, from the top down. Just as with its attempts to restore montane willow scrub and prevent the extinction of some plants at Ben Lawers, the Trust is finding itself once again in new territory, where the best and sometimes only advice it can get is from the experience of its own staff as they pioneer new techniques in restoration management.

On Beinn á Bhuird, at a similar height to the tops of the other mountain properties of the Trust, weather permitting, one can look south-west to Beinn a Ghlo, Schiehallion and Ben Lawers and even to the tops of Glencoe, and west a short distance to Ben Macdui and Cairn Gorm itself. Here the granite bedrock erodes to an acid and porous gravel, supporting only plants such as deer grass, stiff sedge, three-flowered rush, clubmosses and lichens with terracing and wind-patterned waves of vegetation around the west- and south-facing shoulders. To the east the ground drops 50 metres to the beautiful corrie loch of Dubh Lochan, from the crest icy-blue against red granite screes. On the Cairngorm plateaux, at this height is the place to watch for ptarmigan or dotterel, oblivious and almost invisible to walkers against the weathered rock and gravel. Nearer to the Arctic in Scotland one cannot get!

The problems with track restoration at this altitude in Scotland are particularly related to the nature of the climate and the fragility of soil and vegetation. On the upper side of the track the bulldozer has cut a profile into the shoulder of the hill. One of the first steps in restoration is to try and soften this sharp-edged profile; next, to repair and re-vegetate the barren surface of the track itself. Both these objectives have to

Beinn á Bhuird track under repair

be met by returning boulders and vegetation bulldozed off the track. Plant cover may only be of the order of 30–40 per cent at this altitude, so there is not a lot of material available and it is frequently necessary to walk up to 50 metres to find a suitable patch from which small turfs can be carefully uplifted. The first decision to be made is whether or not to use machinery, which although it can move more material about more quickly than someone with a shovel and wheelbarrow and is therefore relatively cheaper, machinery can end up causing just as much damage by its weight and movements as the original track construction. Two things happen when the thin gravelly soil is disturbed. First, rainfall can exploit the smallest runnel and begin an erosion process difficult to stop. Second, the soil is opened up to the freezing and thawing process typical of the arctic-alpine climate, which once again can start erosion processes.

A compromise must therefore be sought between relocating spoil from the track-side for re-profiling purposes, and the risk of losing vegetation from now well-colonised old spoil heaps. The growth of plants in the severe climate around 900 metres is very slow, due both to the short growing season and lack of nutrients. Their natural form of spreading then is by vegetative means, such as rhizomes, rather than by seed. It is equally important then to pick the time of year that will cause the least shock to any lifted tussocks of vegetation and to minimise the time such vegetation may lie, when lifted out of the way, before it is returned to a permanent position flush with the surrounding surface. Because the skeletal soils are so thin and porous, plants can dry out very quickly, so lifting and planting has to be carried out outside the dry months of July and August, in September or October. The general principle is to carry out only short stretches of restoration at a time, and as rapidly as possible.

A small machine working on the track itself, supported by a team of skilled labourers carrying out well-tested and refined vegetation restoration techniques, appears to be the most efficient method of tackling the work. Since the object is also to leave a footpath that will gradually blend back into the hill, but not a path suitable for vehicles, re-settled plants and boulders are scattered randomly on the original track, allowing a new footpath to wind as naturally as possible. It has taken several trial runs to establish the best working methods, and the costs of such work are high. It can take an hour or more for the team to reach the site, before they commence work! Every piece of vegetation or boulder must be lifted and re-settled very carefully. Up to the spring of 1998, some 250 metres of the Beinn á Bhuird track have been repaired at a cost of £17,000, around £30 per square metre, and there are

Dotterel

four kilometres to go! These costs per area may seem very expensive, but are actually not *so* expensive when compared with normal footpath repair, such as has been carried out on the path up to Loch Etchachan.

Loch Etchachan and Loch A'an – the heart of the Cairngorms

Visitor management

Mar Lodge Estate was not only acquired by the Trust for its natural heritage and archaeology but for its 'wild land quality': its large areas of remote, wild and scenic country. The second aim of management that follows the principal aim is:

> *. . . to ensure appropriate access to the land, subject to the maintenance of landscape and nature conservation interests.*

The key word here is 'appropriate'.

There is no general Trust policy yet to guide the management of wild land, but in the Management Plan the Trust suggests several features of such areas, among which are remoteness and naturalness. It is that core of wild and remote landscape, and the fifteen Munros, that draws visitors; and it is the road, track, path and sign that may lead them on, too rapidly and easily, to the fragile plateaux, in numbers that can disturb wildlife, damage the physical and detract from the spiritual aspects of the otherwise relatively remote mountain mass. Removal of the high-level tracks will help to reduce the human impact on both those aspects, otherwise the policy of the Trust is not to make it any easier! Hence there is a presumption against the promotion of the Estate and the adoption of the *long walk in* as the guiding principle for visitor management. No vehicles, other than those of the Trust, will be allowed access to the roads, and bicycles will be discouraged as part of the conditions of the ECT support, though it is difficult to see what harm will be done by the latter on the low-level roads.

One of the features on Deeside, promoted by Tourist Boards, is the Linn of Dee, not far inside the property and adjacent to the track that gives access to the heart of the Cairngorms. In the summer of 1998 this beautiful spot by the River Dee attracted over 200,000 visitors. From the car park it is about an hour's walk up the 5-kilometre track to Derry Lodge and into the native Scots pine forest. However, less than a one-fifth of visitors (fewer than 10,000) entering Mar Lodge Estate get this far. That may not appear many, but with up to 60 tents pitched in this area on a summer night, the continuous removal of brash and even living branches for camp fires and the use of woodland and riverbank as toilet facilities, the impact can be unpleasant at the very least and quite seriously damaging to the natural environment at worst. Half of the number reaching Derry Lodge may then go on and up through the Lairig Ghru, or up Glen Derry and the repaired path to Loch Etchachan and on to Glenmore.

Like the lower slopes of Glencoe and most of Ben Lomond therefore, the lower part of Mar Lodge is also regarded by many visitors as something of a public park. The problem for the Trust is not so much *where*, but *where not*, to provide public facilities. Access, as with all Trust properties, is unhindered, although bicycling and the use of vehicles generally is discouraged on the property, outside the Lodge Policies. The Trust also sensibly discourages mass events on Mar Lodge Estate, such as the fashion for charity walks to the top of the Munros. What should be done at Derry Lodge, apart from addressing the problem of the derelict Victorian buildings there, which is not within the remit of this book? Should camping be prohibited? Should toilets be provided? If facilities are provided at Derry Lodge will they simply attract more people and create more problems, or should all facilities, including the camp site, be confined to the area of the Linn of Dee? No decisions have yet been taken.

How well does the Trust manage to carry on guest-stalking on such a popular mountain property? Fairly satisfactorily but with difficulty, is the answer! Over the stalking season 1997–98 only eight stalks were disturbed and only two cancelled. How is this achieved? First, guest-stalking is largely confined to the southern part of the property which, apart from the footpath from Atholl through Glen Tilt to the Dee, is not greatly used by visitors. Second, the Trust does not carry out stalking at the weekends when the numbers of visitors are highest. On the face of it only eight disturbed stalks in a season is a good record, considering the numbers of visitors, but the disturbance is not only to the stalk. Deer get used to people. Anyone who has walked the roads of Rum has noticed that the deer are little concerned by their presence. However, once people leave the track and their route becomes unpredictable deer *will* take notice and move off. Since there are so many hill walkers at Mar Lodge Estate, often moving off the path, deer move more often than they did in the past. It is now more and more difficult therefore for the stalker to predict where the deer are going to be, resulting in more time being spent on stalking.

Summation

Mar Lodge Estate is in the heart of an area for many generations devoted to sporting management, and although there is now a Cairngorms Partnership and there will be a National Park in 2002, the property is still virtually surrounded by estates managed for traditional purposes – Invercauld and Inchrory for example. Mar Lodge Estate, as we have noted, also depends on the funds and conditions of the Easter Charitable Trust (ECT) for its existence and management as a Trust property. There are therefore inherent potential conflicts for the Trust in managing Mar Lodge Estate for its natural heritage, and in particular for its native Scots pine forest. Because of the many interests of the property, the Trust's founding principles and responsibilities and the conditions of the ECT funding at Mar Lodge Estate, the management rationale and aims are complex and numerous: there are 38 Management Objectives in the current Management Plan! However, as far as the natural heritage is concerned there is one clear, overriding Management Objective (3): *'To manage the Caledonian pinewoods to promote natural regeneration (without fencing).'*

As we have noted, the crucial phrase is *'without fencing'*, for it has a very direct bearing on the Trust's attitude to red-deer management and immediately puts Mar Lodge Estate on a very different deer management strategy to its neighbours. Essentially, as we have seen, the Trust is seeking to establish a very low deer population that will allow the natural regeneration of the woodland, whereas the surrounding estates are managing deer to keep numbers up, particularly hinds, and to produce, through traditional management and additional feeding, stags with good heads. The Trust has ensured, by communication, partly through the Deer Management Group, but also directly with the estates, that it retains good-neighbour relations. However, notwithstanding that the Trust must continue (Objective 5):

> *To demonstrate on a whole estate basis that management of the deer population for conservation reasons can be carried out in harmony with the maintenance of sporting quality and public access*

the end result will be a very different habitat and red-deer population than on the surrounding estates. Where Mar Lodge Estate will be an invigorated and diverse landscape, the former will retain examples of our mismanaged and derelict uplands. It is to be hoped that other estates will learn from the example of Mar Lodge Estate and a few other now radically managed estates, and that the Trust ensures that the 'demonstration' potential of Mar Lodge Estate, as land managed on an integrated and sustainable basis, is fully realised.

However, in order to impress the many Scottish estates that manage their land principally for sporting and particularly red-deer stalking, and to have any effect in changing now ingrained traditional attitudes, the Trust will have to demonstrate that the management at Mar Lodge Estate can be of benefit to the 'sportsman'. The MP mentions developing a 'distinctive approach to stalking' and a move towards improving 'the quality of the experience'. The Trust must also, and crucially, demonstrate the improvement of the quality of the prey – the size and condition of the red deer. This will mean sticking to its principle of low deer numbers – and right across the Estate, not just in the regenerating areas in the face of pressure from the ECT and other traditional estate managers. The Trust must also discard the disproved practices of culling specific animals to 'improve' the quality of the population; it is the quality of the habitat which dictates the quality of the deer. It will also not, however, be enough simply to demonstrate 'quality' improvement. There needs to be hard evidence of the changes and the causes of these changes. To achieve this the Trust must ensure that there is adequate monitoring and recording that will provide unambiguous evidence of the benefits of their management and the radical steps that have been taken.

Unlike all the other properties covered in this book, except Glencoe, Mar Lodge Estate has no tenant or crofting community associated with it. The Trust employs more staff than at any other of its countryside properties and in that sense makes an important contribution to the local community and to local employment, but that is not the same thing as involving the local community in its management. Mar Lodge Estate is also an important tourist attraction on Deeside and therefore indirectly important to those in Braemar who rely on tourism for their living.

Creeping lady's tresses – an orchid of native pinewoods

There is liaison between the Management Committee and the Braemar community, but there is no local representation on that committee. This is a pity when a 'public' body such as the Trust is caring for the land for 'the benefit of the nation', and when so much of the surrounding land is in the hands of very large estates who also have no local democratic involvement in their management. Having taken such radical steps in the management of the land, it would have been fitting if the Trust had likewise taken radical steps in the local participation of management decisions.

On the other hand, Mar Lodge Estate is perhaps an appropriate place to remind ourselves of the *national* and *international*, as against the *local* interests, which all must be taken into account by the Trust. Although just outside Trust property, the Cairngorm funicular development will no doubt have an impact on the high plateau which is part of Mar Lodge Estate. Whatever precautions are taken by the development to ensure that the projected huge increase in visitors are not encouraged onto the plateau, the massive publicity for the funicular will inevitably attract more people to Cairn Gorm and cause disturbance to its wildlife and damage to its fragile soils. Here, natural heritage conservationists have argued, is an example of where the local interest in development has over-ruled the national and international natural heritage interests. However, this was a failure of planning. It is not an argument against local involvement in decision-making, so much as a reason to involve the local community in the management and care of the natural heritage in a much more meaningful way than at present. There is a difficult balance to be struck but, as I have said elsewhere, the local community is as much a part of 'nation' as anyone else.

As a last comment in this chapter, it is interesting to note that Mar Lodge Estate is the first property of the Trust, 60 years after its establishment, to be managed by the Trust for its natural heritage from the outset and that it doubled the area of countryside property in one flourish of the pen. In earlier chapters we have seen that it has taken decades of ownership for the Trust to accept the central importance of the flora and fauna on many of its properties and to change from *laissez-faire* traditional management to positive conservation management. This perhaps leaves St Kilda, which has been awarded the highest accolade of any site in the British Isles for its natural heritage, in a rather anomalous position, in that it is still leased and managed by SNH; but we will return to this in the final chapter.

glencoe
6 Aug 98

Chapter 8

Glencoe

Introduction

Approaching the Glencoe property from the Bridge of Orchy, the road crosses a desolate landscape, winding past just a few of the many lochs and myriads of lochans that lie scattered across the 200 square kilometres of treeless wilderness that is Rannoch Moor. Only occasionally can one see the huge extent of the moorland from the road, but the impression of the flat and open landscape is strong. Part of the way across there are several lochs, close by on either side of the road, whose islets are crowded with birch, but whose shores are bare. These remnants are all that is left to remind us of how the landscape may have looked in the past. After 10 kilometres or so, with the Black Mount looming ever closer on the left, the road begins to be squeezed as it passes between Beinn a Chrùlaiste and the huge mass of Buachaille Etive Mór. Gradually it descends and then, quite suddenly, through the Pass, is the deep and narrow glen that is Glen Coe itself, with the heavy and threatening shoulders of the Three Sisters rising vertically on one side and the three-kilometre ridge of Aonach Eagach looming steeply on the other. After the openness of Rannoch Moor, the atmosphere of Glen Coe, with its towering walls, capped by frequent low cloud, is almost claustrophobic: its myths and stories and its tragic human history adding a feeling of sadness and foreboding.

Glen Coe, because of that one event in 1692 and because of the deep, narrow and moody nature of the glen itself, the backdrop for many a romantic painting, novel and film, is, unfortunately for its managers, one of Scotland's tourist icons. Incredibly, some one million cars or 2,600,000 people pass through it every year, with around 150,000 calling in at the Trust Visitor Centre. The property of Glencoe is also a Mecca for climbers and walkers and has been for many years, with an estimated 150,000 mountaineering visits made annually. In addition, but probably unknown to 99 per cent of those that pass through, it is internationally important for its geology; it has one of the most diverse assemblages of mountain plants outside Ben Lawers and

Facing page
Glencoe: hanging valley

Breadalbane as a whole; and it also has many remnants of the former forest of the area, including a remnant of the Caledonian Scots pine forest. The whole of the Glencoe property (5,811 hectares) is within the Ben Nevis and Glencoe NSA which states so aptly that Glencoe 'must rank high among the most spectacular scenic experiences in Scotland'. Apart from the Dalness end, the property is also an SSSI for its internationally important geology, geomorphology and biology, and a large part is also a cSAC. What it is *not* in 1999, is a National Nature Reserve or a National Park.

It is unlikely that early settlers found much to attract them far up Glen Coe and onto Rannoch Moor except perhaps for hunting, but the relatively fertile ground low down in the glen was probably settled by Neolithic farmers. One of the first historical figures associated with Glen Coe was an Irish disciple of St Columba, around the sixth century AD, who gave his name to Eilean Munde in Loch Leven. In the eleventh century the Glen Coe lands came into the hands of the MacDougalls who, after being on the wrong side of the struggle for power in Scotland, lost them to the MacDonalds following the success of Robert the Bruce in subduing all of Scotland north of the Forth by 1308. The MacDonalds then held on to Glen Coe for another 500 years, the most famous event in their history being the massacre in 1692 by the orders of William III and carried out under the direction of a Campbell of Glen Lyon, about which so much has been written. Later it was the MacDonald chiefs themselves who were responsible for the clearances in

Glen Coe at its moody best!

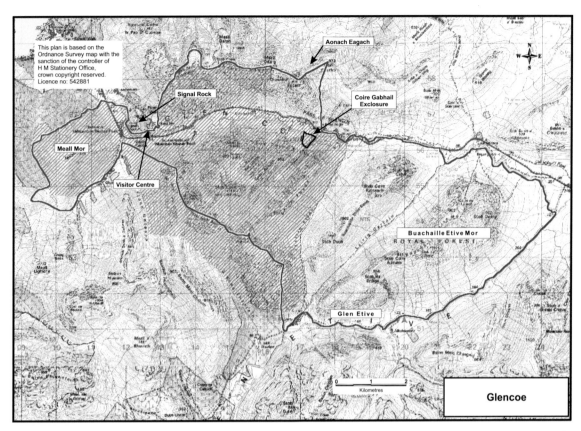

Figure 8.1
Map of the
Glencoe area
(Legend: see p. xviii)

the glen in the nineteenth century when the smallholdings were amalgamated into larger sheep farms. At the time a visitor was quoted as saying that the sheep-farming system had extinguished the MacDonalds more effectively than the 1692 massacre. The first road through the glen was built in 1785 and the glen finally passed out of MacDonald hands in 1837 when it was sold. Almost 100 years later, in 1935, the then owner, Lord Strathcona, sold the estate to the Trust. With the addition of the Dalness Estate and one or two other small areas acquired much later, the total area now under Trust ownership amounts to 5,811 hectares.

On the property of Glencoe there are eight separate Munros and eighteen subsidiary summits over 915 metres (3,000 feet) either in Trust care or approached from the Trust property, plus twenty recognised climbing crags. It is these peaks, ridges and rock-climbs, packed into a relatively small area, that first attracted the early British climbers last century, making Glencoe almost the home of British mountaineering, and that today still attract tens of thousands of walkers and climbers. For example, Aonach Eagach, the magnificent ridge that runs more than 850 metres (2,800 feet) above the north side of the glen, is reputed to be the most difficult ridge on the mainland of Britain. It was the mountains of Glencoe of course which attracted Percy Unna and led him to ensure its acquisition for the Trust: its first large countryside property.

Glencoe was acquired in stages in the 1930s, not long after the Trust was established. First, in 1935, the Trust acquired Clachaig and Achtriochtan on the north side of the glen, and Strone, on the south side, while at the same time it was given Signal Rock, supposedly the site for the signal to commence the 1692 massacre. Then in 1937 it acquired a part of the much larger and adjacent estate of Dalness which included the whole of the south side of the glen east to Buachaille Etive Mór. It was not until 1972 that the Trust purchased Achnacon including Meall Mór right at the west end of the property. The 1935 and 1937 purchases were the result of financial support from several sources, but particularly from the Scottish Mountaineering Club (SMC) and an anonymous donor. It was not until after his death that it became public that the donor was Percy Unna, the then President of the SMC. The reasons for the Trust acquisitions were originally:

1. to safeguard access to the Glencoe mountains;
2. to protect some of the sites associated with the 1692 massacre; and
3. to prevent possible commercial exploitation.

Has the Trust been successful in meeting these aims? It has certainly met the first two, but has it prevented the commercialisation of Glencoe? On the grand scale, yes, it has managed to restrict official visitor facilities to the outdated Centre well down the glen. On the roadside scale, no, but that is as much, if not more, to do with the lack of commitment of others in assisting with the control of roadside parking and the kitsch Scottish pipers. Credit should also be given to the Trust in opposing a hydro-scheme in 1944 which, quite incredibly, would have flooded the glen!

There is no doubt that the acquisition of Glencoe (and Dalness) was almost entirely about mountaineering. Although preventing commercialisation, particularly of the historic aspects, was also important, it was probably considered just as important in relationship to possible detrimental impacts on the wilderness aspects and the enjoyment of climbing and walking. Acquisition was certainly little to do with the flora and fauna. In *The National Trust for Scotland Guide*, as late as 1976, only five lines out of 75 are given to the wildlife of Glencoe. It was not until 1984 that the first action was taken, by erection of an enclosure, to protect any remnant woodland; and it is only in the last year or two, more than sixty years after acquisition, that the Trust has finally taken control of the grazing, the principal factor influencing the vegetation cover and the landscape. Even the Trust's 1994 guide book on Glencoe, which gives ten pages to its history and six to its mountains, gives only four to its geology, wildlife and flora.

The Trust has taken some fifty years to recognise the outstanding importance of the wildlife of Glencoe, particularly its mountain plants and remnant woodlands, and commence action to conserve these interests. Why

Limestone area near
The Visitor Centre

should this have been? I suggest the reason why so little positive nature conservation activity took place here, or on other Trust properties until very recently, was due to the original composition of the Trust's Council, their interpretation of the remit of the Trust and their influence on staffing. The legacy of their narrow view of the heritage of Scotland still lingers and it is only within the last decade or so, with the influx of naturalists and ecologists to the Council and to the staff, that the full remit of the Trust's general purpose as stated in the 1935 Act is being acknowledged. At such an important site for nature conservation, one also has to question why the Nature Conservancy, Nature Conservancy Council and now SNH, did not encourage the Trust to acknowledge and fulfil its natural heritage role.

The current 1992–97 Management Plan has as its principal aim:

to ensure the permanent preservation of a nationally important mountainous property, with significant cultural and historical associations, plants and animal life.

Within that plan, for the first time, the needs of the natural environment are more explicitly addressed, although even now the importance of the plants and animals are still regarded as 'significant' rather than as 'nationally important', as is the mountain landscape. Because of its origins and history then, the property of Glencoe is another illustration of the Trust's changing attitude to the natural environment and the difficulties it has faced, and still faces, in getting this aspect of its responsibilities in perspective, especially when strong traditional forces keep pushing it in the direction of its other competing objectives.

Natural heritage

What are the origins of these mountains though, the ancient events that have shaped them and the more recent events that are responsible for the present vegetation? I have given only very brief descriptions of the geology of most of the properties in this book, but the geology and geomorphology of Glencoe is of such importance that it deserves a little more explanation here.

In the chapter on Kintail we noted that the mountains there were basically composed of sedimentary rocks laid down some 1,000 million years ago, but subsequently metamorphosed into schists. These schists made up much more of Scotland at that time, but some 400 million years ago, as the great Caledonian period of earth movement came to an end, huge masses of magma rose up through the schists and in places poured out as lava on the surface. Much of that lava flow has been eroded away over millions of years, and where today we can see the remnants of that magma it is the deeper granites that are exposed, such as on the Moor of Rannoch and the Cairngorms. It is only at Glencoe, once the world type-locality for 'cauldron subsidence', that we can now see on the surface something of what happened between the lavas and the schists, and at Glencoe it was spectacular! It was also very complex, but to simplify: in the midst of huge upheavals and massive volcanic activity, a ring-fracture around Glencoe, with a diameter of about nine kilometres developed in the upper layers and, like the crust of a gigantic pie, the centre sank some 900 metres (3,000 feet) into the molten body below. Just like the pie, a steep-sided rim was left and, between it and the crust, the molten contents seeped through to form new layers of lava on top of the crust. The temperatures and pressures in this gigantic cooker were enormous and the release of magma was often incredibly violent and explosive, spraying out as incandescent ash. As the crust of the pie stabilised, cooled and contracted it was broken by close-set NNE–SSW fractures that were then re-invaded by magma to form numerous vertical dykes. One of these dykes, subsequently weathered out, is the great vertical slot of Ossian's Cave on Aonach Dubh. After millions of years of erosion the lavas are gone from the surrounding hills and today they are only preserved where they were let down into Glen Coe itself. One arc of the circumference of that ring-fault is near Glen Etive, at the eastern boundary of the property, and the arc on the opposite side runs down the side of An t-Sròn, as a gully, crossing the glen near the road bridge.

Very much more recently, during the last Ice Age, only tens of thousands of years ago, ice from the huge mass accumulated on Rannoch Moor, fortuitously flowed into an incipient Glen Coe and cut the deep and steep-sided glen we see today. It not only cut the wonderful series of hanging valleys with their associated waterfalls and alluvial fans, such as those between the Three Sisters, but in some places exposed all the layers of the ring-fault from the original schists that still form the ground around Loch Achtriochtan, through the various lava flows and even some of the granites that intruded up the ring-fault. It was the great ice sheet of that time, working on the massive and complex mountains surrounding Glen Coe, that sculpted its present spectacular landscape of peaks, ridges, corries, crags and screes.

Today's climate of this area of Scotland is extremely wet with an annual rainfall of around 2,300 millimetres (90 inches). The soils arising from these rocks then, are predominantly leached, acidic, thin at higher levels and blanket-bog at lower levels. The one major exception are the soils on the ancient Dalradian limestones of Meall Mór, outside the ring-fault, which are predominantly base-rich and therefore support a very different vegetation from the bulk of Glencoe and Dalness.

When people first explored Glen Coe several thousand years ago it is likely that the most western and lowest part of the glen floor was dominated by a forest of oak, ash and birch, and that higher up in the glen, birch and rowan dominated outside the areas of blanket-bog. Possibly there was also Scots pine higher up, and willows and alder followed the stream sides from the top

Mountain hare

of the glen to the mouth of the River Coe. The steep, well-drained lower slopes of the mountains would also have been thick with birch, extending, as today, into the hanging valleys and then grading into dwarf shrubs such as heather, crowberry and blaeberry, with rich fern communities in the screes. On the better soils of the limestone massive of Meall Mór there would have been other woods of ash and hazel, grading into montane willow scrub and alpine grassland at higher altitude. In flushes within those woodlands and on wet ledges there would have been tall-herb communities, and where grazing took place there would have been herb-rich limestone grasslands. In addition there would have been a variety of other habitats in total amounting to a very rich and diverse wildlife scene, including many of the native mammals of Scotland that are now extinct. Those that have survived and still occur, such as wild cat, pine marten and red squirrel, would have been far more prevalent than they are today. The bird populations also would have been equally diverse and numerous; perhaps only those of the tops, such as ptarmigan, snow bunting and dotterel, have remained unchanged.

Soon though, the pastoral flocks of primitive sheep and herds of cattle, goats, ponies and pigs, and the torch of the farmer ate into this Eden. The fact that the ancient Gaelic-speaking people named specific places such as Achnambeithach ('field of the birch trees') and Coire nam Beith ('corrie of the birches'), suggests that much of the woodland and scrub disappeared a

Geàrr Aonach and Aonach Dubh and remnant woodland clinging to ungrazed crag and ledge very long time ago and that these were the only outstanding birch woods remaining. Later, very large increases in sheep numbers, plus the native population of red deer, served only to reduce the remnants to even smaller areas and particularly to ledges and crags outside the reach of hoof and incisor. High grazing levels in the past have even been responsible for large-scale erosion leading to landslips in some places! The woodland remnants are now most numerous on the cliffs and in the gorges on the north-facing cliffs of the Three Sisters and, in the wet, cool west-coast climate, enhanced by the high mountains and shading of the steep-sided glens, they support one of the richest collections of Oceanic bryophytes in the British Isles. In Glen Etive there is a small area of Scots pine which may well be a native remnant.

At the end of June, leaving the road and walking across the floor of Glen Coe, with its straggly heather, deer grass and purple moor-grass, up the most popular footpath and across the bridge that spans the gorge of the River Coe, unexpectedly, one suddenly finds oneself in regenerating heather and woodland. This was the Trust's first enclosure, constructed at the foot of Coire Gabhail in 1984. After only fifteen years the regeneration in the enclosure is impressive, giving but a hint of the former woodland cover. It also demonstrates, by comparison, the poor growth of the heather on the dry moorlands outside the fence.

Above the enclosure the path climbs more steeply before crossing the lip of the hanging valley and passing through a mass of huge boulders into the coire itself. In the steep acidic screes below Geàrr Aonach are great clumps of parsley fern, mountain fern and the spreading leaves of lady's mantle with its yellow flowers. On the well-drained slopes are also the small white flowers of wild strawberry and the yellow flowers of bird's-foot trefoil and yellow pimpernel. In some shady places, still flowering rather late in the season, are woodland remnants like wood anemone, primrose and bluebell. Near the summits of these acidic mountains are woolly-hair moss heaths, clubmosses, occasional white flowers of alpine mouse-ear, the inconspicuous Highland cudweed, and very occasionally snow-bed communities with sibbaldia.

A month later on, the steep grassy slopes of Meall Mór and the flushes are full of the flowers of yellow mountain saxifrage, and the scent of thyme hangs heavily in the air. On scattered ledges are tall herbs of roseroot, red campion, golden rod, stiff-stemmed hawkweeds crowned with yellow and the occasional montane whortle-leaved willow. On the species-rich mat grassland on the very top, the early purple orchid is past, but the fragrant orchid is out; also just out is bog asphodel. Other flowers include the fragile harebell, eyebrights, the tiny fairy flax and the eight-petalled white flowers and distinctive crimped leaves of mountain avens. Glencoe also has the very rare drooping brook and alpine rivulet saxifrages; seeds from the latter have been collected to supplement the declining colony at Ben Lawers (see Chapter 4).

Several of these communities are priority 'Qualifying Habitats' for the cSAC; for example the siliceous screes, species-rich alpine mat grassland and eutrophic tall herbs. There are also several other habitats of lesser priority, such as the blanket-bog and wet heath of the low ground, dry heath of higher well-drained ground, the high-altitude siliceous alpine and boreal grasslands and the montane willow scrub. These communities contain some of the most important plants on the property, the majority of which, as on Ben Lawers, are arctic-alpines, of which three are *Red Data Book* flowering plants and three nationally rare bryophytes. In addition there are eighteen vascular plants and 31 bryophytes, all nationally scarce. Including the fauna there are 36 *Red Data Book* and fifteen nationally rare species in total!

Drooping brook saxifrage

The sum of all these natural heritage interests, from the history of the rocks and the landscape to the smallest flowering plant and bryophyte, many of them of international importance, constitutes a very rich and diverse site that must be in the top ten of nature conservation value in Scotland. Combined with the fact that Glencoe probably attracts the largest number of visitors to any Trust countryside property (in the same league as Loch Lomond and the Cairngorms) it might be thought there would be great conflicts and possibly insoluble management problems.

Visitor management

Glencoe is probably the Trust's busiest property, attracting hundreds of thousands of people, predominantly tourists, walkers and climbers. Management up to the early 1980s concentrated almost entirely on visitor facilities. In the 1950s and 1960s two footbridges were built across the River Coe, the first to improve access after the drowning of a member of a mountain rescue party. Since 1971 footpath repair on the 64-kilometre (40-mile) network has been almost an annual event, with around £50,000 spent each year from 1990 to 1995, since when no funding has been available. Because of the sheer numbers of people using them, because the climate is so wet and the terrain so steep, Glencoe more than most places needs annual maintenance of its paths. There have been no path extensions nor signs erected and the one major investment in relation to visitor management, with funds from the CCS, has been the Visitor Centre which was built just off the road near the settlement at Clachaig in 1974–76. This development and the construction of footbridges was seen by some as a breach of the Unna Principles; however, these Principles must now be seen in the very different light of today when the numbers taking to the hills, when compared to the 1930s, are so enormous and still growing. It is also a fact that at Glencoe, bridges over the rivers have existed since people first used the glen, and it is a little ironic that mountaineers themselves make use of huts to improve their own access to mountains, for example the Rannoch Club Hut and Jacksonville.

When I briefly described crossing the glen from the road and walking up the footpath into Coire Gabhail, I omitted to mention that on the well-made path above the woodland enclosure the sound of the traffic on the A82 could be plainly heard. Sitting there, watching cars, caravans and buses disgorging their tourists onto the unofficial car parks and even hearing the bagpipe players, I was reminded more than anything of the view of Princes Street and the gardens from Edinburgh Castle! There are great problems for the Trust in coping with such enormous numbers of people who just want to stop and look at the glen, or perhaps have a break from driving, maybe a picnic or camp – and the Trust is not being helped by others. Once I had entered into

Walkers in the care of a Ranger

Lichen boulder

Coire Gabhail, however, I could no longer hear the traffic and, apart from the occasional discarded can or blackened stumps of a camp fire, I could have been many kilometres away from the crowd. The problem of sheer numbers of people is therefore very much confined to the glen floor, although in 1980 the Hawkins and Mollison report, commissioned by the Trust, expressed concerns about the effect of many people crossing the bridge and entering Coire Gabhail. The report advised that there should be no signing nor encouragement to take people up into the hills. No doubt further footpath repair would reduce the unsightly braiding and erosion, but there is an obvious danger that if paths are improved to too high a standard they will simply make it easier for more people to penetrate further and eventually destroy the wilderness quality of these rugged mountains. However, it has not been demonstrated, relative to the effects of past and present grazing, that walkers or climbers are a serious threat to flora or fauna.

Grazing and woodland management

If one looks at the Trust property on the OS map, the title 'Royal Forest' will be seen imprinted over Buachaille Etive Mór. This refers to the fact that in 1493 the area became a Royal Deer Forest under James IV. Before the advent of modern sheep breeds then, red deer would have been the primary grazer in this area. The last count of red deer on the property was 220 in 1997, giving a density of 3.4 per square kilometre across the property, even less than Torridon. The deer, however, are not evenly spread across Glencoe, being concentrated at the east end of the property where numbers increase in the winter with movement of hinds off Rannoch Moor. There is no sport stalking carried out at Glencoe (Unna Principles) and the present cull is around 40 hinds and calves and 20 stags, or around 27 per cent of the population. The main grazing pressure from deer is in Glen Etive and, as we shall see, special steps have to be taken there to reduce the grazing impact on some habitats, having regard to the fact that the deer spend most of their time on the neighbouring and sporting, Dalness, Blackmount and Black Corries Estates.

The Glen Coe shielings, before the clearances, were at King's House and in Gleann-leac-na-Muidhe, so until the nineteenth century, cattle would have been brought up the glen to the edge of Rannoch Moor in the summer to graze and probably on to the fine grasslands on Meall Mór. On Glencoe today the grazings are either vacant or leased and there are no common grazings. The numbers of sheep through the eighteenth and nineteenth centuries are not very clearly known and it is thought that the peak numbers were not until the 1980s with around 4,000 sheep on Glencoe as a whole. It *is* known that in 1940 there were 350 Blackface, plus cattle, on Dalness Forest. The Department of Agriculture at that time, during the Second World War, recommended that Dalness could carry 800. Subsequently numbers rose to around 1,200 in the winter and 2,400 in the summer! In 1995 the Trust took back the grazing lease on Buachaille Etive Mor and there has been no sheep grazing there since. On Glencoe there were 3,900 in 1995 and 2,749 in 1996. In 1997 the Trust took control of all sheep grazing on Glencoe and sheep numbers fell to 1,007 in 1998, with a further 300 to come off before 1999. Today the Trust has 600 sheep, just 15 per cent of the peak number in the 1980s, and also 30 cattle. So after, historically, some relatively heavy sheep grazing in the latter half of this century, under Trust management, sheep numbers have at last been substantially reduced.

Glencoe is now one of the very few Trust countryside properties where there is full control of the grazing, as most have either some common grazings or leased grazings attached to adjacent farms. At Glencoe therefore, after over 60 years of ownership, the Trust is finally in a position to tackle the issue of grazing and the sustainable management of its internationally important plant communities which it has had as a management prescription for some time. The impulse that is suddenly taking this forward at speed, is the same impulse that is driving forward similar management on other properties discussed in this book – the establishment of the Millennium Forest for Scotland (MFS) with its large financial resources, and the

Coire nam Beith
('corrie of the
birches')

designation in 1996 of over 90 per cent of Glencoe as a cSAC. The goals of these two initiatives and even those for different 'Qualifying' communities within the cSAC are, however, occasionally at odds, as we have already seen elsewhere. Glencoe, like Ben Lawers, is faced with the problem of finding a management regime which will, on the one hand, encourage the natural regeneration of the remnants of woodland and montane scrub, while on the other hand sustain tall-herb and species-rich alpine grassland communities, plus open communities on the glen floor. The former requires the absence of, or minimum, grazing, while the latter, as recommended by an EU LIFE Grazing Plan, requires regular moderate summer grazing and sometimes late summer grazing at least. In finding an answer to this conundrum, Glencoe has two major advantages and one disadvantage when compared to Ben Lawers. The advantages on Glencoe are that the major areas of grasslands are fairly discreet and there is almost complete control of the grazing. The disadvantage is the public perception of the landscape of Glen Coe itself as an open, almost desolate vista that attracts huge numbers of visitors and walkers.

One objective of management is:

The maintenance of the predominantly open landscape, with clear views of the mountains from the road.

Another is to bring about:

an increase in the area of native woodland, based on the existing fragments on the steep glen sides and gorges, to enhance the nature conservation value of the property.

To retain the open fields in the floor of the glen, sheep and cattle will be enclosed there, and there will be no pastoral management of the mountains, except for Meall Mór where the major area of alpine grassland occurs. The edge of the River Coe will be protected from grazing and the natural alder and willow growth will be encouraged to return, which will stabilise the eroding banks. Moderate grazing of Meall Mór will be introduced and a baseline and long-term monitoring programme to record the effects on the important species of the grassland will be set up to guide future levels of grazing. Curiously the LIFE Grazing Plan does not mention a role for cattle which must have been the principal domestic stock grazing this area for at least 1,000 years.

At the present moment there are only two enclosed and therefore protected areas of native woodland at Glencoe. One is the plot below Coire Gabhail amounting to about five hectares, and the other is a WGS scheme on the River Etive at 5.5 hectares: a tiny fraction of the woodland remnants. As red deer will continue to infiltrate from the surrounding sporting estates as long as they are unwilling or unable to reduce their deer population, even though managed to relatively low levels on Glencoe itself, the unenclosed woodland remnants in Glen Etive will have to be enclosed in order to protect them and encourage regeneration. Under an MFS scheme therefore nine plots, mainly for natural regeneration, have been identified, five of which are in Glen Etive, including the remnant area of Scots pine and the WGS plot on the banks of the River Etive, amounting in total to 77 hectares, all of which will be fenced against deer. In addition to Scots pine these plots enclose birch, rowan, aspen, holly and oak.

On much lower ground at the other end of the property, on the west side of Signal Rock by the Visitor Centre at Clachaig, management of an enclosure of both planted woodland and some ancient woodland, of 20 hectares, will be carried out to encourage the regeneration of native species there. Likewise on the east, or lower side of the Rock an enclosure of 10 hectares will encourage the regeneration of alder and willows on the wet ground by the River Coe. Opposite these enclosures, on the slopes of Meall Mór an enclosure of approximately 20 hectares is proposed. It will enclose difficult and exposed ground at around 600 metres (2,000 feet) and is aimed specifically at protecting the few small communities of whortle-leaved willow clinging to ledges, from which the grassland has been derived by grazing. Getting the optimum grazing level here will be tricky as the herb-rich grassland requires moderate to heavy grazing to suppress dwarf shrubs and tussocky grasses, the tall herbs require low year-round and after seeding, late-summer grazing, while the regenerating willow scrub and trees require no grazing!

The last plot will cover an unfenced area of approximately 73 hectares, extending down both sides of Glen Coe itself from the waterfalls at the Pass to the limit of the Trust's western boundary. Its lower boundary will be the enclosed pastures on the glen floor while its upper boundary will be the natural tree-line at around 500 metres (1,640 feet). On the steep slopes and crags of the Three Sisters is the largest extent of remnant birch wood on Glencoe which will very gradually expand in the absence of sheep grazing. Woodland will expand even more gradually on the opposite slopes of Aonach Eagach where there are relatively few seed trees. This is the area where there is concern that the woodland could have a detrimental impact on the popular landscape view of Glen Coe itself. The huge buttresses of the Three Sisters however, will still tower above the tree-line and the uppermost scrub and will still dwarf the impact of the expanding woodland. The change, in the terms of the human lifespan, will also of course be almost imperceptible.

Summation

Of the three great responsibilities faced by the Trust at Glencoe, the first is the management of the footpaths which have to sustain an enormous pressure of walkers and climbers, in the most difficult of terrains and in a very wet climate. A great deal of work has been done, but there remains much to be done. Glencoe, with no endowment, faces difficulty even with the

Volunteers working on path

maintenance of what it has already repaired. At the time of writing the Trust has won an EU Objective 1 bid for about £200,000 for further footpath repair. Unfortunately for the Trust there is serious footpath erosion in the Clachaig Gully on Sgorr nam Fiannaidh, just behind the Visitor Centre and just outside the property, which detracts from the very real efforts being made and, because few visitors know the property boundary, reflects badly on the Trust: a very obvious illustration of the need for the co-ordination and support of others in Glencoe.

The second and most public problem, and responsibility, for the Trust and others, with which I began this chapter, is the sheer pressure of visitors. The Visitor Centre is outside the scope of this book, and suffice it here to note that it is planned to commence a new building in 1999. By far the greatest number of visitors however, in the hundreds of thousands, are those who park on the unofficial roadside car parks and make Glen Coe one of the Scottish countryside's tourist hotspots. The result, in the absence of proper roadside management, is a series of unofficial car and bus parks, picnic sites, eroded verges, litter, fly-camping and other activities that, although they do not threaten the flora and fauna of Glencoe, despoil the glen, turning it into a badly managed public park.

As we noted in the last chapter, Glencoe was recommended as a National Park by the 'Ramsay' Committee in 1945. This committee recognised the need for sympathetic control of developments in areas of high landscape and wildlife value and the need for continuing access for recreation. Radically, they favoured land acquisition and the promotion of the concept of National Parks as tools to revitalise the Highland economy, identifying five potential Parks. The largest of these was to be Ben Nevis/Glen Coe/Blackmount extending to almost 1,600 square kilometres! Fortunately, or unfortunately, depending on one's view, the concept of National Parks in Scotland was dropped after that. However, the 1990 CCS report to the Scottish Office recognised four mountain 'areas of special importance', once again including Glen Coe, Ben Nevis and the Blackmount, and recommended they should be called 'National Parks'.

The Scottish Office response, although not in favour of a National Park, recognised specific site-related pressures arising from visitor use in the Glencoe area, and looked to SNH to seek means of overcoming these, never mind the fact that several other bodies, notably the local authority, Tourist Board and Local Enterprise Company, among others, have responsibilities in this area too. Eight years later, in 1998, once again the Scottish Office asked its countryside advisory agency, SNH, to consult on National Parks. SNH has recommended that there should be 'National Parks' centred around Loch Lomond and the Cairngorms; however it did not recommend that the Glencoe area should be similarly designated. Since 1945 the needs in relation to visitor impact on the landscape of Glen Coe have not diminished; in fact they have become more pressing! Unfortunately, the tardiness of others to accept that they have a responsibility, to co-ordinate their resources and expertise to address the problems, is reflecting badly on the Trust. Glen Coe is such an economic asset to the area that this lack of action is very surprising and rather sad.

Higher up the mountain the principal area of vegetation interest on Meall Mór is coming under grazing management, otherwise the arctic-alpine plants are fairly scattered and not apparently under any visitor or grazing threat: 'apparently', because at present there is only a very limited monitoring of their status. Such an important site as Glencoe, however, requires a much greater investment in this area, akin to that at Ben Lawers.

One day, the paths up into the hanging valleys, over the bealachs, on to the tops, or onto the grassy, flower-rich alpine meadows on Meall Mór, will pass through a variety of woodlands which will echo to the call of woodland birds and be alive with the signs of small and large mammals, and where underfoot woodland flowers and ferns will flourish. All of which will create a new and exciting contrast to the pastures by the river, open areas of wet and dry heath, grasslands, the bare screes, shoulders and ridges of the mountain, as well as hiding some of the worst footpath scars. Of all the properties discussed in this book however, it will be the restoration of native woodland communities on Glencoe which will have the greatest impact on Scots and tourists, as its restoration will be very visible on this, the most public of the

Trust's countryside properties. When the Trust gets round to replacing the interpretation panels in its Visitor Centre and rewriting its Glencoe literature, it should bear this in mind.

Chapter 9

Ben Lomond

Introduction

Ben Lomond is the most southerly of the 'Highland' mountains, lying just north of the Highland Boundary Fault that runs from Stonehaven on the east coast right across Scotland to near Helensburgh on the west. From the eastern banks of Loch Lomond, across which the fault runs, Ben Lomond rises fairly steeply to its summit at 974 metres (3,195 feet). Although physiographically in the Highlands, Ben Lomond, on the initial approach from the south, has a feel of the Lowlands. One passes first through arable farmland, then along the gentle loch side through oak woodland and the Queen Elizabeth Forest Park, before the footpath takes off uphill at Rowardennan. Being so close to Glasgow and its numerous satellite towns, as well as adjacent to Loch Lomond with its many recreational facilities and, like Glencoe, a site associated with folk songs, poems and nostalgia, Ben Lomond has always attracted a large number of people. Ben Lomond is one of the most accessible of Scottish mountains and became popular for visitors from the eighteenth century onwards. For example, Pennant visited in 1790, and William and Dorothy Wordsworth, accompanied by Coleridge and Dr Johnson later in 1803, while Sir Walter Scott based his famous romantic poem 'The Lady of the Lake' here, as well as the novel *Rob Roy* on the area. The works of writers such as these popularised Ben Lomond for a large audience. Ben Lomond is also, more than any other Scottish peak, the 'people's' mountain. Even before the Second World War, in the 1920s and 1930s, 10,000 Clydesiders made the journey to Loch Lomond and took the path to the summit annually.

Having set off from the car parks, picnic tables and paddling children by the lochside, it is a five-kilometre walk of variable gradient to the summit. The first and last sections are the steepest, and it is not really until one stands on the top that one appreciates being *in* the Highlands, for there they are laid out in a wide panorama, well described by the Reverend William Freeland in the 1845 Statistical Account:

Facing page
Loch Lomond

When you reach its conical summit, overtopping every surrounding eminence, and elevated 3,000 ft above the level of the sea, you have on the north an endless succession of mountains, like the billows of the stormy ocean; and on the south, you have presented before you, as on a map, the riches and beauty of the central district of Scotland, from the Western Isles to the Firth of Forth.

To the north and north-east are the Breadalbane mountains and Ben Lawers, of which Ben Lomond is a westerly outlier. Glencoe and Ben Nevis lie further to the north, and away beyond Ben Lawers lie the Cairngorms. A careful look at the plants around one's feet will also confirm that Ben Lomond *is* a mountain and that the climate is very different from that by the banks of the loch below. As well as being so attractive to walkers, Ben Lomond, being a Munro and probably the second most popular peak in Scotland, is a site of both landscape and nature conservation interest; and it is also a working hill farm, supporting a family.

As with all the other sites we have discussed, the Ben Lomond area would have been settled very early in the history of human expansion into Scotland following the retreat of the ice some 10,000 years ago. The fresh waters and the islands of the loch would have offered food and refuge and the opportunity of easy travel over its length. There is no doubt, though there are no scheduled archaeological sites on the property, that the lower slopes have

Walkers on Ben Lomond in winter

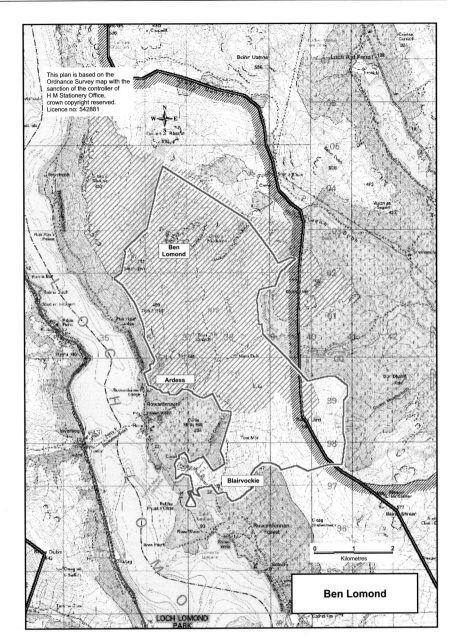

This plan is based on the Ordnance Survey map with the sanction of the controller of H M Stationery Office, crown copyright reserved. Licence no: 542881

Ben Lomond

Ardess

Blairvockie

0   1   2
Kilometres

Ben Lomond

LOCH LOMOND PARK

Figure 9.1
Map of the
Ben Lomond area
(Legend: see p. xviii)

been continuously occupied and that from Neolithic times the woodland would have been cleared and the hill ground used for pasture. In the middle of the first millennium AD this was an area of human turbulence, occupied by British tribes who were hemmed in by the Scots of Dalradia to the north and west, the Picts to the east and by the Angles of Bernicia to the south-east. Unlike the other Trust properties to the west and north, it was not involved in the turbulence around the turn of the first millennium AD when much of the west and north was occupied by the Vikings, but it was absorbed early into the new nation of Scotland.

By the thirteenth century most of west central Scotland had been transformed into a feudal state with large areas of land being given to the new aristocracy by the incoming Normans. The farm soils were fertile and the oak forests of great value for their timber, charcoal and game. For the next 200 years times were fairly settled, but there then followed more turbulence through the Reformation and the Jacobite wars. Several powerful families owned the land around Ben Lomond at this time, including the Buchanans and Drummonds, but towards the close of the seventeenth century the land fell under the ownership of the Marquess of Montrose (the first Duke of Montrose) and in the middle of the nineteenth century that family also purchased Blairvockie, the present farm, and Ben Lomond itself. In 1925, when the 5th Duke of Montrose died, large portions of the huge estate were sold off.

Just after the Second World War, because of the importance that Ben Lomond had held for so many years for the people of Clydeside and because so many of them gave their lives for their country in both World Wars, the National Land Fund, in their memory, purchased a large area of ground around Rowardennan, including Ben Lomond itself. The land was then put in the hands of the FC to manage it for the people. The FC interpretation of that responsibility was to plant up a great deal of the land as commercial plantation, in some locations underplanting the existing oakwood. In 1984, after selling off Cashel to private hands, the FC put Blairvockie Farm and Ben Lomond on the market, retaining the planted forests. This aroused much concern among those who remembered why the land had been purchased in the first place! In order to keep the 'people's' mountain and access to it in public ownership, the then Countryside Commission for Scotland, considering that the Trust was the ideal owner, gave a grant to the Trust to enable it to purchase the property. There is a strange untold story here as to why Ben Lomond, bought by public funds for the people, was bought a second time 30 years later with funds from another public body! The Trust then, through a public appeal, which included a large sum from the National Heritage Memorial Fund (NHMF), established an endowment fund for the property. In 1985 the Trust formed a Limited Partnership agreement with the Firm of Messrs J. Maxwell to whom they let Blairvockie Farm. In 1995, on the forty-fifth anniversary of the purchase of the property for the people, Ben Lomond, along with the adjacent FC property, was designated as a National Memorial Park to those who gave their lives in both World Wars.

The property, of 2,173 hectares, covers Ben Lomond itself and the high ground south to Blairvockie Farm, only touching the Loch Lomond shore for a couple of hundred metres north of Rowardennan. There are several designations which cover the property. Over two-thirds (1,638 hectares) is notified as an SSSI, of which the citation states:

Ben Lomond is the most southerly hill massif in Scotland with an altitude exceeding 3,000 feet. It is distinct from the other hills in the Southern Highlands in that it retains remnants of the full range of upland plant communities from low to high altitude, a feature which has been lost from neighbouring hills.

The property is also wholly within the ESA established first in 1987, almost wholly within the Loch Lomond Regional Park which was created in 1988, and wholly within the NSA established in 1972. The Regional Park was created for the purpose of conserving natural beauty and wildlife, promoting enjoyment of the countryside and encouraging the social and economic well-being of the area, and is administered by a Park Authority.

The landscape of the area and its recreational importance had, however, been recognised some time ago, by the 'Ramsay' Committee in 1945 when it was recommended, like Glencoe and the Cairngorms, as a National Park (NP). The 1990 report of the CCS to the Scottish Office also recognised the need for co-ordinated management of the area and similarly recommended NP status for this area. In 1992 the Secretary of State established The Loch Lomond and Trossach Working Party to report on the pressures and problems facing the area. This report noted that there were now four to five million visitors annually to the area and recommended co-ordinated management. Most recently SNH has once again recommended an NP for the area, which recommendation has at last been accepted by the Government which intends to bring legislation to the Scottish Parliament to enable Loch Lomond and Trossachs National Park to become operational by 2001, almost fifty years after the original recommendation!

Natural heritage

Belonging to the Highland side of the Boundary Fault, the geology of Ben Lomond is mainly that of schistose grits and mica-schists which are metamorphosed rocks of the Dalradian, just a little younger than the Moine rocks of Kintail, but hundreds of millions of years older than the softer sedimentary rocks of the Devonian that commence just a few kilometres south, on the other side of the Fault. The soils derived from the schists of Ben Lomond are mainly peaty with sandy loams and occasional loam and silty loams. Such soils, in conjunction with altitude, steep slopes and in an area of high rainfall and humidity, are generally poor and make the upland agriculturally suitable only for rough grazing. In places though, there are flushes and springs that support more diverse plant communities, and at higher altitude there are scarce species-rich montane communities, notably on cliff-ledges.

Ben Lomond from across Loch Lomond with native woodland and commercial plantations

The last Ice Age did not have such a spectacular effect on the relatively simple shape of Ben Lomond as it did on the complex mountains at Glencoe, or at Torridon or Kintail, but a large post-glacial rock slide can be seen on the west side of the summit. Post-glacial plant colonisation of Ben Lomond, even at its relatively southern position in Scotland was, however, of much the same species as at other Scottish mountains, and a few of these arctic-alpine and montane species still survive there as we will see. Following the succession of vegetation types that occurred due to the amelioration of the climate during the first few post-glacial millennia, the subsequent effects of a deteriorating climate and the arrival of people created the vegetation pattern that we see today. Before the forests were cleared and the upland pastures established on Ben Lomond however, birch and willow scrub would have been found up to around 600 metres (2,000 feet) and the latter beyond that height. This would not have been complete cover of course, as blanket-bog, whose formation was due mainly to the climate becoming cooler and wetter, covers almost a third of the property.

Nevertheless, looking across to Ben Lomond from a high point on the opposite side of Loch Lomond around 4,000 years ago, the scene would have been very different from that of today. Instead of seeing open moorland and grassland from Beinn Uird at the south end right to the Ben Lomond summit, all that would have stood out as unforested, dwarf-shrub heath and summit moss-heath would probably have been the summits of Ptarmigan,

Ben Lomond itself and the ridge to Sron Aonaich. By the opening of the first millennium AD however, farming activity had basically established a stable pattern of very much reduced forest and a landscape dominated by open dwarf-shrub heather moorland from well below the tree-line, which was to last for almost another 2,000 years. It is only in the last couple of hundred years or so that the stability of the dwarf-shrub dominated moorland and the very survival of a number of other upland communities has become so seriously threatened.

This has happened, as we have seen elsewhere, because of changes that have taken place in our management of the uplands. After hundreds of years of traditional mixed summer grazing at Ben Lomond, predominantly by cattle, but also by goats, Blairvockie Farm in 1780 was converted into an upland sheep farm. The number of sheep on the hill from that time is not accurately known, but we do know from the *Statistical Account* in 1845 that there were around 16,500 Blackface ewes, plus 240 milking cows and 840 black cattle grazing along the upper side of Loch Lomond in the Balmaha parish, which would have had access to the hill pastures *and* the many lower areas of the hill now fenced off and forested. Today there are 1,800 ewes and followers with access to only 2,000 hectares; however, that is not a heavy stocking level, at least on paper.

In 1986, with much of the property and its vegetation communities being designated as an SSSI, the Trust contracted NCC to carry out a survey of the vegetation of Ben Lomond. This resulted in a report, *Blairvockie Farm – Ben Lomond SSSI*, from the NCC which analysed the present condition of the various plant communities, the impact of present management and made recommendations for future management. Since the implications of the report have such a widespread applicability in Scotland we will return to it shortly in some detail under 'Management'. Meanwhile we should have a look at the status of the other communities and particularly those that heather moorland gradually replaced over a long period of time.

The original forest cover of the Ben Lomond area was a broadleaf woodland dominated by oak, ash and birch, with also holly, hawthorn, blackthorn and rowan among other trees, which extended from the loch side well up the mountain. Within the western perimeter of the Trust property, which as we have noted only briefly touches the loch side, there are only scattered woodland remnants left, very often as fingers stretching up the hillside, clinging to steep stream banks. In total however, the many fragments may total as much as 100 hectares of native woodland. On the lower slopes this woodland would have been managed for building timber and fuel for a very long time. In the eighteenth century charcoal was used in iron smelting and in the nineteenth century the woodland was managed by coppicing and planting for its bark for tanning and in the production of dyes. At this relatively low altitude on damp soils there are now communities with the

Oakwoods

distinctively sweet-smelling bog myrtle, grassland dominated by purple moor grass and, on the drier ground where once there was woodland, stands of bracken.

In flushes within the woodland relicts, all along the lower west slopes, are also shrub communities mostly of heather, eared and grey willow, but also with taller goat willow and the prostrate creeping willow. These communities are rather rare today in Scotland as they are very susceptible to damage from traditional moorland burning and grazing practices. Below the natural tree-line dwarf-shrub moorlands and grasslands have been created from the woodland by burning and grazing. Above the tree-line the montane dwarf-shrub heaths – of heather, crowberry and blaeberry for example – are semi-natural, but some of the grasslands have been created from the original dwarf-shrub heath by similar grazing and burning management, for example the mat-grass community which dominates the hill at mid-altitude. This mosaic of semi-natural and altered moorland and grasslands now covers the hill to not far short of the summit. Of these, dry heather moorland, which is so characteristic of the uplands of Scotland, is particularly valuable as it is becoming increasingly scarce.

A large proportion of the property, above and below the tree-line, has therefore been modified by management to a considerable extent. However, within that area, as we have noted earlier, covering about 30 per cent of the property, is blanket-bog, a community that has probably been very little modified. This is dominated by heather, hare's tail cotton grass and sphagnum moss and is one of Scotland's and Britain's specialities, a fragile habitat created in oceanic, cool and wet climates and supporting a range of plants and invertebrates adapted to living on its wet and acidic surface.

Finally, on the summit, as on the tops of all the other mountain properties, are the oldest communities that were more widespread just after the close of the Ice Age, but have become restricted by the encroachment of more temperate communities that have crept up the hill as the climate improved. On the summit at Ben Lomond is the typical woolly-hair moss heath, a fragile community very susceptible to trampling damage. On the coldest part of the mountain, the north-facing crags just below the summit, is another

The sweet-smelling bog asphodel

moss heath (here reaching its southern limit in Britain) and also the montane variety of mat grassland, of which only fragmented examples can be found further south. Both these communities are typical of mountain areas where there is prolonged snow-lie, and here must be under threat if climate change implies more moderate winter temperatures in the west of Scotland.

It is the presence of *all* those plant communities, from the shores of Loch Lomond to the summit of the Ben, that makes the vegetation of the property so unique in the Southern Highlands and that is the principal reason for the SSSI designation. There are no 'protected' upland plant species on Ben Lomond, today at least, although there are a few species with a restricted distribution, just as there are a few restricted upland invertebrates. Climbing the hill in early July through the bog myrtle and bracken and up into bent grassland, the fragrant orchid is in flower and living up to its name, and on the blanket-bog the under-rated asphodel, just out in Glencoe a week earlier, is also smelling sweetly. Close to the summit the alpine mouse ear is in flower, looking much smaller and greener than the arctic mouse ear on Torridon. Also at this altitude are the restricted alpine saxifrage and vernal sandwort, the less conspicuous montane rushes – three-leaved and three-flowered – a few other restricted montane plants and several other that are more widespread, but nonetheless extremely attractive.

The change in vegetation management

We have covered the significant changes that have occurred since the Ice Age to the vegetation of Ben Lomond and highlighted the dramatic change in land management that occurred only 200 years ago, namely the introduction of intensive sheep grazing. Dwarf-shrub heath, both wet and dry forms, and blanket-bog were probably the dominant vegetation types from below the tree-line to the summit heath at the period when Blairvockie became a sheep farm in 1780. So how did the changes come about? As we noted in Chapter 1, sheep require to feed on heather shoots in the winter months when grass is not available; this necessitates the burning of heather on a periodic basis to ensure that there is always a supply of tender young heather shoots. If the grazing pressure is too great for the heather it cannot grow fast enough to re-establish its dominance after burning and can be replaced by grass and rush species. Burning also kills those other 'woody' plants – trees, willow shrubs and juniper for example. It seems that on Ben Lomond much of the blanket-bog, which also supports heather as a dominant, was probably not severely burned or grazed, partly because the wet ground makes it difficult to burn and partly because, if there is drier ground available, sheep will avoid the wet ground. Where there *has* been burning on blanket-bog, the heather has partly been replaced by cotton grass, deer grass and heath rush. It is estimated that around 20 per cent of the vegetation of Ben Lomond has been modified in this way.

On dry moorland with heavy grazing, heather can become replaced by the unpalatable mat grass, as at Ben Lawers and Kintail. On Ben Lomond this type of grassland is now by far the most common. At lower levels on Ben Lomond where both bog myrtle and purple moor grass are components of heather moorland, burning has favoured the purple moor grass, allowing it to replace the shrubs. At this level too, which was once woodland, bracken has spread through the bent grasslands.

Nearly all the plant species mentioned above that replace heather under an over-intensive grazing and burning regime, such as mat grass, heath rush, purple moor grass and bracken, are unpalatable to sheep. If burning and high grazing pressure is sustained, a vicious circle sets in, whereby a decreasing area of heather moorland becomes more and more of a focus for winter grazing and spring burning and a larger and larger area of unpalatable vegetation replaces that moorland. Unfortunately for nature conservation, the replacement vegetation is also very much poorer in wildlife terms than the moorland that is lost. This story is common across Scotland and has not yet reached its conclusion. At Ben Lomond there is a further element in the tale of the vegetation though.

Having said earlier that Ben Lomond has a *few* restricted montane plant species, I have to say that this was not always the case. This mountain, like Ben Lawers, has actually been a Mecca for botanists for over 200 years and there are records of a number of flowering plants, grasses, sedges, ferns and clubmosses, that no longer occur. Even allowing for the fact that there may have been mis-identification, or later quotation without verification, there can be little doubt that many plant species, not just a few, have disappeared from Ben Lomond since the late eighteenth century. In the past the summit heath was described as species-rich; but it certainly cannot be described as such now. There is no doubt that some, apparently extinct before the twentieth century, probably disappeared in the vasculums of ardent collectors in the eighteenth and nineteenth centuries and that possibly one or two that apparently disappeared *this* century went the same way. However, some species, such as blue moor grass and russet sedge, were described as 'plentiful' by early botanists and it is surely no coincidence that these two species, and interrupted clubmoss, all grew in open habitats where they would have been vulnerable to increased grazing levels. It seems very probable therefore that a number of these losses were also due to the change in management to intensive sheep grazing. Even today there are plant species that are becoming harder and harder to re-locate.

Heather

So the changes that have occurred to the vegetation over the past 200 years have not just been about the modification of communities, but also about the total loss of species. It must also be borne in mind that the records of change just discussed refer only to the flora; there are not, relatively speaking, such good records for the fauna. It can easily be surmised however, that waders, grouse and ptarmigan, and possibly hare populations, would have been higher before the agricultural changes took place. It is also very probable that the populations of a number of montane invertebrates have also been impoverished and in some cases become extinct.

Present and future vegetation management

The 1986 Report from the NCC on the condition of the vegetation of Blairvockie Farm on Ben Lomond has been the basis for much of the above description of its present state. The Report, however, went on to recommend that, although there has been a deterioration in the condition and diversity of the vegetation in recent years through heavy grazing, prior to Trust ownership, Ben Lomond still has the remnants of its original vegetation types, fragmented though they may be, and that 'this trend can be reversed'. The Report acknowledged that simply fencing off the SSSI from the farm and managing it separately could allow restoration of the vegetation; however, more radically it suggested that, with appropriate management, Ben Lomond could set itself the goal of demonstrating how upland farmland and wildlife could co-exist, and this the Trust has accepted.

The principal aim of Trust management at Ben Lomond is to:

Ensure the permanent preservation and enhancement, for the benefit of the nation, of Ben Lomond as a property of high landscape, nature conservation, cultural, recreational and educational value.

The dilemma on Ben Lomond for the Trust and the Blairvockie Farm tenant who runs 1,400 Blackface ewes and followers, plus around 25 Galloway cattle and followers, was that the Report stated that the detrimental changes to the vegetation discussed above were continuing. It had been estimated that on about 20 per cent of the property, predominantly on the lower ground, heather was still being over-grazed and eliminated from dry heath, wet heath and blanket-bog. Likewise, growth of eared and grey willow, and bog myrtle was being suppressed, and tree and shrub regeneration was being held in check. On the highest ground it was also apparent that the woolly hair-moss summit heath was being colonised by grasses, such as wavy hair grass and sheep's fescue, at the expense of the naturally dominant moss species itself. This was occurring most probably by the trampling of sheep and the importation of grass seed via their feet. Clearly if the Trust intends to meet its principal aim, while sustaining a viable hill farm, there has to be agreement on grazing management between the Trust and the tenant.

In 1989 therefore a 50-year Management Agreement was concluded between the Trust, the tenant farmer and NCC, which included conditions on grazing stock. Under the terms of an Agreed Management Policy the management objectives are:

a)   *to maintain the land in an uncultivated and unimproved state;*
b)   *to maintain and enhance the special scientific interest of the land.*

A specific objective includes:

the protection and regeneration of heather moorland and native woodland and scrub over prescribed areas and the restoration of the summit heath.

In 1990 the NCC produced a Management Plan for the SSSI, in agreement with the farmer, whose first and second operational objectives are:

1.   *To maintain, enhance and extend to their more natural state the site's semi-natural habitats and communities including wet and dry heaths, blanket bog, willow scrub and summit heaths with an associated lower altitude native woodland.*
2.   *To maintain and enhance the population of rare species of animals and plants native to the site.*

This was the first and only Management Plan for Ben Lomond until the Trust produced the present five-year plan in 1994, ten years after its purchase, in which it included the objective to:

Maintain and enhance the nature conservation and natural heritage value of Ben Lomond.

Gradually, therefore, the Trust has come to recognise the importance of the nature conservation element of Ben Lomond.

At the time (1989) of the agreement with the tenant farmer, the boundaries of the site were not stock-proof, allowing 60 to 100 neighbouring ewes to move onto and graze the property. A march fence has now been erected with the agreement of the neighbour on the north end of the property which will reduce grazing pressure on the cold north-facing slopes which support the moss and grass heaths associated with snow cover. The other high-altitude vegetation community of interest requiring some protection is the summit moss heath. Excluding the few sheep which graze at this altitude should not incur any economic loss to the farm and would benefit this slow-growing vegetation; but on the other hand, fences at this altitude would be an intrusion on the landscape. At the present moment therefore the Trust has erected some small experimental enclosures to monitor the effects of grazing reduction. Such monitoring is also being carried out on the other (unenclosed) main grass and heath communities, and in 1998 results have shown a reduction in the grazing of heather from 45–50 per cent to around 32 per cent of that available. The aim is to get that down to between 20–30 per cent, at which level the individual plants will begin to put on growth.

At the present moment the bulk of the sheep graze the northern two-thirds of the farm, which includes the north-facing slopes and the summit heath. Advice from the Scottish Agricultural College (SAC), after examining the grazings in that area, has been to reduce that by 300. The Trust and the tenant farmer, conscious of the poor condition of the heather, have reduced this by a further 100. The other, slightly less controllable, grazers of Ben Lomond, are red deer. It is estimated that about 200 graze the hill, sheltering in the surrounding plantations and woodland where they are under the management of FE. That number is rather high and must be having a significant effect on the vegetation. This has been recognised by the Trust and FE, and the annual cull is to be increased.

The widespread mat-grass community, conversely, requires heavier grazing, at least in the short term. Here it is recognised that there is an opportunity to use cattle (as at Ben Lawers) which are so much less selective in their grazing preferences than sheep. If some of the finer grasses and even heather can be restored to this community this could attract the sheep and reduce grazing pressures elsewhere. Another opportunity for spreading the grazing pressure will be to carefully burn areas of old heather on dry moorland, so making the heather more palatable to sheep. A suggestion in the MP that there might be burning of 'rank' heather on blanket-bog for the same purpose, in contrast to the non-burning policy of this community on

Young wheatear

Enclosure at Coire Corrach after seven years, showing heather and birch regeneration

Mar Lodge Estate, should be ignored, as much damage can be done to the living surface of the bog. Burning of the areas dominated by purple moor grass would also have a negative effect by killing off any regenerating trees and shrubs and simply encouraging more moor grass.

To meet the objective relating to protection and regeneration of native woodland and scrub, which occupies about 1 per cent of the property, one large enclosure of 25 hectares and two smaller ones totalling 10 hectares were erected in 1989/90 around remnants, and there has been a general policy to remove exotic tree and shrub species. At Coire Corrach, where there are post-twelfth-century shieling remains, there has been some spraying of bracken using ESA funds. Here and at another enclosure there has been vigorous regeneration of birch, growth of willow and bog myrtle, and even some oak regeneration, all now freed from grazing. In the third there has been regeneration of hazel and aspen from suckers. Once the growing tips of these shrubs and trees are above grazing height sheep may be introduced for short periods. One of the other principal aims of management is to maintain and improve the landscape quality. Naturally there is a concern that increasing the cover of woodland will have some effect on the landscape. A more natural woodland extending gradually up towards the tree-line, accompanied by an improvement in the health of the dwarf-shrub and grassland vegetation within and beyond the woodland should, however, enrich the quality of the landscape.

Apart from management of the vegetation by fencing or burning, a third method of reducing grazing pressure at a critical time, has been to remove some 530 sheep from the hill in the winter months. This should gradually allow the heather, and therefore future winter feed, to recover, to the benefit of both the sheep and wildlife such as grouse and mountain hare. This, however, will be the most expensive element of management as far as the tenant farmer is concerned.

Summation

Although only a few, and rather simplified, examples of vegetation management have been given, for example by grazing manipulation and burning, we have noted that the situation in reality is very complex and that monitoring of all the components of the vegetation and herbivores, including deer, will be required to provide a guide to grazing management over the whole farm. There are no fences compartmentalising the mosaic of vegetation communities, apart from the three woodland enclosures, and therefore the logistics of grazing management will not make differential grazing easy. This means that the grazing levels on each component of the vegetation will need to be continually appraised against the economic viability of the farm. These problems do not exist at Glencoe where all the grazing is in hand and have been approached on Ben Lawers in a less holistic way by a very large-scale division of grazing management. They do exist however, over a wide area of upland Scotland and that is why it is right in this specific situation, that the Trust, in addition to having the support and advice of NCC and now SNH, is seeking the advice of the agriculture experts. Finding the finance to support this management in the long term is not going to be easy.

In this chapter we have concentrated mostly on the vegetation and agricultural management; however it should not be forgotten that the Trust has had to invest heavily in footpath management at this property, taking over from the voluntary efforts of the Friends of the Ben. Between 1993 and 1996, of the 30,000 people who visited Ben Lomond annually, as many as half climbed the Ben. Some of those will have been walkers taking the West Highland Way which passes through the property by the loch shore. Most visitors use the Main Path, but a fair proportion also use the Ptarmigan Path, often using both as a circular walk. With that number of users it is not surprising that ten years ago the paths were in very poor condition. Since 1991 however, a programme of path repair has been carried out by the Trust (£50,000) annually with the support of grants from SNH (circa £210,000 over ten years), the Royal Bank of Scotland (£75,000) and the SMC (£10,000). It is estimated that around £350,000 has been spent on completing the capital work to the footpaths on Ben Lomond over the past ten years. Now that this has been accomplished, SNH is funding 60 per cent of a seasonal post whose principal task is the maintenance of these paths. The footpath work and that on the enclosures, and monitoring now being carried out, could not be continued without a resident Ranger and a Ranger Base. The Trust has therefore very recently also made a substantial investment in a Base for its full-time Ranger at Ardess.

The principal aim of the Trust at Ben Lomond, as we have seen, is the conservation and enhancement of the natural heritage while continuing the

Footpath repair
discussion

long tradition of hill farming. This is yet another example of the other side of
the new coin of natural heritage conservation thinking – of the central place
of people and community – which the Trust has adopted. The challenge at
Ben Lomond to achieve the balance is relatively simpler than that on the
islands of Fair Isle and Canna where there are additional transport and
communications costs, and elsewhere where there are also crofting
communities, as at Torridon and Kintail. Nonetheless the principles are the
same and the solutions potentially equally applicable to many similar hill
and mountain properties in Scotland, whether under Trust, other voluntary,
state, or private hands.

Ben Lomond is yet another excellent example of the deterioration of the
vegetation resource of the hills of Scotland, particularly over the past couple
of centuries, a resource both aesthetic and economic. It is an ambitious Trust
plan to restore both elements, and as we have seen, a complex plan that must
remain flexible in its grazing patterns for at least another generation and
maybe a minimum of 100 years. Because of past records, Ben Lomond has
the evidence that demonstrates, even more than Ben Lawers, the gradual
impoverishment of its flora, and inevitably its fauna also. Along with
Glencoe these properties support a significant number of our rare arctic-
alpine and montane plants. So tenuous is the hold of some of these species
that they could already be on their way to extinction without direct efforts of
restoration, such as is being carried out with the alpine rivulet saxifrage on
Ben Lawers. If, as is probable, the Trust do not have enough information on
the exact status of these species, there is an urgent need to carry out the
detailed monitoring required, to investigate the genetic relationships
between the various populations, and co-ordinate the effort on at least these
three properties.

Chapter 10

St Kilda

Introduction and Description

July is the season for seabirds and their young, when colonies overflow with sound and activity, when there is a continuous traffic of birds of all shapes and sizes from nests and ledges to the horizon and back, and, if the season is good, off-duty birds laze and preen, or endlessly and effortlessly promenade the streets of the air adjacent to the cliffs. Nowhere in the British Isles, nor in Europe for that matter, can compare with the sheer scale of the seabird colonies on the magnificent islands of St Kilda. Looking down on the enormous gannet colonies from the summits of Boreray, or up from the heaving deck of a boat on the Atlantic swell, it is as if a giant duvet has burst and filled the sky with feathers, swirling haphazardly in the invisible eddies of the wind. But there is even more to St Kilda than that!

On most days, approaching by sea, one loses sight of the Hebrides before fully seeing and appreciating the size and shape of the St Kilda archipelago. The islands are surrounded by empty ocean out of which they erupt from the depths like the heads of leviathans, or in the case of Boreray, like a cathedral of Atlantis. The abruptness of their appearance above the surface of the sea is accentuated by the fact that, with one exception, there are no beaches on the islands, and the cliffs and grassy flanks, towering to over 380 metres (1,250 feet) in places, also plunge vertically 50 metres beneath the sea to an ancient shoreline. There is no softening therefore of the boundary between the land and the sea, and their meeting is uncompromising. If one wants to land anywhere but on the shore of Village Bay one is either clutching the heaving gunwale of a boat, leaping in the air, scrabbling for a grip on slippery, seaweed-covered slabs of rock, or in no-man's-land – the cold Atlantic! Like the seabird colonies they support, there is no other coastline in Britain or Europe to match St Kilda. The cliffs of Foula and St John's Head on Hoy rise to around the same height, but only over a short distance: St Kilda is almost totally surrounded by such cliffs.

There was no saint called St Kilda and the name appears to have been mis-spelt and misplaced, possibly pertaining to another Hebridean island near the west coast of Lewis. The islands, of which there are four, and the main stacs – Stac Lee, Stac an Armin and Levenish – lie some 60 kilometres west of North Uist, with only the lonely outpost of Rockall breaking the surface of the North Atlantic some 300 kilometres further west. They cover a total area of only 830 hectares, similar in area to the other two islands (Canna and Fair Isle) discussed in this book. In order of decreasing size they are Hirta (637.4 hectares); Soay (98.8 hectares); Boreray (76.5 hectares) and Dun (32 hectares). Hirta is the main island on which the village was situated, Soay and Dùn are adjacent, while Boreray and the two most spectacular stacs lie some 7.5 kilometres to the north east.

There are a number of very accessible descriptions of St Kilda, its wildlife, its human history and the final evacuation of the indigenous population in 1930 and I will only dwell here on those aspects pertinent to its present and possible future management. It is, perhaps, the very remoteness of the place, the fact that the islands rise so heroically against the elemental power of the sea and that it is green and once supported a human settlement, that so entrances those lucky enough to visit it, and that gives even its name – like other far more remote islands such as Tristan da Cunha or Pitcairn – a special human resonance. But therein also lies a danger, as the spell of St Kilda can suspend rational debate and judgement when it comes to managing for its future.

Hirta from the sea, with Village Bay sheltered by the cliff ramparts

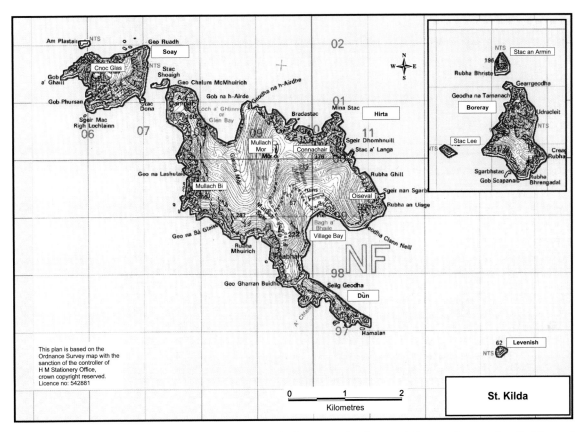

Figure 10.1
Map of the
St Kilda area
(Legend: see p. xviii)

The rocks of St Kilda belong, as do those of Canna, Rum, the Cuillins of Skye and many other places on the west coast of Scotland, to the Tertiary volcanic era of about 60 million years ago. A ring drawn through Soay, along the south and west of Hirta, Dùn, Levenish and continuing around Boreray, represents the perimeter of an ancient volcano.

During the last Ice Age Hirta had its own thin glacier which, however, did not cover the whole island. Unlike the other Western Isles and the mainland of Scotland there was no depression of the land and subsequent re-emergence above sea level and therefore there are no raised beaches. Following the retreat of the ice, Hirta, like other areas of Scotland, came under the influence of another brief and very cold period – the Loch Lomond re-advance – which resulted in much periglacial activity (freezing and thawing of soils and splitting of rocks) giving rise to the screes at the foot of the steep hills that surround Village Bay. If it were not for those screes and the massive reservoir of stone they provide for buildings – for human and animal accommodation and for storage of food – it is unlikely St Kilda could have been settled by people without a great deal more difficulty. It is remarkable to note that the difference in colour of the bedrock, between the blacks of the diorite hills to the west of Village Bay and the whites of the granophyre hills to the east, which is reflected in the colour of the screes, is also mirrored in the buildings of the village. One can almost draw a line through the village that separates the use of the two rocks as building materials. The slowly crumbling village is now such a natural part of the landscape that it seems to metamorphose out of the screes where the steep slope levels out, as if seawards the struggling boulders are evolving into buildings and walls.

The soils of St Kilda that have been derived from the bedrock and some till resulting from the limited glaciation are generally poor in nutrients. With intense leaching of these nutrients in the cool, wet climate, acid, peaty soils and peat predominate. In the Village Bay area where there has been a long history of cultivation, slightly less acid and better agricultural soils have been developed. The more freely draining and acid soils of the granophyres are also reflected in the vegetation, and the brown-coloured, heather hills of Conachair and Oiseval stand out against the green grassy hills of the remainder of the archipelago.

Analysis of peat cores has shown that in the period around 10,000 BP dwarf willows, purple saxifrage and mountain sorrel, grasses and sedges predominated, indicative of a tundra-like terrain. Thereafter the vegetation developed into a mosaic of grasslands and moorlands whose areas and components varied in extent under the influence of varying climatic patterns, with formation of peat in some areas from about 6000 BP, until around 4000 BP.

The principal factors that govern the vegetation of St Kilda today are its geography, isolation and climate. The climate is oceanic, similar to that of Fair Isle, with its higher than expected (for the latitude) winter temperature and cool summer, which allows the growth of montane plants, such as moss campion and purple saxifrage, on sea cliffs; yet also southern plants, such as the Mediterranean-Atlantic liverwort (*Fossombronia angulosa*), growing far to the north of its next most northerly station in Donegal in Ireland. In fact

St Kilda field mouse

St Kilda is a degree or so warmer in the winter months, but just a little less warm in the summer, than Fair Isle. It also has a significantly higher rainfall at approximately 1,400 mm, compared to Fair Isle's 918 mm. The wind on St Kilda is rarely absent, with around Force 3 (gentle breeze) or above, for 85 per cent of the time, and with gales around 20 per cent of the time, or 75 days a year. That almost makes Fair Isle, with 58 gales days per annum, seem relatively calm!

Such exposure to constant maritime winds has a profound effect on the vegetation of both islands. St Kilda is dominated by species-poor maritime and sub-maritime grasslands. Only on Hirta, where there are areas relatively free of the influence of spray, are there sub-montane grasslands and heaths similar to those on the lower hills of the western Highland seaboard. Such grasslands, supplemented with constant inputs of salts and nutrients from sea-spray and from seabirds, has provided a surfeit of grazing for the Soay sheep which helped support the islanders for so long. Almost all the plant communities of St Kilda are anthropogenic, only the most sheep-proof cliff ledges and the island of Dùn have any luxuriance of growth – in July, white with the flowers of scentless mayweed, sea campion, angelica and lovage, intermingled with the tall and rust-red heads of common sorrel.

The islands, being relatively small and so isolated from the mainland of Scotland in the direction of the prevailing winds, have a limited terrestrial flora and fauna – many seeds and spores just never reach St Kilda. There are only about 180 flowering plants and ferns here compared with about 600 on Skye and 2,000 on the British mainland. The flora of St Kilda in fact is almost more notable for its absentees. In July the yellows in the inbye grasslands of the village are of meadow buttercup and lesser spearwort, but there is no cat's ear, nor bird's-foot trefoil and there are no marsh marigolds in the few wetland areas. However this also presents opportunities for some species to occupy a wider range of niches; for example the meadow buttercup, in the absence of the creeping and bulbous buttercups, can be found also in both the wet and dry extremes of the inbye grassland.

Biologists have sometimes described the limited diversity of the flora and fauna of such islands as St Kilda as impoverished compared to the mainland. However this is misleading and it would be better to describe the ecology as simplified. The only terrestrial mammal indigenous to the islands is the St Kilda field mouse (*Apodemus sylvaticus hirtensis*) which, it has been variously suggested, may have survived the Ice Age, may have been introduced by early settlers from the Hebrides, may have been introduced by the Norse, or may be descended from all three sources. Whatever the explanation, it is double the size of the mainland field mouse and larger than any other Scottish island field mouse. There used to be a St Kilda house mouse (*Mus musculus muralis*), but it became extinct following the departure of the St Kildans, its demise possibly hastened by competition

Anemone, just one example of St Kilda's colourful marine life

from the larger field mouse. The other well-known mammal of St Kilda is of course the Soay sheep, but we will come back to it a little later.

The only other existing sub-species native to St Kilda is the wren (*Troglodytes troglodytes hirtensis*) which, like the field mouse, is larger than its mainland relative. Both sub-species are similar to their Fair Isle counterparts and are of great interest and value, telling us something of the processes of evolution and adaptation in isolation. In July, the resident wren at the factor's house was very busy feeding three young and, like the field mice, hopping in and out of the dry-stone walls; not surprising that its Faeroese name is *mùsabródir* – which hardly needs translation! Also around buildings of the inbye and its rocky ground were wheatear, but surprisingly few. The most common birds of both the grasslands of the inbye and of the hill were meadow pipit, snipe and oystercatcher. The last also breeds on the steep flanks of the coast and is very aggressive in July. Maybe such behaviour is necessary when one's neighbours are the large gulls and bonxies! There are few other regular terrestrial breeding birds, but in the past there would have been several more associated with agriculture, such as corn bunting and sparrow.

To an extent the limited flora and fauna of the land is reflected in their marine counterpart on the submarine cliffs of St Kilda. These are the cliffs of a drowned landscape that has been subject to the immense and unhindered forces of the North Atlantic storms for millennia and they are pitted with caves and tunnels. Although the forces of the sea are most obvious on the surface where we see the swell crashing against the coast, the turbulence produced actually extends many tens of metres below the surface. The submarine cliffs are therefore, like the exposed tops of mountains, tough places in which to live and where only a limited number of adapted species can survive. Such is the surge on the coast that kelp, the usual sub-littoral seaweed of the slightly more sheltered coasts, cannot hold its grip on St Kilda's rocks above a depth of 30 metres! In the main the fauna that occupy this area are anemones, hydroids and sponges, colourful creatures that, because of the great clarity of the pristine seas around St Kilda, descend to much greater depths than on mainland coasts.

Almost the same distance, 60 kilometres, to the west of St Kilda as the Hebrides are to the east, lies the edge of the Continental Shelf. North along this edge flows the warm Slope Current from the Bay of Biscay. Where it meets the less saline and slower-moving waters of the Continental Shelf the two volumes of water mix, bringing nutrients to the surface in which, in season, thrive vast numbers of plankton and on which, in turn, feed the fish, seabirds and whales. St Kilda itself is a stubborn and lonely impediment on the Shelf and it too causes disturbance and upwellings in the sea around it, adding locally to this nutrient supply. The seas adjacent to St Kilda are therefore rich in food resources and, with its great cliffs and stacks, it is not surprising that it has become a most natural home for vast numbers of seabirds. St Kilda's marine flora and fauna is therefore very important to its native terrestrial counterpart and, as we shall see, more fragile too. Both are inexorably linked and, without many of the features of each, it is unlikely there could have been much of a human history either.

Human settlement and ownership

From the pollen record of around 4000 BP there appears to have been an increase in ribwort plantain which is usually taken as an indication of pastoral agriculture and therefore of the presence of people. The earliest archaeological record are fragments of Neolithic pottery found in Village

Cleitean and Soay sheep

Bay, although this may not indicate continuous occupation. Notwithstanding, one can imagine the earlier Mesolithic hunters who probably
travelled throughout the Hebrides visiting St Kilda during a settled climatic
period and appreciating the value of its summer seabird larder. And if
Mesolithic people did not visit St Kilda, Neolithic people must have, or how
else has St Kilda ended up with the Soay sheep whose skeleton so closely
resembles that of the primitive sheep found in European archaeological sites
of that period? Perhaps the Neolithic people continued a tradition of
exploiting the St Kilda seabird larder. Perhaps they took a few sheep and left
them so that the following year they would have some easy meat to subsist on
when they were there. And perhaps eventually, again in a stable climatic
period, they took the risk of settling.

For the human inhabitants there could only be one initial area of
settlement and that is in Village Bay where the hills of Mullach Sgar, Mullach
Mór, Conachair and Oiseval shelter the bay, where there is the only relatively
flat area suitable for cultivation, where the screes provide building materials
and where lies the only beach on St Kilda. For at least 2,000 years people
have worked at clearing the rocks from the lower ground and have built an
incredible concentration and number of buildings and walls in Village Bay
with a scattering also all over the rest of Hirta and on the other islands. There
is not space here to describe the human historical remains of St Kilda which
represent a once vibrant and unique culture, now gone. However, there is a
uniquely St Kilda building which does deserve some comment here, the cleit.
This type of building was so vital to human survival that there are over 1,000
of them on Hirta alone!

The St Kildans had a self-sufficient and sustainable culture right up to the
beginning of this century. They grew grain crops and hay, burned peat and

Tagged Soay sheep
and lamb

divot, got milk, wool, leather and meat from their cattle and sheep, and did a little fishing. But critically, they relied on seabirds, particularly fulmars, puffins and guga (young gannets), for eggs, oil, footwear from the skins, and meat; the last particularly important to them through the winter months. They paid their rents in many of these products and exported woollen cloth from the sheep, and oil and feathers from seabirds. Grain, hay, fuel and seabird carcasses all needed to be stored and preserved in a wet and windy climate. The St Kildans therefore developed the cleit. Cleitean are stone buildings, loosely constructed to allow the wind to blow through the walls, but rain-proofed with a deep earth and divot roof placed over capping stones. These buildings were the larders and stores, without which St Kildans could not have survived through the winter on the archipelago.

The story of the people of St Kilda, apart from the last few hundred years and its final capitulation, is not well known. There were, possibly, early Christian settlements, and the Norse were certainly familiar with the islands – hence the mixture of Norse and Gaelic names for the islands, stacs and hills. The Norse may also have brought their own sheep and cattle to St Kilda, the former possibly being crossed with the St Kildans' sheep on Hirta. The first comprehensive account of the islands was that of Martin Martin after his visit in 1697, when there were approximately 180 people on Hirta. He described their way of life and particularly their fearless prowess on the cliffs when fowling. In the eighteenth century the population was stricken by a smallpox epidemic in which almost 100 died. In the late nineteenth century a number emigrated to Australia, from which the population never recovered. Finally, in the twentieth century, modern alternatives reduced the demand for the exports of St Kilda, resulting in the mass exodus of 1930.

When the last inhabitants pulled away from St Kilda they left behind them a history in stone, a record of structures for the living and the dead dating possibly from the Neolithic. Some of these structures have disappeared under the soil, some have been robbed for stone, some robbed in the name of archaeology for their artefacts and bones, some are roofed with divots and some are inexplicable. The most recent had glass in their windows, oil on the hinges, embers in the fireplace. Elsewhere, on the mainland of Britain, there was an accumulation of written history and description put together by many intrigued visitors and occasional residents over many years. Together, these records, paper and stone, amount to an irreplaceable collection of documented history and artefacts, of an Atlantic island community over a period of several thousand years.

Over all these years a number of small areas, in addition to Village Bay, were cultivated and now all have reverted to grassland, and every accessible corner of the St Kilda archipelago has become grazed. In the absence of cattle and the presence of sheep only, over the last 70 years at least, there will have been some changes to the species composition of the grasslands. No doubt there is now less of some of the sweeter grasses encouraged by cattle which must have been more prevalent around cultivated areas and the shielings. There will be more mat grass and it may be that the present tussocky nature of some of the grasslands is due to the absence of cattle. It is clear that heather is held in check in some areas, but there are no indications of overgrazing.

Undoubtedly too, the level of harvest of the seabirds must have kept some populations in check. For example it has been calculated that some 10,000 fulmars would have been required to produce the 566 gallons of fulmar oil in 1875 alone. As with the vegetation however, there is no indication that any of the seabird populations were endangered, with the exception of the particularly vulnerable great auk, which, due to hunting, had been declining all over its range anyway and which became extinct for the same reason at St Kilda in 1840.

The earliest record of the ownership of St Kilda refers to that of John MacDonald, the Lord of the Isles in the fourteenth century. In the middle of the fifteenth century it passed to the MacLeods of Harris, in whose hands it remained until it was sold to Earl of Dumfries (later the 5th Marquess of Bute) in 1931. He was a keen naturalist and managed the island as a bird sanctuary, actually employing a St Kildan, Neil Gillies, as the first Warden. When the Earl died in 1956 he bequeathed St Kilda to the Trust, which only accepted it after much debate. In 1957 a lease, passing management of the islands to the Nature Conservancy (subsequently SNH), was drawn up. In the same year the Air Ministry (now MoD) began the construction of a radar base for the tracking of test missiles fired from the Benbecula Range.

Although St Kilda and a large part of Mar Lodge Estate and Ben Lawers are NNRs, the major difference in the management of St Kilda compared to those properties, is the fact that effectively the natural heritage of St Kilda is managed by SNH. There are no objectives in the Trust's Management Plan relating to the natural heritage except within the first aim, which we will return to under the last section in this chapter.

Soay sheep

Earlier, in the Ben Lawers chapter, I spent some time describing the vegetation, and the monitoring and radical management of the rare plants. I did this to illustrate the importance of this part of that property's natural heritage and therefore the Trust's responsibilities there. Likewise in St Kilda we need to take some space to examine the place of its unique Soay sheep before considering what the Trust's responsibilities are for them.

Soay sheep are the most primitive living sheep in Europe, closely resembling both the original wild species and the domesticated sheep kept in

Village street

Bronze Age times over 3,000 years ago and perhaps much earlier. Sheep were an indispensable part of Neolithic farming giving wool, meat and milk, and must have been brought from Europe at that time to all the inhabited corners of Britain including St Kilda. Their closest living relative is the Mouflon of Corsica, and the breeds in Britain that most resemble them today are the North Ronaldsay and the Shetland sheep; the latter being close to the Scottish shortwool long since superseded on the Scottish mainland. Like Soay sheep, both are hardy breeds, used to surviving under harsh conditions. Soay sheep, however, are only light or dark browns, not multi-coloured like the native Shetland sheep, and are longer in the leg. Significantly also they do not flock like modern sheep when attempts are made to gather them, but scatter. They eventually ended up on the island called Soay (Sheep Island), hence their modern name.

Initially, after they were introduced, they were probably present on all the St Kilda islands, possibly right up until the introductions of the early Blackface sheep. In the 1850s when modern Blackface were brought to Hirta, the St Kildans requested that the owner allow them to introduce the Blackface to Soay, to improve the breed, but the owner refused. He owned the sheep on Soay and there was a higher price in that period for the Soay wool. Otherwise, after surviving for thousands of years, the Soay sheep might have gone the way of all the old breeds and have been lost to us only 150 years ago!

At the time of the evacuation of the people of St Kilda in 1930 the Blackface-Cheviot sheep then on Hirta were rounded up and also left the

St Kilda wren

island. Two years later any stragglers remaining were shot before over 100 Soay sheep were re-introduced from that island to Hirta by the Earl of Dumfries and left, as on Soay, to their own devices. There may have been one or two Blackface-Cheviot left on Hirta, but there is little evidence of this in the physical characteristics of the present Hirta sheep. Numbers increased rapidly to over 1,000 and up to very recently the population varied between about 600 and 1,800. There is also a smaller population (200–650) of sheep – an early Scottish breed of Blackface – on Boreray, which were left behind by the St Kilda people in 1930.

Reading the accounts of management of the Soay sheep by the St Kildans it is obvious that they were never managed in the modern sense. Apart from the fact that the sheep scatter rather than flock, the physical nature of the landscape of St Kilda – hectares of steeply sloping and isolated ledges of coastal grassland, often separated by cliff face or massive buttresses and frequently only accessible by dangerous paths – precludes the modern approach to gathering sheep. The sheep were in fact individually and physically run down and tackled by man and dog, after which the wool could be harvested and/or the sheep slaughtered. No doubt also, ewes with lambs were brought in to shieling and inbye and there tethered and milked.

The sheep on the three islands of Soay, Hirta and Boreray – there are none on Dùn – do have one thing in common with modern hill breeds: they are hefted. In other words there are different groups of ewes and followers that stick to particular areas. Unlike modern managed breeds however there is no control of numbers today, reflecting a very long tradition which could not, on the terrain of St Kilda, have limited the population. Instead, as has probably happened on Soay since the sheep were introduced over 2,000 years ago, there is an irregular fluctuation in the population, followed by a crash, which is followed by rapid population growth once again. It has taken many years of study to establish this – not long ago it was thought there was a four-year population cycle – and just when we thought we knew the answers, the unexpected happened. But we will come to that.

The Soay sheep, besides being the closest living link surviving on St Kilda that we now have to the St Kildans themselves, are unique in Europe. They are therefore of great interest to science, for pure conservation reasons, for innate characteristics which may be of value to modern sheep breeding and in terms of the lessons we might learn from the nature of their adaptation to their environment in the absence of management. They are therefore of national and international importance. There are few Trust properties where there is basic research, not necessarily directly related to management, and it is therefore worth examining the results of such research in this chapter in some depth.

In 1957, when the Nature Conservancy (NC) took over the management of St Kilda it was recognised that if the natural regulation mechanism of the sheep population on Hirta could be understood it could have considerable implications for the management of both wild and domestic sheep. Thus began one of the very few long-term studies of a mammal population, led by J. Morton Boyd and P. A. Jewell. Up to 1972, on an apparently four-year cycle, the sheep population of Hirta increased from the original 1,000 or so in 1932 (Figure 10.2). These fluctuations were the result of large-scale deaths of the young, the old and males, in the early spring, apparently mainly due to malnutrition and heavy parasite loads.

Following this study there was a gap for several years until in 1985 the study was resumed by a research group from Cambridge University. This

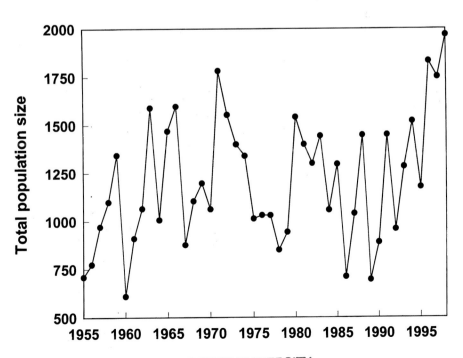

Figure 10.2
Population of Soay
sheep 1955–1995

Reproduced by
permission of the
Large Animal Research
Group, Cambridge

group, under T. Clutton-Brock, had been studying another unmanaged herbivore – red deer – on the NNR of Rum in the Small Isles for two decades. There the natural regulation of the population is basically through density-dependent mortality and there are no 'crashes'. In fact crashes do not occur in any other wild sheep either (except to mouflon introduced to the Kerguelin Island), but they do happen in some of the small-mammal populations of the Arctic and sub-arctic; such as the lemming, snowshoe hare, muskrat and one or two other small rodents. Studies of these populations show that the smaller the mammal, the shorter the population cycle.

The study by Cambridge is on a very intensive level, and along with an impressive list of other research groups from Edinburgh, London and Stirling Universities, the Institute of Zoology, London, ITE Banchory and MLURI, covers many aspects of the life of Soay sheep and their relationship to their environment. To be able to study the population in some detail and over several generations, all the sheep hefted to Village Bay have been tagged so that individuals and their offspring can be identified. Every year there is at least one census of the whole of Hirta as well as many counts of the study area in Village Bay. Also once a year, all the tagged animals and their lambs are caught and various measurements taken. When opportunity allows and in conjunction with the Warden, censuses have also been carried out on Soay and Boreray.

On St Kilda the mild, wet climate, salt from the sea and nitrogenous waste from the many seabirds results in rapid and ample grass growth. Although

The island of Soay

there is more than enough grass for the sheep in the summer, by late autumn growth has ceased and all that the sheep have to survive on is heather and any grass surviving. By the early part of the year there is little grass left and the weak, the old and the young begin to die. The 'crash' is caused, it appears, by several factors. At a certain population size there is too much competition for the limited winter food. This, combined with a heavy parasite load and a wet and windy spring – which increases heat loss, making the cost of grazing away from shelter high – induces the crash. However, what is the relative weighting of each factor? A curious fact has emerged which may shed some light on this. Counts of sheep on Hirta and Boreray, over a 40-year period, have revealed that both populations, of different breeds and on separate islands, seem to crash in the same year; in other words the population fluctuations are synchronised. There is also evidence that the sheep population on Soay also fluctuates in synchrony. The only obvious factor common to the three islands is the climate. It has been suggested then that above a certain population threshold it is the climatic factor which becomes most critical. In the academic world of ecological studies there is a keen debate on the relative importance of intrinsic factors such as population density and food availability, and external factors such as climatic variation, in determining fluctuation. For 'fluctuation' rather than 'crash' seems to be the recent pattern of the Soay sheep population. Since the early 1990s the population appears to be 'stabilising' at higher levels, reaching an all-time peak of 2,000 in 1998. There has not been a 'crash' involving the death of half the population since 1989.

So how does the sheep population recover so quickly? Soay sheep are relatively fertile and produce a high proportion of twins when the population is low, and a Soay lamb born in April can conceive in the autumn and produce a lamb itself when it is just over one year old! Following a crash the population can recover to its former level in just two years. The population then rapidly reaches a peak, at which level competition for grazing between the sheep themselves reduces the rate of growth of the population.

In examining the sheep that die over winter and comparing them with those that survive it was found that those that had lower burdens of parasitic worms in summer were less likely to die the following winter. Soay sheep therefore experience strong selection for resistance to nematodes, and it is possible that they are among the most worm-resistant sheep in the world. Other research has shown that Soay sheep on St Kilda have appreciable levels of genetic variation, hardly what one would have expected from a population isolated for thousands of years! It seems likely that these two observations are linked. Already, it has been established that more outbred members of the Soay population are more resistant to worms, which acts to maintain the level of genetic variation after population crashes. Also, there is some evidence for high genetic variation in those genes thought to be involved in combating parasites, which may be the signature of a long-running evolutionary battle with genetically diverse parasites. Nematodes are a world-wide threat to cattle and sheep husbandry, particularly since they have evolved resistance to drenches used by farmers, and Soay sheep may yield important information about genetic resistance to parasitic worms. Management of Soay sheep on St Kilda however, could have substantial effects on the parasitic resistance and other unique features of Soay sheep. For example, if management reduced population density to prevent crashes, this would immediately relax selection for worm resistance, the population might then evolve to be less resistant and we would lose this, and probably other unknown research opportunities that could have benefits for the husbandry of our domestic stock.

One might conclude from the fact that, as the unmanaged population is able to reach a maximum population – the carrying capacity in the winter – the vegetation must be over-grazed at times. Over-grazing is actually a function of management, when more animals than can be supported naturally by the vegetation resource are kept (often by additional feed) and the effect is to damage the grazing resource. Because of the sheer amount of annual grass growth on St Kilda however, the sheep are dependent on the productivity rather than the total biomass of the vegetation. In other words St Kilda sheep are only consuming the annual production. There is no evidence of a loss of plant diversity, no evidence for loss of heather since the human inhabitants left, and no evidence of erosion: all signs of overgrazing.

Is it not cruel to allow the sheep to die of malnutrition? Well, the size of many African ungulate herbivore populations is dictated by food resources and not predators, and we do not attempt to manage all of them. Although the people of St Kilda will have always culled sheep for their needs, it is likely that it was never at a level that prevented winter mortality, i.e. a situation similar to that at present has been happening on St Kilda for a very long time and occurs elsewhere in naturally-regulated populations. We humans, as a species, are actually very selective in what species we consider require culling to prevent suffering. We justify some blood sports by stating it is better to die in one's prime than of starvation, but of course we do not apply that to all species, especially not to ourselves.

There are of course pragmatic reasons against attempting management on St Kilda. For example, as the very dangerous and awkward terrain precludes access to many sheep and they cannot be shepherded, how would one control numbers – by shooting? Even shooting goats for conservation reasons is hardly publicly acceptable, and what would one do with the carcasses? Then there are moral dilemmas. For example, if the Hirta sheep are to be managed then so too, on the same principle, should the sheep on Soay and Boreray, but these islands are relatively inaccessible compared to much of Hirta.

The current phase of research on Soay sheep is also providing a useful lesson for species conservation – after all, as an isolated population with frequent population reductions, the Soay population mimics the worst-case scenario for wild populations. The long series of population data is being used to improve methods for assessing the risk of extinction in endangered species and the ongoing genetic studies are overturning previous perceptions. Geneticists usually worry that when populations experience sharp reductions in numbers, genetic variation is lost, but on St Kilda, natural selection (via parasites) removes the most inbred portion of the population in each crash, so that the surviving population actually contains much more variation than expected. Geneticists need to think harder about the factors causing population declines and the selection process that might be operating during such declines.

From the foregoing it is plain that Soay sheep are not domesticated in the modern sense. These are virtually wild animals whose management has been opportunistic over a period of thousands of years and who have, over that period, adapted to their environment, initially on Soay itself and latterly on Hirta. It is also clear that the Soay sheep of St Kilda are a hardy and fecund breed with many special characteristics and that they are both a unique research, and specifically genetic, resource which we should not compromise by management. In the next section on seabirds we will also come across the dilemma of whether to manage or not *and* where the evidence is pretty unequivocal. Perhaps the last word on the subject should be left to J. Morton Boyd, one of Scotland's foremost conservationists in the second half of the twentieth century and whom it could be said initiated the original study of the Soay sheep: 'The balance is delicate and interference, no matter how well-intentioned, might set the sheep against their habitat, setting in train changes in the soil, vegetation and in the sheep themselves' (*The Hebrides*, 1990).

Seabirds

In July, the seabirds are all busy feeding and defending their chicks. The gannets are having yet another successful season and the young, the guga, on Boreray and the stacs, are growing large and fluffy, and the bonxies (great skua) are finding returning adults easy pickings. The bonxies themselves, though, seemed to being having a mixed season with some dive-bombing intruders on their territories with their usual aggression, but many showing no concern at all. Kittiwakes, unfortunately, appear to be struggling to find food for their chicks and many have abandoned their nests. Their colonies are sad places dotted with mute and inactive adult birds who should be lively, busy and shrill at this time of year. The guillemots seem to be more successful

and by the third week of the month many of their chicks are already off the ledges and paddling with their parents out to sea. During the day, the huge boulder-field on the steep coast at Carn Mór on Hirta is thick with puffins, whirring in from the sea or standing about in small groups looking embarrassed as only a puffin can. During darkness, the night air of the same boulder-field is filled with the dark shadows of storm petrels, Leach's petrels and Manx shearwaters. The storm petrels flit about silently and jerkily like bats, but call out from their burrows, and the larger Leach's petrels emit maniacal high-pitched chuckles that pass in the dark as if from one hidden speaker to another. It is exciting and a little unsettling to sit by a boulder in the dark listening to these calls and sensing wings brushing the side of one's face or one's hair.

Scotland is a very small country compared to most of our neighbours in Europe and we have few natural heritage features that we can boast are unique or even the best examples of those that are widespread: peat bogs and dwarf-shrub heaths come to mind. It is the geographical position of Scotland (and that of the British Isles more generally), on the Atlantic fringe, adjacent to cool seas, rich in plankton and fish in season that gives us perhaps our one natural feature that is not excelled anywhere in Europe – and that is our seabirds. There are of the order of four million pairs of seabirds of 24 different species that breed in the British Isles. There are many seabird colonies around the coasts of Britain but by far the largest are in the north and west of Scotland and these are at St Kilda, Westray in Orkney and Foula in Shetland.

Undoubtedly the huge seabird colonies of St Kilda have been known to people since at least the Neolithic. Between 1930 and 1956 a number of seabird counts were carried out, but the first comprehensive survey was not carried out until 1957 by Kenneth Williamson and J. Morton Boyd, confirming the archipelago's importance as the largest 'single' colony of

Table 10.1   Selected breeding seabirds of St Kilda: current population estimates and national importance.

	Numbers		% British Population
Fulmar	62,800	AOS	11.7
Manx shearwater	>1,000	Pairs	Small
Storm petrel	Present		?
Leach's petrel	>1,000		Large
Gannet	60,400	AOS	30.9
Great skua	230	AOT	2.6
Kittiwake	7,800	AON	1.6
Guillemot	22,700	IND	2.2
Razorbill	3,800	IND	2.6
Puffin	155,000	IND	34.5

AON – Apparently occupied nests.
AOS – Apparently occupied sites.
AOT – Apparently occupied territories.
IND – Individuals.

Reproduced, with permission, from Thompson, K. R. and Walsh, P. M. (1997) 'Seabird Monitoring on Hirta and Dùn, St Kilda, 1987–1996.' Joint Nature Conservation Committee Report No. 276.

seabirds in the British Isles and Western Europe. The latest census of seabirds (Table 10.1) puts the total at well over half a million birds of fifteen different species.

Concern at the lack of a baseline for our seabird populations, which were under threat from North Sea oil, fishing and industrial pollution, resulted in the formation of the Seabird Group in 1965. In 1969 this Group organised Operation Seafarer, the first national census of seabirds in the British Isles. Following that event monitoring trials were set up which eventually established standard methods for counting each species. In 1987 a Seabird Colony Register of Britain was set up, and in 1989 the JNCC took up the responsibility for organising annual monitoring at a selected suite of colonies. While Fair Isle and Canna are key British seabird monitoring sites, St Kilda has a much more limited monitoring programme, both in the number of species that are covered and the regularity with which they are counted.

The most numerous seabird on St Kilda is the puffin which makes its burrow on the sloping grassy cliffs and island's summits. A quarter of a century ago it was estimated that the St Kilda colony of puffins was of the order of two to three million pairs, but since then there has been a decrease, of unproven cause, but probably related to oceanographic changes. At present there is no annual monitoring of puffin numbers on St Kilda, but over the last 25 years we know that there has regularly been poor breeding. This has been established by catching and weighing the newly fledged puffins that, having left their burrows in the dark of the night in late July, have been attracted to the lights of the MoD base and come to ground around the buildings. Fledging weight is good indication of breeding success; the greater the weight the better chance of survival, and conversely low fledging weights indicate poor feeding and poor breeding success. It has been the latter that has been found to be the case in recent years.

The next most numerous seabird is the fulmar which has nested on St Kilda since at least the seventeenth century and may even have been the first resident at the end of the Ice Age, as it is an Arctic species whose only known colony in temperate seas before 1878 was on St Kilda. It was at that date that the fulmar began nesting elsewhere in the British Isles when it bred for the first time on Foula (Shetland). Since then it has rapidly spread around the whole of the British Isles and on St Kilda it is still increasing at around 3.6 per cent per annum. Incidentally there is a new piece of research taking place on St Kilda designed to throw more light on the fulmar spread from the beginning of the twentieth century. Using similar techniques to those used on some of the rarest arctic-alpine plants of Ben Lawers, genetic investigation is being carried out to determine how close the link is between the St Kilda fulmar and those of the rest of the British Isles. Could it be that the dramatic spread of fulmars on the latter did not come from St Kilda via Shetland as has been widely assumed for many years? For why did the fulmar not colonise the rest of the British Isles much earlier? Could the remainder of the British Isles population have colonised directly from the Arctic instead?

The third most numerous seabird is the magnificent gannet, which appears to still be slowly expanding at just under 1 per cent per annum. On Fair Isle where it began breeding only recently, it is expanding more quickly. All three species have their largest British colonies on St Kilda and in fact the gannet and puffin colonies there represent 30 per cent of the total British populations.

One of the advantages of St Kilda's isolated position, well away from the coast, is the opportunity to monitor the levels of pollutants reaching the area, that arise from industry and agriculture on mainland Britain. Every two years eggs of gannets are examined for organochlorines (DDE from DDT) and derivatives of the insecticides aldrin and dieldrin, as well as mercury. The levels of these pollutants in the eggs reflect those in the body of the female, which in turn reflect the levels in the fish prey species within a known area of the Atlantic. Such regular monitoring is a valuable tool in policing and measuring our efforts in reducing our pollution of the seas.

Two intriguing species are the storm and Leach's petrels. These are oceanic birds feeding many tens of nautical miles from St Kilda and so we do not see them inshore often. The former is our smallest breeding seabird not dissimilar in size to a swallow; and the latter is only a little larger. These secretive birds return to their nests in burrows, boulder-fields and drystone walls in the darkness at night, as they are vulnerable to predators. Because of

The gannets of
Stac Lee

their nesting habitat their colonies are quite difficult to find and very difficult to census. The storm petrel has a number of colonies in the north and west of the British Isles, and a few are probably of the estimated size of that on St Kilda. Leach's petrel, on the other hand, is much more restricted in the British Isles, there being only eight known colonies of which St Kilda is undoubtedly the largest. In terms of European conservation then, St Kilda is a very important site for the latter, but we must also remember that in global terms – in the Western Atlantic and the Pacific in addition to the Eastern Atlantic – Leach's petrel is relatively more common than the storm petrel which is confined to the Eastern Atlantic and Mediterranean.

A seabird of limited numbers on St Kilda, but in global terms one of Britain's most important, is the bonxie or great skua. The bonxie first bred on St Kilda in 1963, only increasing very slowly up to the early 1990s. However, very recently, the population on Hirta has been increasing at the rate of 29 per cent per annum, which is far too great a rate of increase than can be accounted for without immigration. In fact several birds ringed as chicks in Shetland have turned up to breed on St Kilda. In most of its (northern hemisphere) colonies, such as one of its largest on Foula, the bonxie feeds mainly on fish which to a large extent they obtain from other seabirds, but on St Kilda 55 per cent of bonxie diet is other seabirds. Of those, 43.2 per cent were petrels, of which the majority were Leach's petrels. There is obviously some cause for concern here, but without knowing the size and breeding success of the colony of Leach's petrel, we cannot judge how concerned we should be. However, even if bonxies are reducing the breeding success of the Leach's petrel colony – even if the colony is declining because of this – we should not be tempted to take action against the bonxie.

The balance of seabird populations, the resources on which they live, and both the effect of exploitation of these resources by ourselves and the natural effects of climate which govern the production and availability of these resources, is a very complex set of inter-relationships over which we have no control. For example we have sometimes regarded the large gulls as having detrimental effects on populations of the smaller and more attractive seabirds – puffins and terns. Yet on Dùn where there has been plenty of evidence of great black-back gulls preying on puffins for many years – and where there might have been the temptation to control them – even though there is no shortage of puffin prey or nest sites for the gulls, the latter's population has actually declined over the last 30 years. Most of the time when we interfere we do not know exactly what we are doing and we may well be exacerbating a problem rather than solving it. As with the urge to manage Soay sheep, we need to examine our motives carefully and objectively.

Essential in determining the health of seabird populations, is regular, and preferably annual, monitoring of numbers and breeding success. Unless we know the baseline for the populations and the annual variation in numbers and breeding success we will not be able to pinpoint changes, never mind causes. For seabird conservation it is important also to monitor their food sources (fish stocks), to research their diet and to make contingency plans in the event of oil spills. Monitoring of populations is of no value in itself, of course, in telling us what it is that is actually causing fluctuations in populations. St Kilda, although it is arguably the most important seabird site in the British Isles, does not get the monitoring or research level that it deserves. We will come back to the conservation of seabirds in the next chapter.

Designations

It may seem rather superfluous – after considering all of St Kilda's wonderful natural features, which speak so adequately for themselves, and the variety of survey and research carried out in order to understand its ecology – to add labels; unless, of course, they provide some additional protection for the features, stimulus and support for research, or access for enjoyment.

In the same year, 1957, that the Trust became the owners of St Kilda and leased (initially under a 'Minute of Agreement') the islands to the Nature Conservancy, the latter drew up plans to schedule St Kilda as an SSSI and declare it a National Nature Reserve, which it did in 1964. One of the purposes of an NNR is to provide: 'special opportunities for the study of and research into, matters relating to the fauna and flora of Great Britain and the physical conditions in which they live . . .'.

The next designation to be awarded, that of Biosphere Reserve (1977), was the first to recognise the world standing of the natural heritage of St Kilda. The main purpose of a Biosphere Reserve is to promote the conservation of the site, including the genetic diversity of its species; provide areas for ecological and environmental research, and provide facilities for education and training. Another purpose is to gather and to communicate the findings, for the general purpose of sustaining the earth's natural and managed ecosystems. In 1981 St Kilda became an NSA, and in 1990 a Marine Consultation Area which acknowledges that the surrounding sea is just as important to the interests of St Kilda as its cliffs, and simply means that SNH is consulted on any marine development in the area. In 1992 St Kilda became an SPA and more recently a cSAC for its vegetated cliff areas, its reefs and sea caves. Both these European designations, as we have seen elsewhere, require more positive action in regard to protection of features than does the SSSI designation. In addition to these designations for its landscape and natural history, a number of areas and buildings have been scheduled as ancient monuments, including most of Village Bay.

However, the greatest accolade that has been bestowed on St Kilda is its listing as a World Heritage Site by UNESCO in 1986 for its outstanding universal values, such as its natural characteristics and in particular for its superlative natural features, its habitats for rare and endangered species and its impressive populations of seabirds. Listing means that each state has to recognise its international responsibilities in conserving the site; but in addition, all states as members of the international community should co-operate in the site's protection. One requirement of the WH Listing is that the marine habitats should receive more protection. SNH has proposed St Kilda as a Marine Nature Reserve, but as yet it has not been designated. Like Fair Isle, the other great seabird station discussed in this book, despite all these designations, there is as yet no statutory protection for the outstanding marine environment of St Kilda. Fair Isle, having a human population, seems better able to articulate this need, as we will see in the next chapter!

In St Kilda's case it is important to note that although the archipelago was nominated (by the Secretary of State for Scotland) for both its cultural and natural features, it was only for the latter that it has been listed and, in 1999, it still remains the only World Heritage Site for the natural heritage in the United Kingdom! The Trust is still pressing for inclusion of the cultural features which undoubtedly are of universal value. It is also important to remember that, although not a statutory designation, and although there are no written obligations, the UK Government as signatory to the Convention, and the Trust as owner, both have particular responsibilities to ensure the strict protection of the site and, as stated in the Trust Management Plan 1996–2001, among other things, 'to develop scientific research and studies'.

It is interesting that in the Technical Evaluation of St Kilda for WH nomination by the International Union for the Conservation of Nature (IUCN) for UNESCO, it states that the MoD base 'has not resulted in significant impact', but does not make clear whether this insignificant impact is to the landscape, wildlife or the cultural heritage, or all three. It is also important to note that the Evaluation recognises that 'The feral Soay sheep are also an interesting rare breed of potential genetic resource significance.'

The designations that have been conferred on St Kilda, possibly the most 'decorated' natural site in the British Isles, therefore should not only be protective, but proactive and specifically in regard to its natural, rather than its cultural, features.

Visitors and public access

Staying on St Kilda is a unique and privileged experience. The islands are so small and rise so steeply from the sea, so far from any other land and so apparently lost in the ocean, as to make their very existence under one's feet, insecure. And in the middle of this insecurity the predominant sign of human existence, huddled at the foot of screes and embracing virtually the only arable ground, sheltered bay and beach, lies abandoned. There is a strong feeling of the last outpost and a heroic, but ultimately useless, struggle. Away from Village Bay, it is the awesome physicality of the stupendous cliffs, the endless susurration of the ocean swell against its flanks, the cities of seabirds and the incredible unawareness of it all of the grazing sheep, that fascinate and almost hypnotise the visitor. The only level pieces of ground are in Village Bay, on the top of the hills and, where they are chopped off, the clifftops. Walking anywhere else is either up or down; for example to get to Gleann Mór (the adjacent glen) from Village Bay involves a climb of 250 metres (900 feet), so that by the end of a day or two knee-joints are complaining sorely.

On the cliff tops, without a reference, it is very difficult to grasp scale and it is only when a toy yacht or launch skirts the base of the wall at one's feet that one realises just how high are the St Kilda cliffs. The spectacle is equally imposing from the sea, looking up and up and up, and with binoculars,

Soay sheep

realising that the brown speck ambling ever so slowly and unconcernedly across a steep grassy slope below the last rise to the summit, is a Soay sheep. One of the most incredible sights is the approach to Stac Lee from Hirta, at the point when one suddenly realises that the apparently whitewashed surface of the rock rising 172 metres (564 feet), is actually alive and made up of thousands of gannets.

Because of its isolation, lack of a very secure anchorage, and exposure to Atlantic weather including regular windy weather with oceanic swells, St Kilda is unfortunately not an easy, nor inexpensive, place to visit. Most people visit on small charter boats or in private yachts which can be very uncomfortable on the long haul out from the Outer Hebrides. Otherwise there are occasional cruise ships. The only way visitors can stay on St Kilda is to camp, carry out approved research or survey, or be a member of a Trust work party, the last of which are always over-subscribed. The work parties, of which there are several every year, carry out archaeological work under professional supervision, and maintenance of buildings.

From the mid-1980s to the mid-1990s annual visitor numbers have been around the 1,000 mark. In 1995 they reached 1,693 due to the visit of six cruise ships, and through 1996 and 1997 numbers have risen to 1,900. However, these numbers are relatively very low and because of the physical nature of the archipelago, such numbers of people cause little harm or disturbance; that is, except for those who might want to climb the cliffs and stacks and whose activities in the breeding season would certainly cause disturbance. Part of the reason for the general increase may be due to the publicity given to the previously little-known but spectacular marine environment and the resulting increase in the popularity of the islands for diving.

Summation

As far as the natural heritage is concerned, St Kilda, of all the Trust's Highland and Islands properties discussed in this book, although no less managed in its history than any of the others, is now managed with the minimum of intervention, which is right. It should perhaps also be the most intensively monitored and researched, which it is not.

St Kilda does not require intervention management as its terrestrial biological features are largely in balance. The only major threat to the biological features of St Kilda are, like Fair Isle, to the marine environment and to the seabirds which it supports. First there is the continuing and, to an extent, unknown effect of the fishing industry, which appears to be having both positive and negative effects on several species. All we can do here is to press for a sustainable industry that does not waste the resource unnecessarily nor directly endanger seabirds by the type of equipment it uses.

To an extent a Marine Nature Reserve around St Kilda will protect some of this resource, but to a large extent it would be only symbolic protection, as many of the seabirds of St Kilda (unlike Fair Isle) feed far beyond any potential Reserve boundary.

The more serious threat to the marine environment is from the oil industry, both from exploration and production to the west, and from tanker traffic immediately to the east. The threat is not only from large-scale oil spillage, which is unlikely going by the record of the North Sea oil industry production and transportation to date, but from small-scale and possibly chronic leak and spillage, which will have an irreversible effect on the present pristine marine environment surrounding St Kilda. Once contaminated there is no going back.

As far as tanker traffic is concerned, the Donaldson Report *Safer Ships, Cleaner Seas* (1994), following the *Braer* disaster in Shetland in 1993, recommended that loaded tankers over 10,000 Gross Registered Tonnage and other large vessels carrying significant quantities of bunker oil should avoid the Minches and use the Deep Water Route to the west of the Hebrides. This no doubt would remove some of the threat of oil spillage between the Hebrides and the mainland of Scotland, but it simply places such a threat further out and nearer to St Kilda.

Following consultation by the Trust with the British Government and various conservation bodies on the oil exploration blocks nominated under the 1984 Licensing Round, a block to the immediate west of St Kilda was removed from consideration. This may have had more to do with missile testing than conservation though! However, there is still the possibility of oil exploration and production in other blocks to the west, north and south of St Kilda, the nearest being 37 kilometres to the south. Oil spills in any of those areas will affect St Kilda seabirds and could, under fairly average conditions, be on the cliffs within a day or two. Although SNH (as manager of St Kilda) will be in consultation with the Department of Trade and Industry in advising on working practices and contingency plans, there will be little anyone can do if a spill does occur, as it will be almost impossible to deploy booms, and treating oil spills by dispersants around St Kilda may well be more damaging than leaving them alone.

At the time of writing, Greenpeace has been drawing attention, in its usual spectacular way, to these threats from oil developments and lobbying UNESCO to include St Kilda on the World Heritage in Danger List, thereby putting more pressure on the British Government to take action to protect St Kilda from the industry. Greenpeace's agenda is really against the global profligate use of an energy resource that may be promoting the greenhouse effect and global warming. Since the ultimate result of global warming may be an effect on sea temperatures to the detriment of the food resources for seabirds, Greenpeace is doing St Kilda a good turn!

Having said that there are no major threats to the terrestrial biological features, we cannot overlook the presence of the MoD base on the island and its effects on the environment. There is no doubt that once the MoD (the RAF at the time) decided, in 1956, that they wanted to use St Kilda as a tracking base, nothing could have stopped them. The Trust and SNH (Nature Conservancy at the time) then could only mitigate the effects as best they could. Most photographs of St Kilda, particularly of Village Bay and the village itself, are carefully taken to omit the grey, squat buildings, the rock-filled wire gabions propping up part of the shore, the connecting road to the landing craft ramp, the helicopter pad and the radar domes placed on the summit of one of the hills. They also, with greater difficulty, seek to avoid the large quarry used to provide the material for the roads, in the very face of the surrounding hills.

There is no getting away from the fact (despite the IUCN Technical Evaluation) that the cultural landscape of Village Bay on Hirta has been brutally shattered by the infrastructure of the base. If that landscape is valued for the story of its long human history of settlement and the sustainable and almost self-supporting use that the St Kildans made of the natural landscape and resources, then the MoD, who presumably have made financial provision, must remove the base, lock, stock and barrel, when its term of life is over. There must be a wealth of written and illustrative information concerning the MOD base for its future study by historians and therefore there will be no need to retain the buildings. If anything is put in its place to provide the modern facilities that make temporary sojourns so pleasant, it must be with far great empathy for the physical landscape and spirit of the place.

On landscape grounds the damage is done and until the MoD leaves there can be no amelioration of its impact. However, chronic fuel leakage onto the beach from the base, which has been occurring for a number of years, and the future of the gabions and their effect on other parts of the shore, must be addressed, especially in a location whose natural heritage is of world status.

As noted earlier, there are actually two Management Plans for St Kilda, that of the Trust itself and that of SNH (in preparation), the manager. The Trust's primary aim states that:

The Trust should ensure the permanent preservation of the natural heritage, cultural heritage and landscape of the islands of St Kilda, given the designation of the islands as a World Heritage Site, the Trust has an added international responsibility to ensure that all aspects of this heritage are conserved, whether under direct management of the Trust or otherwise.

The SNH Management Plan covers only the natural heritage, and to paraphrase, its objective is: to maintain and enhance (where appropriate) habitats, seabirds, sheep, endemic species, earth sciences, landscape and archaeological features.

Other objectives of the Trust include: to continue to allow access to the public, but not to promote the islands, and to provide for greater understanding and appreciation, both for visitors and the wider public. The fourth and final aim states:

The Trust must ensure that Aims 1, 2, and 3 can be met with or without the presence of the MoD on St Kilda.

Taking the first Trust aim at its face value, the Trust, as owner, accepts responsibility for the environmental management, even though it is being carried out by SNH. The lease with SNH expires in 2001 and the Trust has acknowledged this in its Management Plan (1996–2001) highlighting that it will become increasingly involved in the management of the natural heritage.

The general management policy of SNH is one of non-intervention and in research non-manipulation, which seems entirely appropriate for an environment that has not been managed for the past 70 years and whose conservation features show no deterioration nor damaging conflict. The

Village Bay, the MOD base on the right and Boreray in the distance

Trust goes so far as to say in its lease to SNH, regarding the Soay sheep, that 'sheep numbers must not be reduced and they must be treated as wild animal'. However, in its own (later) Management Plan it states that 'Concern has been expressed by visitors to the islands that this high mortality indicates an uncaring approach by Trust and SNH to the welfare of the sheep.' The Trust therefore needs to provide more information to explain the reasons why there is no management of the sheep. A similar concern, regarding an apparent need to manage, could arise with the bonxies and their apparent impact on other seabird species. Both issues must be approached rationally by the Trust and will be a real test of its credentials as a manager of the natural as opposed to the 'cultural' environment. The Trust must resist any Siren calls for humane management of the Soay sheep.

There is no indication on St Kilda that the environment that sustains the sheep has changed a great deal over a very long period of time, nor that the environment with fewer sheep would be of greater diversity. In the absence of sheep, plant diversity would actually decline, but the vegetation would be taller and more impressive. One just needs to look at Dùn to see what the rest of the environment could be like without sheep. The question is – what is more important, the Soay sheep or the vegetation? I would suggest that there is no contest!

St Kilda, to a great extent, exemplifies the position in which the Trust finds itself today. In St Kilda the Trust has responsibility for a site which has the most important heritage designation that can be bestowed on any site in the world. The designation, however, is for the natural heritage. What resources does the Trust put into the conservation of the natural heritage on St Kilda, and what resources does it put into the conservation of the cultural heritage, that is not designated? Does the Trust actively support research, survey and monitoring of the designated natural heritage as expected under the NNR, Biosphere Reserve and World Heritage designations? Compare and contrast the Trust resource input to the natural heritage of Ben Lawers. How much longer can the Trust continue to rely on the resources of other, usually statutory bodies, to manage the natural heritage for it? More than on any other property – since World Heritage Listing puts the onus for care on the owner – the Trust is faced in St Kilda with making the decision as to whether or not it is a body that truly embraces a holistic approach: that puts its resources equitably towards all of the elements of its responsibility, the natural heritage included.

There is one final major problem facing the Trust on St Kilda. The MoD has undoubtedly caused a great deal of damage to the fabric and spirit of St Kilda, but without its presence it is very unlikely that the Trust could itself have built up such a presence there. However, if and when the MoD depart, the Trust will be faced with enormous costs of transport if it is to continue its restoration and archaeological activity at the present level, and with the problem of how to protect that investment in the winter months from visiting fishermen. If Trust staff are to be present on the island throughout the year, the Trust will need to find substantial new funds and meaningful activities for staff in the long, dark and wild winter months. Two potential solutions may be available. First, the MoD should be persuaded to contribute towards an endowment fund which could be built up before it departs, in return for the invaluable contribution St Kilda has given to the development of missiles and Britain's defence. Second, if the Trust accepts a new role for itself in the promotion of research and monitoring of the natural heritage appropriate to St Kilda's global natural heritage status, other research and monitoring partners might share some of the staffing and logistical costs in lieu of rents.

Chapter 11

Fair Isle

Introduction

Fair Isle, perhaps meaning 'Truce' island, is truly 'fair' nonetheless in August, with tall herbs still flowering in the meadows and neat rigs green with oats, potatoes and kale. For an island as small and remote as Fair Isle, it is surprising and pleasing to see so many cattle, milking cows and calves on the croft land. However, not only the land, but the croft houses and newly built homes look in good order, a productive and positive atmosphere reflecting a community with confidence in itself and its landlord.

The Trust acquired Fair Isle in 1954 from George Waterston, one of the founding fathers of the Fair Isle Bird Observatory Trust (FIBOT). He had bought the island from the Sumburgh Estate in 1948, after more than a decade of involvement in the study of the migrant birds which alight on Fair Isle in the spring and autumn. However, the study of migrant birds on Fair Isle, for which the island is probably predominantly known to naturalists, goes right back to the early part of the century and to Dr William Eagle Clarke, Rear Admiral James Stenhouse and George (Fieldy) Stout of Fair Isle – but that is another story! Today there is an active and modern observatory which plays a very important part in the life and natural heritage of the island, through its work on seabird research and monitoring, as we will see. Additionally it plays a very important part in Fair Isle's economy, providing accommodation just as much for the more general visitor as for the ornithologist.

In the early 1950s however, it was obvious that one man could not solve the problems of a tiny and remote island community which was struggling to survive. George Waterston therefore offered the island to the Trust. Although, on the face of it, the Trust stepped in to secure the future of the bird observatory, the Trust knew well that taking on the administration of Fair Isle would involve far more than that. Fair Isle is one more anomaly in Trust properties, in that it was acquired as much for the Trust's potential to help the island community, as for its observatory, its landscape and national

Facing page
Fulmar and Fair Isle cliffs

heritage value. From the beginning then, the overall aim of the Trust's management of Fair Isle has been the survival of the community, that:

> *the Trust should ensure the permanent preservation, for the benefit of the nation, of Fair Isle, as an example of an island where man and nature work in harmony, having particular regard to:*
> - *the maintenance of a viable, balanced community;*
> - *the protection of the natural environment;*
> - *the cultural identity of the island.*

This is a principal and single aim shared with no other Trust property, although contained within more complex principal aims at Balmacara, Canna (and Iona), but not Torridon. How much would the Trust's approach to management on these (and other) properties change, I wonder, if they adopted the principal aim in Fair Isle?

I have touched on this aspect of the Trust's responsibilities in other chapters, but on Fair Isle and Canna the communities depend, for their very survival, on the Trust as a benevolent and supportive landlord. On these properties the well-being of the community is central to good management of the natural heritage; so, as with Canna, we need to take into account the investment the Trust has made in the infrastructure of the island. First, however, we should look at the history of the natural heritage of Fair Isle.

Natural heritage

The island is set almost exactly halfway between Orkney and Shetland, but politically, culturally and geologically it is part of Shetland. It is composed almost entirely of old red sandstones similar in age and structure to the south end of Shetland, supporting soils of sufficient quality to allow the development of crofting in the lower-lying south end of the island, while the higher northern two-thirds, rising to 217 metres at Ward Hill and separated by a hill dyke, provide the common grazing. In size the island is slightly smaller than Canna, being just under five kilometres in length and nowhere more than two kilometres in width. Being so far north relative to the rest of the British mainland, but in the track of both the Slope Current travelling from south of Britain and the low-pressure systems that sweep across the North Atlantic, the temperature is relatively cool and even, but the winds are boisterous and ever present. Gales occur on average on 58 days in the year, while precipitation occurs on average two days out of three: a climate described as submontane oceanic. In fact Fair Isle has the highest relative humidity and, along with St Kilda, is probably the windiest place at such altitude in the British Isles. Because the archipelago is relatively isolated, the

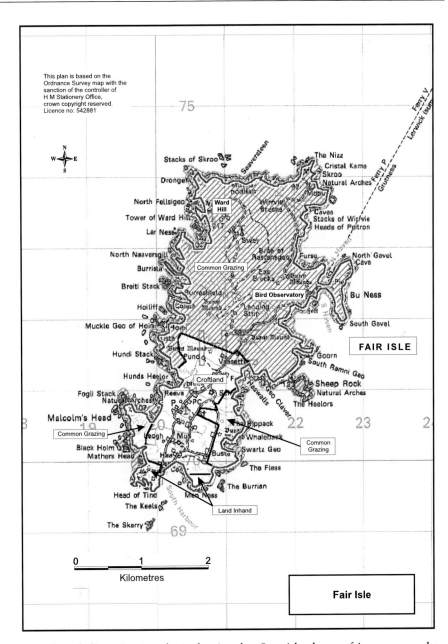

Figure 11.1
Map of the
Fair Isle area
(Legend: see p. xviii)

vegetational diversity is relatively simple. Outside the crofting area and to the north of the hill dyke, it is predominantly heather moorland on peat of varying depth, with a band of maritime grassland skirting the cliff tops.

Physically the island is very impressive; perhaps the coast is not to the scale of the St Kilda cliffs, but apart from two low and accessible shores in the north east and at the southern extremity, Fair Isle is virtually cliff-bound with the western and northern coasts being the most impressive and holding most of Fair Isle's seabirds. The NSA designation describes the landscape of Fair Isle thus:

. . . a combination of green fields, moors and sandstone cliffs, all related to the coast. Remote from the mainland of Shetland, it has a great diversity of cliffs, geos, stacks, skerries, natural arches, isthmuses and small bayhead beaches. While it lacks absolute relief, it has the distinctive features of Sheep Rock and the several eminences of its west coast which add further variety to the coastal scenery.

In fact the coast of Fair Isle makes for the most wonderful walking, with breathtaking new vistas of cliff and sea around every corner. In some places the bedding of the red sandstone is almost vertical and the erosive power of the sea has fashioned from it magnificent sharp-edged stacks and promontories, arches and caves.

Like St Kilda, it is Fair Isle's geographical position, close to rich, natural marine resources, that has ensured its attraction for settlement from earliest times and which today is just as vital for its present human community of around 70 adults and children. The first settlers were the Neolithic farmers who brought with them their grazing stock of sheep, very similar to the Soay, cattle and possibly ponies as well as their arable skills. They must have had good sea-going skills to have made the crossing with their stock and belongings and knowledge of fishing and the exploitation of seabirds. Unlike the St Kildans, who were seabird exploiters *par excellence*, the Fair Isle people relied far more on the sea, not just in relation to the fish resource, but also in intercepting passing ships to barter fresh food for manufactured

Skylark and croft fields

Prostrate Juniper on
the hill grazings

articles they could not make themselves. This book is not the place to describe all the archaeological remains on Fair Isle – a recent survey recorded 750 sites – suffice it that there is a wonderful and varied record of the Bronze, Iron, Pictish and Viking Ages still extant. This small island, then, has supported people for at least 5,000 years and it is a remarkable testimony to their management of fairly limited resources that the arable land is still in good heart and that the moorland is one of the very few places in the Northern Isles that still contains a fair proportion of prostrate juniper, a sure sign that it has not been over-grazed or artificially improved in all that time.

The ratio of croft land to rough grazings on Fair Isle is approximately 1:7, with the nineteen crofts occupying about 157 hectares, of which only 34 hectares – less than half a square kilometre – was put down to arable in 1991. It is this tiny area of arable land that has supported the Fair Isle population over recent decades. In the past, under the pressure of a larger population living on the edge of starvation at times, the area under arable was much greater, although its quality would have been much less. In 1861 for example, the population was over 350 and there were 38 crofts! So high was the population that the island could not sustain all the people and there was a mass emigration the following year, with 23 families going to New-foundland. It was the inability of the land, and gradually of the sea through international exploitation of its rich fishing grounds, plus the rising demand for a better standard of living, that led to the steady emigration and decline in Fair Isle's population. It was this continuing decline, right up into the 1950s, that led George Waterston to the conclusion that the island needed a landlord with much greater resources than were available to him. It was this decline then that faced the Trust when they acquired the island in 1954.

From the beginning of its tenure of ownership, the Trust has appreciated the importance of the infrastructure in supporting the Fair Isle community. Initially the Trust used its own funds in improvements, but gradually it has had to seek funds from other bodies, using its considerable influence and connections. In 1962 it installed a diesel generator to provide the first community-wide electricity for the island, and in 1982 an aerogenerator was installed, the first commercial aerogenerator in Britain. The Trust also set about improving the housing stock and, with the islanders, encouraged improvements to the communications facilities with Shetland, so that by the

The island boat, the
Good Shepherd IV

early 1990s Fair Isle not only had a new boat, the *Good Shepherd IV*, but a breakwater sheltering a new pier. Trust volunteers have also rendered much physical assistance to the upkeep and repair of many aspects of the infrastructure, such as dykes and buildings, as well as making a substantial social input. At the same time the Trust, along with other funders, contributed to the establishment of a new bird observatory which was opened in 1969. To a great extent it has been the provision of improved facilities and the commitment shown by the Trust to the welfare of the island which gave confidence to other funders, which has halted the population decline and even seen islanders returning and newcomers settling. Perhaps, if the vision of the Gaelic study centre on Canna can be fulfilled, it would have an equally positive benefit for the community there. Very much part of the empowering process on Fair Isle has also been the establishment of partnership committees between the Trust and the islanders, which have taken over responsibility for the running of many aspects of the island.

In mid-August Fair Isle's flowering plants are still at their best. Along the ungrazed roadsides grow statuesque angelicas, accompanied by the purple of devil's-bit scabious and the yellows of autumnal hawkbit and bird's-foot trefoil, while the wet hayfields and meadows are bright with ragwort, ragged robin, kidney vetch, buttercup, self-heal and many more herbs. The most subtle and beautiful plant community though, is that of the herb-rich heath within the hill dyke. These and the inbye grasslands still survive as rich and diverse habitats, as little fertiliser or pesticide is used in management – a rare situation in today's agriculture elsewhere. Here grazing pressures trim the vegetation to the texture of tapestry, a weave of ling, bell heather, crowberry, occasional juniper, creeping willow and lichens in which are stitched the tiny flowers of the dwarf shrubs, the flat yellow petals of tormentil, eyebrights, thyme and the almost washed-out lilac flowers of the sheep's-bit scabious. By and large the produce of the rigs (narrow fields) is yet to be lifted, so they are neat and green. The oats are sometimes cut green and fed along with the haylage to the cattle and the sheep in the winter, the former needing to be fed for the six months they are kept inside in the winter months. In wet summers only some of the fields are cut as hay and the grass heaped into coals.

By this late in the year the breeding season for Fair Isle's terrestrial birds is virtually over, the local starlings and twite are flocking and there are occasional small flocks of passing waders such as knot and sanderling. Regular August visitors such as a ruff and a few barred warblers have arrived. On the hill the wheatear is still vocal and both the bonxie and arctic skua are still hanging around, but they no longer bother the walker. Of the seabirds, the guillemots and puffins are well away to sea and only the fulmar and the gannet are on the cliffs and stacks, still with young on the nest. The gannet first bred on Fair Isle in 1975 and has expanded fairly rapidly compared to the established gannetries close by on Noss and Herma Ness. On the sea are shags, tysties, eider duck in eclipse, a few grey and harbour seals, and a minke whale feeding close inshore.

An element of the natural heritage that Fair Isle shares with the other remote Trust island of St Kilda, but which is absent from Canna due to its close proximity to other islands and the Scottish mainland, is its endemic fauna. Like St Kilda. Fair Isle is sufficiently isolated to have allowed the evolution of its own subspecies of field mouse (*Apodemus sylvaticus fridariensis*) and wren (*Troglydytes troglydytes tridariensis*). The former, like other island mice, is larger than its mainland counterpart and second only in size to those on St Kilda which can be twice the weight of their mainland cousins. Fair Isle too then, provides fairly unique opportunities for the study of colonisation and adaptation. The only other Fair Isle terrestrial mammals are the house mouse, the rabbit and, unfortunately, feral cat; but no other wild mammals have managed to colonise the land.

Crofting and the environment

Fair Isle is one of a diminishing number of places where traditional crofting is still very active, not just in terms of agricultural management, but in terms of community – part necessity, part a way of life. The average size of a croft on Fair Isle is only eight hectares and, as with all agricultural units of this sort

Traditional
haymaking, now a
thing of the past?

of scale, it is hardly worth investing in specialised machinery, such as a small
silage baler, to manage only a part of that: so on Fair Isle there is co-
operation between the crofters in sharing the costs and maintenance of such
machinery. As at Drumbuie, in the Balmacara property, there is much arable,
as well as pastoral, management. Such management not only sustains the
health and productivity of the soils, it also supports the diversity of wildlife,
only hinted at above.

Although the corncrake is an annual migrant on Fair Isle it rarely stays for
long and has not bred since 1966. The ESA was established in 1994 and the
grant towards corncrake habitat, requiring no cutting of hay until 1st August,
has not yet therefore had the success it seeks. On Fair Isle, as elsewhere, there
are inflexible aspects of the ESA that need to be addressed. For example, if
corncrakes are not present there is no reason not to graze the fields or cut them
earlier – which would be of enormous help to crofters already working at the
margins of such agriculture, as well as helping to maintain botanical diversity.
The regulations can also lead to unnecessary additional fencing which gives
extra work to crofters and detracts from the crofting scene. In addition, the
ESA scheme does not give enough support to cropping, essential if cattle are to
be encouraged and for sustaining the fertility of arable fields. Although there
are problems with the ESA regulations, the form of low-intensity agriculture
that it encourages undoubtedly brings positive benefits to the Fair Isle
landscape and to the birds, such as ringed plover, snipe, lapwing, curlew and
skylark, all species declining in areas of more intensive farming in Britain.

Because the environment is so well ordered and so very obviously cared for,
it also results in the promotion of well-being (a particularly apt old-fashioned
phrase) in the community. With such positive management it is not surprising
then that Fair Isle won the Crofting Township of the Year in 1995. The future

for the typical low-input, low-yield crofting on Fair Isle though is not assured. The cost of transport of both feedstuffs and animals, and inflexible EU regulations, threatens its viability, and there is a desperate need therefore for the right financial incentives to continue such good stewardship.

Crofting in the northern isles has also relied on access to the *scattald*, or common grazings, where crofters have traditionally had additional rights to win materials essential to their form of agriculture. In the past this included turfs, heather and rushes for building materials and as bedding for animals, but today only peat is cut for fuel. Fair Isle, like the rest of Shetland, has had to exploit these resources on the hill for many, many generations, and the hill soil has suffered some erosion in places from such use. In some situations however, scalping has produced dry heathland habitat, rich in juniper. In a situation where the climate is such that the islanders are virtually living on a hill, though at sea level, and where salt-laden winds regularly lash fragile growing tips of plants, such exploitation, sometimes accompanied by a high grazing pressure, has exacerbated the climatic pressures on the vegetation, resulting in stunted growth and even soil (peat) erosion in places.

In recent years there has been some concern on Fair Isle as to the state of the heather, an important winter food source for the islanders' sheep. In 1992 therefore the Macaulay Land Use Research Institute (MLURI) was contracted by the Trust and SNH to carry out a survey of the heather and to report on the effects of sheep grazing. Indeed, the heather was found to be in poor condition with low growth and much dieback. The reason for this was mainly due to management in the last century and earlier, and to present climate, rather than present sheep grazing pressures. The results indicated that the sheep grazed mainly on the maritime grasslands and on the heath-grassland mosaics, rather than on areas of pure heather. Heather in the northern islands is in fact reaching its climatic limits. The conclusion of the report suggested that the present grazing level of approximately 1,000 breeding Shetland ewes, or roughly one per hectare, only led to heather loss in localised areas and was therefore sustainable for the immediate future. This conclusion is supported, as mentioned earlier, by the continuing presence of prostrate juniper within the moorland, some of which was found to be over 160 years old! The MLURI report went on to suggest a need for the monitoring of the health of the heather on the hill, and there is now such a programme in place.

Some years earlier another local controversy arose concerning sheep on the hill, which could have blown up into a conflict between the crofters and conservationists. Because of the partnership approach on Fair Isle however, a proper investigation was carried out and no action was found to be necessary. Of the seabirds which breed on Fair Isle, two species breed on the moorland and these are the bonxie (great skua) and the arctic skua. The colony of the latter is the fourth largest in the British Isles and is therefore of national conservation importance, while the former is one of the most important of Britain's seabird species in global terms. Both species are aggressive towards intruders in the breeding season, both human and animal. Their attacks are exciting, frightening or annoying, depending on one's perspective! On the NNR of Noss in Shetland bonxies make it very difficult to use dogs to round up sheep, but on Fair Isle it seemed that the arctic skuas were also preventing sheep from grazing on some of the best grassland. This inevitably led to the danger of islanders taking the law into their own hands: the law, because of course these birds are protected. Obviously this could have led to real problems if there was genuine and serious disturbance to sheep grazing, as it was, it was found that the skuas only had a very limited effect on sheep grazing.

Seabirds

Fair Isle, like St Kilda, as we noted in the last chapter, lies in an area rich in plankton in the summer months which provide the food resource for its large and varied seabird populations; Fair Isle's sandstone cliffs and stacks, near-vertical coastal grassy slopes and its moorland, provide a range of nesting habitats. In total on this small island, breed seventeen of Britain's 24 seabird species, two more than St Kilda. From the table it can be seen that most of the species mentioned are at least of national importance.

   Although each seabird species has its preferred diet, there is a great deal of overlap. Some, such as the petrels, feed directly on the plankton. Others, such as shag, the auks, the terns and kittiwakes, depend to a very great extent on sandeels, which can also be a large component of the bonxie and gannet diet. The sandeel is also the prey of some other larger fish, seals, and fishermen. As its name suggests it requires a sandy substrate in which it lives when not shoaling through the water column. To the immediate west and

Table 11.1   Approximate breeding numbers of selected seabirds in recent years.

	Numbers		% British population
Fulmar	43,317	AOS	7
Gannet	1,116	AON	<1
Shag	1,100	Pairs	3
Arctic skua	98	AOT	3
Great skua	152	AOT	1
Kittiwake	11,650	AON	4
Arctic tern	1,730	Incubating adults	1
Guillemot	32,300	IND	3
Razorbill	3,400	IND	2
Black guillemot	254	IND	<1
Puffin	23,000	IND	2

AON – Apparently occupied nests.   AOT – Apparently occupied territories.
AOS – Apparently occupied sites.   IND – Individuals

Arctic skuas

east of Fair Isle are two sandeel spawning grounds. The sandeel, of course, is not the only fish species that brings seabirds (and other marine life) into conflict with fishermen; for example both the herring and mackerel can be important prey for the gannet. On the other hand some seabirds, fulmar and bonxie for example, may have almost come to rely on the wasteful fishery practice of dumping offal and whitefish discards.

While the gannet is able to switch prey in times of shortage, the puffin, and to a much greater extent the kittiwake – reflected in its fluctuating breeding success over recent years – are particularly dependent on the natural availability of sandeels during the breeding season. The gannet and the fulmar populations in the British Isles are therefore continuing to expand and in fact the former has comparatively recently established new colonies on Fair Isle (1975) and Foula (1980). The kittiwake (and the arctic tern) on the other hand, unlike the diving auks (puffin, guillemot and razorbill) depending on sandeels near the surface, suffered heavily in the 1980s in the Northern Isles from lack of availability of sandeels in that part of the water column. Because of the perceived conflict between seabirds and the sandeel fishery, much research and investigation has been carried out on the biology and behaviour of sandeels. The conclusions reached suggested that, in Shetland at least, the lack of sandeels was due to changes in their population and movement and was not directly the result of the fishery. There are natural fluctuations in the breeding success of seabirds, and most species, due to their longevity, can have poor breeding performances for several years without any harm to their populations. However, the fishery could limit the number of sandeels available to seabirds in time of shortages. The lesson, as if we need it repeated, is that we need commercial fisheries that take into account the legitimate needs of the other natural marine predators, such as seabirds, cetaceans and seals.

Although the total numbers of seabirds is relatively high in international terms, the populations of several species are decreasing and the breeding success of a number has been average or below average in recent years. Due to the very wet weather of 1997 only one arctic tern chick hatched! How do we know this? Fair Isle is fortunate in having

Seabird monitoring

the FIBOT, which from its beginning has gradually widened its remit from recording and investigating migrating birds to becoming involved and supporting seabird research and monitoring. Through the presence of FIBOT the seabirds of Fair Isle have been subject to the longest continuous study of any colony in Britain. FIBOT is presently contracted by the Seabirds and Cetaceans (whales) Team of the UK Joint Nature Conservation Committee (JNCC) to carry out detailed monitoring of several seabird species. The JNCC carries out and co-ordinates work, such as that concerning seabirds, that is UK-wide. Seabird work is a very important part of JNCC responsibility because of the international importance of Britain's seabird populations. Monitoring of the size and breeding success of these populations has become increasingly important over the last couple of decades, first because of the development of the marine oil industry in the North Sea and the Atlantic, and the accompanying dangers to seabirds from oil pollution; and second, because of the increasing pressure on our diminishing fish stocks, particularly the industrial fishing of species known to be essential to the breeding success of several seabird species, such as sandeels. Fair Isle is one of just four key seabird monitoring sites in Britain which are closely monitored annually. The others are Canna, Isle of May (in the Forth) and Skomer (Wales). Long-term monitoring of less intensity, under the aegis of JNCC, also takes place at St Kilda, Orkney and in Grampian. The Trust has responsibility for three of these sites!

FIBOT plays a very important role on Fair Isle. Its contract with the JNCC does not just concern itself with seabird numbers or breeding success, but is seeking to look behind these data to try to understand why they both may fluctuate by examining the diet of the birds: changes in diet can indicate the lack of availability of certain food sources and therefore the lack of their presence in the marine environment. FIBOT also had contracts with SNH to monitor the spread of the tern colony near the runway in relationship to aircraft safety, and is in partnership with SNH in the provision of an island-wide Ranger service to which FIBOT contributes 50 per cent of the costs. The observatory accommodation is an important element in the support of research on the island. In 1997 the observatory supported a team of researchers from Durham University, who studied aspects of the foraging ecology of Fair Isle's seabirds as part of a European collaborative project to investigate the impact of fisheries on seabirds.

In addition to this, FIBOT continues its recording and ringing of migrants and providing accommodation for the general-interest visitor and those who come in the hope of seeing regular migrants and rarities well off their usual migration path. FIBOT and its wardens over the years have contributed substantially to our understanding of the mechanics of bird migration. For example it was originally thought that Fair Isle was simply on a major migration route, but the data collected by of one of the early wardens, Kenneth Williamson, from assiduous trapping, recording and weather study over a number of years from 1948, led him to establish his theory of *drift migration*, which is still accepted today. In 1968 Fair Isle was in the headlines when the first attempt to re-introduce the white tailed or sea eagle to Britain from Scandinavia was attempted. Unfortunately it failed, but much was learned and applied to the more successful attempts that began on Rum, adjacent to Canna, from 1972.

Designations, the sea and the future

An objective in the Fair Isle Management Plan is to:

> *Conserve the marine environment, by appropriate methods giving particular consideration to the establishment of a Marine Protection Area.*

Until only the last couple of decades, the seabird populations of Britain have generally been on the increase this century and we have therefore been very complacent about their long-term prospects. The recent history of several seabird species on Fair Isle and elsewhere however, particularly the kittiwake, has underlined the critical link between the seabirds on the cliff and the health of the surrounding seas. Up to now, we have been content to confer on seabird cliffs, such as those of Fair Isle, Canna and St Kilda, statutory protective designations such as Site of Special Scientific Interest (SSSI) and more recently Special Protection Area (SPA). The latter requires maintenance of population levels through appropriate conservation measures, but these have not yet been spelt out. In the case of St Kilda, its seabird populations come under the protection of World Heritage listing. None of these designations, however, confer any protection on the seas

Croft

surrounding the seabird colonies on which they rely for their food, nor any regulation of the fisheries there, without which statutory protection of the seabirds is meaningless. The protection of the sea is critical to Fair Isle where the main seabird food resource is proving very elusive in recent years, causing regular catastrophic breeding seasons, and yet it is still fished commercially. There has been a statutory designation available since 1981, the Marine Nature Reserve, which *can* confer protection of a marine area up to five kilometres offshore. However, it requires the agreement of all interested parties, including the fishery interest. As a result only three have been declared in the UK so far.

Where do the Trust and the Fair Isle people fit into this complex picture? In the past this community lived partly off the sea through fishing, but alas the scale of commercial exploitation has not left enough to make this a viable avenue of income any more. The islanders therefore, as all islanders must, have had to look today to other sources of subsistence. Earlier, I mentioned some of the forms of employment available on the island including B&B and the FIBOT. Visitors to Fair Isle are extremely important to the island economy and they come not only for the migrants, but for the unique atmosphere of the island and particularly for the seabirds. So it is of the utmost importance to the future of the island and to the Trust, that some form of protection and control is found for the seas around Fair Isle, and not just for its own sake.

In 1985 the Council of Europe awarded Fair Isle the European Diploma. The original recommendations of this award related almost entirely to terrestrial management, although it highlighted the need for control of oil prospecting and development. With the renewal of the Diploma of Europe in 1990 new recommendations were included stating:

Protection should be reinforced and extended to the seas around the island, if possible through the creation of a total marine reserve, and there should be scientific study of the development of the sandeel population near the island.

Further, in renewing the Diploma for the second time in 1995, the recommendations were expanded to include:

The possibility of applying a 10-mile 'Voluntary Exclusion Zone' for oil tankers, as applies to other parts of Shetland, should be examined, as well as the restriction of fishing to island inhabitants within three miles of its coasts, limited to artisanal and selective methods. The sandeel fishery should remain closed.

These marine additions to the Diploma recommendations were the direct result of the Fair Isle community recognising the importance of their wildlife and pressing for its protection. On the initiative of the Trust, along with the community and FIBOT, the Fair Isle Marine Environment and Tourism Initiative (FIMETI) was launched in 1996, to recommend appropriate action to protect the marine environment surrounding Fair Isle and was the first step to bring together all those who need to reach agreement if some sort of protection of Fair Isle's seas is to come about.

In 1997 and 1998 a partnership of the FIBOT, Fair Isle Committee and Community Association (FICCA), the Trust and RSPB, published two reports. The first was an illustrative management plan for the island's inshore and adjacent offshore waters designed to present the case for an integrated approach to the management of the surrounding marine environment. The second, *Safeguarding Our Heritage, The Fair Isle Marine Resource: A Community Proposal for its Sustainable Management*, drawn up within the community, sets out the case, aims and objectives to achieve the goal, identifying all the players and defining the areas and degree of protection and control required around the island (Figure 11.2).

Within the innermost protected marine areas, Zone 1, the community, with the support of the Trust and FIBOT, seeks the reinstatement of the old exclusive fishing rights which extended up to 4.8 kilometres offshore until as recently as 1984 (Scotland Inshore Fisheries Act). The proposed perimeter is set at 5 kilometres as that is the range within which most of Fair Isle's seabirds feed. The next Zone (2), extending from 5 to 16 kilometres, is proposed to be an area of much improved fishery management which would protect spawning grounds of several species. Zone 3, recommended by the Shetland Fishermen's Association (SFA), extends to the south east to ensure better protection of the major haddock nursery area. Zone 4, it is suggested, should be promoted as unsuitable for oil and gas exploration and

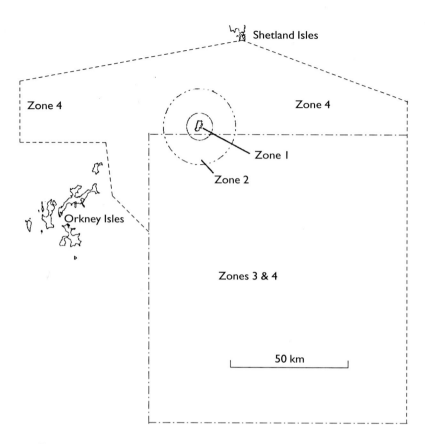

Figure 11.2
Illustrative boundaries for proposed Fair Isle marine protected area

Reproduced, with permission, from Riddiford, N. J. (1998) 'Safeguarding our heritage – the Fair Isle marine resource: a community proposal for its sustainable management, FICA, FIBOT and NTS, Fair Isle and Inverness'.

Zone 1: Inshore waters up to five kilometres from Fair Isle coastline
Zone 2: Adjacent waters up to sixteen kilometres from Fair Isle coastline
Zone 3: Proposed haddock nursery box
Zone 4: Outer waters within proposed protected area

production, while a 16-kilometre limit should be placed on ships carrying potentially polluting cargoes such as oil. (Note: in June 1999 a fully laden oil tanker passing around the north of Scotland broke down while just 9 kilometres off Fair Isle!) This limit relates particularly to oil tanker traffic leaving the busy oil terminals at Sullom in Shetland and Flotta in Orkney, or passing by Fair Isle from Norway en route to the Atlantic.

Summation

The proposals above may appear at first reading to be rather grandiose. However, it might be remembered that:

1. the principles in the Diploma are recommended by the Committee of Ministers of the Council of Europe and have some support from statutory UK bodies;

2. the Government has already withdrawn a block (close to St Kilda) from oil exploration in an Offshore Licensing Round in 1994;
3. inshore exclusive fishing rights used to exist;
4. the Donaldson Report (*Safer Ships, Cleaner Seas*), after the loss of the *Braer* at Shetland in 1993, recognised that Fair Isle was a Marine Environmental High Risk Area;
5. fishery management is supported by the SFA;
6. the publishing of the FIMETI report was actually sponsored by an oil exploration company which had carried out exploration work just 25 miles offshore!

There is already then a great measure of sympathy and support for what is virtually a prospectus for ensuring the survival of Fair Isle as a living community through the sustainable use of their marine environment. If their vision can be successfully turned into reality, it will give hope and spur to many other small and remote Scottish communities and a template for action which the Trust might apply, possibly in other forms, to other communities for which it has responsibility.

There is one anomaly in the community management of Fair Isle, and that is the status of the FIBOT. On a small island where every opportunity for survival must be exploited and where such opportunities should be fully co-ordinated, FIBOT is part of and yet separate from the community and Trust control. FIBOT contributes enormously to the economy and life of Fair Isle, but it needs to be integrated into the management structure. It also contributes the seabird and migrant science for which the Trust has not the capacity. Elsewhere I have argued the case for the Trust's greater commit-ment to the conservation of the natural heritage; on Fair Isle the Trust could demonstrate this through seeking closer ties, even partnership, with the FIBOT, a partnership that could benefit both organisations.

There are so many near-moribund crofting communities in Scotland, where management has been reduced to a minimum and where the inbye has been sacrificed to sheep, where communities are dwindling and the scene is beginning to look like the first stages of abandonment – fences neglected, machinery rusting, buildings derelict, little human activity – that it is more and more important to try to learn lessons from places like Canna, Drumbuie, Balmacara, Torridon and Fair Isle. On Fair Isle there appear to be several reasons why crofting is so active and productive and, like all these things, it stems from the community. No matter what support might be available, the community must first want to make use of it. The primary reason for the environmental, economic and social success which is Fair Isle today has to lie with the present highly skilled and enterprising local community, exemplified by their united efforts in taking forward the marine initiative with the aim of taking control of their own resources and their own future.

Wet meadow,
aerogenerator and the
hill beyond

In Fair Isle there is also the Trust and its contribution, and it is not only that contribution *per se*, but the manner in which it was, and continues to be, delivered that is important. The Trust has set about supporting the restoration of the infrastructure and establishing committees and partnerships, involving the islanders, giving them a real sense of ownership of their own island. This has given the islanders confidence in the long-term support of the Trust and in turn, more confidence in themselves. That is not to say that enterprise was lacking in the islanders before the arrival of the Trust, but that the Trust's support, its additional range of skills, national standing, financial and political clout, helped the islanders to channel that enterprise into activities that could ensure their future. On St Kilda, perhaps, the innate enterprise, that had kept that island alive for so long, in the face of decline and without outside support directed to their long-term needs, was channelled into short-termism that only resulted in the hastening of their decline.

On Fair Isle there are also three other factors which are not always applicable everywhere. First, the island community is large enough to require an infrastructure that itself requires maintenance by the responsible authorities. So there are some full-time and a number of at least part-time jobs – on the roads, water supply, in the school, maintenance of their own power supply, boat crew, post office, telephones, etc. Then there are the bird observatory, guest houses, and numerous forms of craft and other skilled self-employment, of which Fair Isle knitting is the best known. The existing Management Plan lists almost 40 employment opportunities! Such part-time or full-time employment for at least one member of the family is essential to crofting. Second, Fair Isle has a leavening of recent incomers and returning islanders, who have brought new skills and qualifications, and fresh enthusiasm to the island. Third, the Trust owns most of the houses – a position with which the community is quite content – and which ensures there are no absentee crofters, while preventing houses from being sold as holiday homes.

Each of the Trust properties discussed in this book has its own history and therefore its own unique present administrative structure. With new land ownership structures arising, almost annually, *pace* Assynt, Eigg, Orbost, Knoydart, and with a Scottish Parliament and Land Reform on the horizon, the Trust and other landlords are going to have to look to how they will administer their properties in the future. Perhaps in certain circumstances, in order to avoid 'take-over' by communities, if that is not what they want. Coincidentally, some of the best opportunities for a radical change in management of large areas of Scotland, from exclusive, narrow and sometimes exploitive regimes to more inclusive, diverse and sustainable forms, are arising through the new ownership structures. The course that the Trust has taken on Fair Isle is perhaps closest to an ideal model of a landlord–community partnership that may avoid conflict and take advantage of the complementary contributions that tenants and landowner can bring to each other.

At the moment several committees and partnerships between the Trust and the community have been set up to run various aspects of Fair Isle, while the first Management Plan was initiated by the islanders themselves. When meetings are held on the island it is by the medium of a committee; on the other hand, decisions are also taken off the island by the Trust without community involvement. There is no island representation on the Trust's Fair Isle Management Committee, because it does not exist! Will the Trust address this? Partnerships can allow the Trust to tap into funding not otherwise available. Much more radical, however, would be for the Trust to set up a full Fair Isle partnership with the community. The Trust *has* moved towards empowerment of the community through the formation of the electricity company, and perhaps this is the first step of many. However the desire for partnership has also to come from the community itself, and in the meantime the community also sees advantages in 'final' decisions on several aspects of management, notably in relation to housing, coming from the 'landlord'. It is handy to have someone else to blame! It will be interesting to see what happens next.

What is most important to emphasise about the whole unique initiative on Fair Isle, is that it is a community-led effort to exercise control over its own resources on a sustainable basis.

Chapter 12

The Future

The community and environmental management

I have described some of the recent changes in our approach to countryside management in Scotland, which the Trust must recognise and apply. In this book I have specifically concentrated on the management of the natural heritage, but in acknowledging that wider issues impact on that management, I have included, for example, discussion on the role of the community. To reiterate briefly: conservation, enhancement and restoration of the natural heritage of Scotland, as by and large it has been shaped by management, requires continuing management, and that increasingly has meant the involvement and support of the local rural community and not merely unilateral management by a private, public or voluntary body. In addition I have suggested that the local community is as much 'the nation' for whose benefit Trust land is managed – as are Trust members and the rest of the population of Scotland.

With the advent of a Scottish Parliament, the issue of the role of local communities in the management of the land on which they live, has been absorbed into the political arena with a recognition that local people have little say in the management of the land or access to its resources; such is the history of land ownership in Scotland. The Land Reform Policy Group (LRPG) set up by the Secretary of State for Scotland in 1997 and chaired by the Minister for Agriculture, the Environment and Fisheries, published its *Recommendations For Action* in January 1999. These are recommendations for the future Scottish Parliament to address and the most pertinent here is 'increased community involvement in the way land is owned and used'. Under the section (7) Action Without New Legislation: Private Landowners, the recommendations state:

A Code of Good Practice for rural landownership should be developed, compliance with which should wherever possible become a condition of public assistance. The Code should provide that major landowners

Facing page
West side of Unst

(including non-Governmental organisations which are major landowners in Scotland) should be known locally and as far as possible should be readily available to the local community or, if not available personally, should have *clearly identifiable and accessible local representation.* (my emphasis)

It should be said that the Trust is generally ahead of the field here, but there is still some way to go.

In February 1999 the Secretary of State when launching proposals for access to the countryside and new SSSI arrangements stated:

We therefore propose a stronger voice for local authorities and local communities in the management of SSSIs. A new emphasis on community involvement in land management is consistent with our land reform proposals.

Exactly how widely this will apply – to all SSSIs or just the very large ones – we do not yet know, but there is a principle here that deserves some attention from the Trust too.

The implications of these recommendations for all large estates, including Trust properties and particularly those with SSSIs, and their local communities in Scotland, are revolutionary for private landowners. As far as the Trust is concerned, this should translate into the direct communication and involvement with the local community on a property before any management steps are taken. One of the first questions raised is how will future management of the property benefit the local community as well as the natural environment, and what are the wishes of that community? Lest one should think that such implications of local involvement should be threatening, one need only look to the Trust property of Fair Isle, to see how positive such involvement can be and what creative energy can be released.

For most Trust properties however, there is no Management Committee that includes 'official' local representation. That is not to say that the Trust does not consult and liaise with local communities. This lack of official local representation on Management Committees is apparent on all the Trust properties discussed here and is most obvious, in its absence, on those properties where there are communities living on and trying to make a livelihood from the property, namely Fair Isle, Canna, Torridon, Balmacara and Kintail. Since staff living on Trust property, such as Mar Lodge Estate, can also legitimately be considered part of the community, they too should be represented.

Situations on Mar Lodge Estate, Ben Lawers, Ben Lomond, Glencoe and of course St Kilda, are quite different, but is it easier to address the issue of involvement of the local community with these properties?

All hands to haymaking on Fair Isle!

The Trust is not unaware of the situation and it is heartening to see the many recommendations made in the Trust's own *Crofting Working Group Report* (1997), for example 'Appropriate steps should be taken to ensure that the local community, crofters and non-crofters alike, have an effective system for greater involvement in the management of each property', which is already being taken forward at Balmacara Square. The report went on to make a number of further recommendations which would benefit the natural environment of its croft land. All of them entail positive encouragement and support for crofters, from advice on species management, to support for crofter forestry and diversification, to establishing a fund to finance joint initiatives.

A recommendation of the Land Reform Policy Group (LRPG) is that there should be 'Legislation to give all crofting communities who create a properly constituted crofting trust, a right to have ownership of their croft land transferred to that trust on fair financial terms.' This recommendation and that relating to encouraging the involvement of crofting communities in the management of the land is echoed by the Crofters Commission discussion paper, *The Role of Crofting in Rural Communities* (1998). However, if the recommendations of the Trust's Crofting Working Party are taken ahead it would be unlikely that any of their crofting communities would want to swap a benevolent and supportive landlord for a more precarious existence on their own. Note that if a crofting community on Trust land really wanted to buy their land, the apparent protection provided by inalienability is unlikely to be used to prevent them. For all the distance the Trust has gone on the issue of crofting – and one must recognise that it is a long way – the Trust needs to press on to the ultimate step of real partnership with

Abandoned croft

communities, perhaps by setting up Trusts such as at Balmacara with real democratic power sharing. If successful, such partnerships could be valuable demonstrations for other charitable bodies, public bodies and private estates. Co-operation and even partnership with tenants is, of course, not confined to crofting communities, as we have seen at Ben Lomond and Ben Lawers.

Before we leave the agricultural aspects of environmental management it is worth returning for a moment to the LRPG report and further recommendations for crofting legislation which could have exciting benefits for marginal agricultural land on Trust properties, particularly where communities are small and fragile. It is recommended that there should be 'Legislation to allow the creation of new crofts by removing the barrier to the creation of crofts in present legislation and allowing landowners in crofting areas to create crofts and new crofting common grazings on land which is not currently in crofting tenure . . .'. If such legislation is passed by the new Scottish Parliament, the development of such projects as that at Balmacara Square would be much easier, while it would open up the option of creating new crofts and common grazings on Canna which could increase the Canna population, make available new sources of grants, and bring more land back into positive management for the environment. There are possible implications for Torridon too.

I could be accused of over-emphasis of the importance of community involvement in the management of their own local natural heritage, and I would acknowledge that as far as the Funicular development on Cairngorm is concerned, the best solution for the natural heritage was not achieved. However, I would point out that the wider interests of the Trust – its individual members, skiiers, walkers, climbers, naturalists, historians, archaeologists, foresters, agriculturists, conservationists, local authorities (through COSLA), etc., are represented through the Trust Council and staff, whereas local interests are not. I would also, again, simply point to the example of Fair Isle.

Hill, moorland and woodland management

In Chapter 1 I described the general state of the hill lands, moorlands and native woodland in Scotland and the issues that arise in their management. In the individual property chapters – which have not included *all* the Trust's countryside properties – I have covered the different approaches taken on each within the Trust's overall aim of the promotion of the conservation of their natural features. The crucial issue, as we have seen on each one of the sites, is very often the level of grazing in relation to the aims of management of each. On only two sites could it be said that the grazing level was in balance with the aims of management for the vegetation, and those are St Kilda and Fair Isle. Elsewhere, past management combined with present grazing levels has significantly impoverished the native flora, fauna and natural landscape, and it is only through reduction of these grazing pressures, diversification of grazing, or by protection by fencing in the short term, that damaged or lost natural features can be restored. In the case of several properties, this has been mainly due to high levels of domestic stock, specifically sheep, and on others the problem has been predominantly red deer. As pointed out in earlier chapters, this problem *was* recognised by the Trust in 1992 when it set up its Grazing Working Party.

We have seen that on some properties – Mar Lodge Estate, Glencoe, West Affric and to a large extent Canna – the Trust has total control over the grazing levels, both domestic and wild, while on others grazing is particularly a domestic stock problem and the Trust must either bow to tenants' grazing rights, encourage tenants to make use of agricultural conservation grants, or enter into management agreements with them. In some cases, Ben Lawers for example, grazing tenancies have been acquired by the Trust by the simple but expensive expediency of buying the relevant farm as it came on the market and then re-selling it without the hill grazing. On Ben Lomond the Trust must come to an amicable compromise with an individual tenant; and on the crofting properties discussed here – Kintail, Balmacara, Torridon and Fair Isle – the Trust must have the support of the whole community.

As far as domestic stock is concerned the Trust need only concern itself with its tenants and lessees within the boundary of a property. The control of red deer however, which ignore boundaries, involves co-operation with neighbouring estates, raises moral issues, access issues, a number of practical management difficulties and challenges outdated and traditional views of their place in nature and Highland culture. All of these we have discussed in several preceding chapters. The central point however, that a countryside manager, concerned for the conservation and enhancement of the natural heritage in its totality, must bear in mind, is that the red deer and its management cannot be considered in isolation. The red deer, though spectacular, must be treated as just another grazing animal among many. In other words it is the aims for the habitat that should dictate deer numbers and not *vice versa*, as it has been in most of Scotland for a very long time. The Trust has recognised this in its own Deer Management Policy in 1999:

> The Trust will undertake a full assessment of each relevant Trust property to determine the status of the habitat, the required grazing regime and the culling level required to reach the aims and objectives for flora and fauna, and historic/archaeological remains, which will be specified in the property management plans.

On a number of properties such as Glencoe, Kintail and Ben Lawers, due to Unna funding, it is assumed that there can be no sport stalking, although as I have pointed out elsewhere the Unna Principles should not in fact be a bar to commercial stalking as long as there is no effect on access. On others, notably Mar Lodge Estate, sport stalking is actually mandatory because of Easter Charitable Trust funding. It is on this last property that the Trust has its greatest challenge as far as red deer are concerned, for here, as we have seen, on one half of the property there is to be a red-deer population for sport stalking, while on the other the population must be low enough to allow natural regeneration of woodland without fencing. Are these management aims compatible, or will it all end in tears? The odds must be heavily weighted on the latter, but we will just have to wait and see!

The natural regeneration of woodland and scrub, without fencing wherever possible, is another Trust policy which is being enacted across several of the properties we have discussed such as Mar Lodge Estate, most of Glencoe and parts of Ben Lawers and Torridon. Elsewhere, due to the presence of others with grazing rights (Ben Lomond, Balmacara and Canna for example), fencing for woodland and scrub regeneration is essential. In other situations, Kintail for example, although grazing numbers of both sheep and deer may be low, fencing may still be necessary, at least initially. At West Affric the opportunity to proceed with restoration without fencing has just arisen. In situations where the Trust lacks grazing control and where the remnants of native woodland and scrub are so small and attractive to grazers

Red deer stag in pinewood – we can have both!

that unless there are virtually none the trees and shrubs will never regenerate and eventually die out, fencing may be necessary in the short term. However, there must be a parallel strategy to reduce grazing pressure substantially before fences are removed, or the hard-won growth will be destroyed.

On all the Highland properties that we have covered there are management programmes to significantly expand native woodland and scrub. This is happening also on many sites under the care of SNH, the RSPB, SWT, JMT, WT, and is being promoted widely by bodies such as Trees for Life, Reafforesting Scotland, Scottish Native Woodlands, Highland Birchwoods, Tayside Native Woodlands, in many cases supported by the FA and the Millennium Forest for Scotland (MFS). Relatively small in area in comparison to the total area of Scotland, it is still almost impossible for us to imagine the scale of this woodland expansion and the impact it will have on the landscape. Possibly more importantly, we cannot prejudge future perceptions of the place of native woodland in the landscape of our descendants. The Trust is undoubtedly a major contributor to this exciting restoration and, as we have seen in the case of montane willow scrub, is pioneering management techniques. But the Trust must be careful not to be driven to fencing as a relatively quick and easy way to spend the funds available from MFS.

We have been discussing the negative impact of heavy grazing on tree and shrub regeneration, but it should not be forgotten that heavy grazing has also further modified and impoverished moorlands and grasslands, often to the detriment of the quality of the grazing, as at Ben Lomond and Ben Lawers. In these situations grazing pressure can be both reduced and diversified to improve the situation, for example with the introduction of cattle. What we must also not lose sight of are the positive effects of grazing

Buzzards and ravens

and the fact that many of today's attractive grassland and moorland communities have actually been created by agricultural grazing, for example some of those of Ben Lawers, Canna and Fair Isle. If these wonderful herb-rich grasslands, machairs and herb-rich heath are to survive the pressures of modern agriculture, the Trust needs to ensure that the appropriate grazing levels are continued.

The ideal long-term goal for all the Trust properties, outside the inbye or home farm, must be a level of grazing in balance with a diverse and dynamic range of semi-natural plant communities including woodland, sub-montane scrub and montane dwarf-shrub, without fencing. Monitoring of the effects of manipulative grazing management at Ben Lomond, Mar Lodge Estate and Ben Lawers particularly, will be invaluable in informing the required grazing regimes in many other parts of Scotland.

Having discussed the needs for managed grazing, to allow semi-natural vegetation to redevelop towards its 'natural' climatic climax, bearing in mind all the modifications that have happened to it since we first began to manage it over 8,000 years ago, let us look briefly at the grazed island vegetation communities of Fair Isle and St Kilda, which have slightly different histories and requirements. As we have noted in the relevant chapters, the position and exposure of Fair Isle so far north means that the climate at sea level is already sub-montane. In addition Fair Isle, like St Kilda, is relatively isolated from mainland Scotland and is also subject to regular gales which bring salt spray whipping across the land. On the moorlands of these islands there never were very many trees or shrubs. There are no indigenous terrestrial mammals on these islands, so grazing only began with the introduction of domestic stock around 5,000 years ago. The climatic climax vegetation in these situations is not a great deal more diverse than it is at present. Fair Isle, with its prostrate juniper and willow among the more common dwarf shrubs, is one of the least grazed areas in Shetland.

St Kilda is probably one of the very few places in the British Isles where there is no management of its 'domestic' stock and yet there is no evidence of over-grazing! Ironically, without management of overall numbers, which as we saw must have always been almost impossible on islands much of whose grazing is of the vertical coastal kind, this is the only place we have covered where grazing pressures are apparently in balance with the vegetation resource. This is entirely due to Soay sheep that have evolved and adapted over thousands of years to a superabundance of summer grazing and a late-winter of serious want. The lessons from our mismanagement of the grazing on the hills of pretty well all the rest of Scotland should be rather obvious – in St Kilda leave well alone!

Restoration, monitoring and research

The theme of the preceding section has been restoration and enhancement: the re-creation of diversity and richness in our wildlife and landscape. At Ben Lawers we saw that this was being taken a step further to include action to save plant species from extinction. Such is the state of health of many of our native species, animals as well as plants, that the Trust has now a Species Recovery Officer whose remit covers all the endangered species on the Trust's properties. A major part of that post's work at the moment is with the restoration of habitat for the corncrake on the west coast crofting properties. As noted on Ben Lawers, we cannot tell which species are endangered without survey and monitoring in assessing, first, the present status of certain species and, second, their state of health and future prognosis.

We have seen that detailed and regular monitoring has been occurring on Ben Lawers and a few other properties for some time – the seabird monitoring at Fair Isle, Canna and St Kilda, red-deer counts at Mar Lodge Estate, Torridon, Kintail and West Affric, and the Soay sheep research on St Kilda, to name but a very few. The importance of monitoring, discussed in several chapters, cannot be over-emphasised and must become an increasingly larger and more co-ordinated part of the Trust's investment in its countryside properties. This point has been recognised by the Trust within its proposal for a Nature Conservation Strategy by the year 2000, in the draft Corporate Plan 1998–2003.

The need for a range of conservation policies, similar to those for red deer and woodland, and the importance of research and academic involvement in it, is also given official recognition by the Trust in that document. As far as research into the natural environment is concerned, its promotion within the Trust has been closely linked, first, to Ben Lawers where the Trust made its first real acknowledgement of its responsibility to restoration of the natural environment; second, to those properties most recently acquired such as Mar Lodge Estate; and third, where such research has been initiated by other bodies, such as seabird research on Fair Isle through FIBOT and JNCC and the Soay sheep research through the encouragement of SNH and the involvement of the Large Animal Research Group.

Globeflower, rarely seen because of grazing pressure, but one of our most beautiful native flowers

The impulse to write this book came from the innovative and pioneering environmental management at Ben Lawers. On Ben Lawers, monitoring and research of the natural environment has been a growing proportion of Trust effort over the past two decades, but oddly at the equally important natural heritage properties of Glencoe and St Kilda the investment to date by the Trust in this area of work has been somewhat limited. It could be said that because the management of the natural environment of St Kilda is leased to SNH it has not been the Trust's role there to encourage or invest in such research. I have argued in the St Kilda chapter that the fact that St Kilda is a World Heritage site for its natural heritage, puts an overwhelming onus on the Trust as owner, not the lessee, to take responsibility for the natural heritage.

The anomaly in the Trust's attitude to its responsibilities to the natural heritage, as against its very well-known and successful investment in the other equally important areas of its original remit, is most apparent at its most important natural heritage property in world terms. How does the Trust's investment in St Kilda compare with that of its only World Heritage site for the cultural heritage, Charlotte Square? Just as what happened at

Ben Lawers in the early 1980s was the impetus for the very positive changes that have occurred within the Trust towards the natural heritage of its countryside properties over the last fifteen years, so St Kilda could be the impetus for an even more radical change for the Trust. Which now brings me to my final thoughts on the Trust's future role in the management of Scotland's nature.

Conclusions

I return now to the theme of the opening pages of the first chapter. The British designation for our natural heritage areas of national importance are the NSA and the SSSI. It has proved difficult to get exact figures for either, but taking the latter, the largest voluntary conservation body in Scotland devoted entirely to natural environment management is the RSPB which owns approximately 45,000 hectares of land. Approximately 69 per cent or 31,000 hectares of that land is designated as SSSI. The SWT in comparison has approximately 22,000 hectares, 10,000 of which is SSSI. The Trust is a body with a much wider remit than the RSPB or SWT and a landholding double that of the former. Coincidentally though, at approximately 31,000 hectares, or 45 per cent of its total holding, it has almost exactly the same amount of SSSI land as the RSPB! Each body holds almost 4 per cent of all SSSI land in Scotland. Who would have thought that the Trust, *at the very least*, is just as important a manager of our natural heritage in Scotland as the RSPB?

Scots pine and Ben Alligin

The SSSI is not the only natural heritage designation of course, nor need it be the only reason to manage the natural heritage sustainably, *pace* large parts of Kintail and West Affric, Torridon and the croft land at Balmacara, Fair Isle etc. In addition, the Trust sites discussed are also covered by NNR, cSAC, SPA, NSA, ESA, MCA, Ramsar, proposed National Park, Biosphere Reserve, Council of Europe and World Heritage listing! My point is that the Trust in 1999 has responsibility for a very significant portion of the most important land of natural heritage value, and the most important individual site, in Scotland if not the British Isles!

At this point it is important to remind ourselves of one of the general purposes of the Trust as stated in the 1935 Act: '. . . as regards lands for the preservation (so far as is practicable) of their natural aspect and features and animal and plant life . . .'. It is not possible, nor necessary, to try to place the various Trust responsibilities set out in the Act, in a hierarchy of importance: they are all important. However it is fairly clear from the figures (1998) that the proportion of the Trust's annual resources that go towards the natural heritage of £1.7 million (revenue as opposed to capital costs) compared to the total of £8.5 million (again revenue), including mainly the cultural heritage, is relatively small and that this area of its responsibilities is heavily dependent on external funding, for example the recent £3 million over three years from SNH. In other words less than 25 per cent of Trust (revenue) resources go towards the conservation of Scotland's natural heritage.

It was the intention of the essays on each property to illustrate just how much the Trust *is* now contributing to the management of Scotland's nature, as well as to be critical. The Trust *is* playing an increasingly important role, but one might say that the Trust has been a late developer in the field of natural heritage management. We noted that, although the Trust was established 60 years ago with a remit that covered the natural heritage, its attitude for many years was that the land would simply look after itself. It was only with the purchase of Ben Lawers in 1950 that a property was acquired primarily *for* its natural heritage value, and even then actual management to begin protecting and enhancing that interest did not begin until the late 1980s, some 40 years after the Trust's establishment. The Trust's slow recognition of its responsibilities picked up after that with the establishment of the Nature Conservation Working Group in 1990, which led to the appointment of the Countryside and Nature Conservation Committee and the Ecologist in 1991/92, later a Director of Countryside and a Species Protection Officer, to support property staff. The recognition of the need for management of its countryside properties is further illustrated by the fact that the number of full-time Rangers has more than doubled from twelve in 1990 to 27 in 1999. A new turning point for the Trust has been the acquisition of Mar Lodge Estate in 1995, which not only almost doubled the total area of countryside held by the Trust, but also almost doubled the area of SSSI land under Trust management.

That property and Ben Lawers have been given substantial investments to ensure that their natural heritage is managed to the highest degree; others such as Torridon, Ben Lomond and Glencoe are not so well endowed or staffed and have to compete with other properties of lesser importance for funds from the Trust General Fund. I would suggest that the present proportion of resources invested by the Trust more generally in the natural heritage, considering its portfolio, is not yet enough. In the parlance of business management today, the Trust should not see this as a problem so much as an opportunity. The choice it has to make will certainly be a difficult one because it will mean either a new perspective and a shift in the allocation of resources, or a retrenchment of its remit. The Trust must decide whether it is a body with a truly holistic remit in which the natural heritage plays an equal part or whether it is a body more concerned with the cultural environment. St Kilda epitomises its present quandary, where Trust resources are directed only to its cultural heritage, whereas the island has world-wide recognition for its natural heritage.

To manage all of its countryside properties to the level of Mar Lodge Estate and Ben Lawers however, will require not just a better balance of funding and of staff on the ground, in terms of numbers and ecological management experience and qualifications, but back-up in terms of specialist advisers and the encouragement of greater involvement of academic research. If the Trust decides to take this road it will be the only voluntary Scottish body able to manage the natural heritage under a holistic remit, not just covering birds, trees, access and wilderness, but community and the cultural and historic elements in addition. For example the Trust is the only voluntary conservation body that employs an archaeologist and it is the only body carrying out a series of Historic Landscape Assessments of all its properties to guide its restoration management. Such an extended breadth of appeal would undoubtedly attract new members and more finance if it was better known: the success of the Tarmachan appeal at Ben Lawers is evidence of that.

The Trust has an additional and key advantage over the other voluntary bodies and over the Government's own advisory body SNH: the Trust's land is held inalienably for the nation. Would the land ever be wrested from it for development or any other purpose? I think it very unlikely that the MoD would be able to have such an impact on St Kilda today. Because of inalienability the Trust has also all the time and security it needs and therefore it need not rush into management, nor rush to change management if the expected results are a little slow in coming. On the other hand we have noted just how little positive management of the natural heritage can take place over a long period if the prevailing political culture is simply to maintain the *status quo*. The Trust must use the advantage of its security, which others do not have, to take the lead in radical holistic management of its properties.

To an extent the maturing of the Trust as a natural heritage manager has been recognised by the government's official adviser on the subject, SNH. In the recent Concordat between the two bodies, one proposal suggests exploring the opportunity 'for the transference of management responsibilities for NNRs to NTS where there might be operational benefits in so doing'. What about St Kilda returning to the Trust's responsibility when the lease to SNH expires in 2001? Or uniting the management of the Torridon

Great skuas defending territory

property with Beinn Eighe NNR, Loch Lomond NNR with Ben Lomond, or Cairngorm NNR with Mar Lodge Estate?

In 1998 the Trust acquired around 1,800 hectares of mostly hill land in Unst (Shetland), the most northerly inhabited island in the British Isles. There is nothing of exceptional natural heritage interest on this property, though its landscape and wildlife is very attractive and undoubtedly there are valuable archaeological and cultural features. Much of the property is hill grazings with some blanket-bog on which breed bonxies and red-throated divers. There are some semi-natural and herb-rich sedge grasslands, which in late August are full of the deep-blue heads of devil's bit scabious, flowering eyebrights, tormentil, self-heal, fairy flax, thyme and autumn gentian, and the papery seed-heads of mountain everlasting and sea pink. There is one tiny area of plantation woodland – the most northerly in the British Isles – a sycamore copse that shelters a house called 'Halligarth', once the home of two of Shetland's earliest and best-known naturalists. There is also a community that needs to make use of all its natural resources to survive.

Here is a clean slate and time – the Trust does not yet have full control of the property – for the Trust to apply the best of all of its varied experience elsewhere and to consult the local community. Here is an opportunity for the

Trust to demonstrate that it spreads its resources equitably across all of its responsibilities. But where does the Unst property fit into the jigsaw of Trust countryside properties scattered across Scotland? Does it complement the natural heritage of Mar Lodge Estate, is its serpentinite sedge-grassland unique in Scotland, is there a cultural landscape that requires conservation management, and what role will the Trust give to the local community? Perhaps the Trust should now look at its countryside portfolio to see if it has a balanced representation of Scotland's natural heritage, and if not draw up an acquisition strategy to achieve this.

I began this book with reference to an American organisation, the Trustees of Public Reservations in Massachusetts, from which the Trust originally took its blueprint. Today, the Trust with its holistic remit could be much more than that body in its role in managing *Scotland's* natural heritage. It might now look to another voluntary American organisation, the Nature Conservancy, as another possible role model and become *the* manager of the natural heritage in Scotland. But the Trust could go further even than that, if it has the courage to develop not just a national, but a community partnership. Whither the Trust?

Halligarth and sycamore copse. The most northerly woodland in the British Isles

Appendices

Appendix I: Percy Unna's Letter

23rd November 1937

To the Chairman and Council of the National Trust for Scotland

Dear Sirs

As the movement initiated by a group of members of the Scottish Mountaineering Club to acquire Dalness Forest and hand it over to the National Trust for Scotland, to be held for the use of the nation, so that the public may have unrestricted access at all times, has now materialised; as subscriptions to that end were invited not only from the members of the Scottish Mountaineering Club, but also from the members of all the other mountaineering clubs in Great Britain; and as the funds so subscribed enabled the forest to be handed over free of cost to the Trust, together with a surplus to be used as an endowment fund; it is considered desirable that what are believed to be the views of the subscribers as to the future of the estate should be expressed in writing, and recorded in the minutes of the Trust. This is all the more necessary, as in the attached circular which was issued for the purpose of inviting these subscriptions it was stated that the land 'would be held on behalf of the public and preserved for their use', and 'that the Trust' would 'be asked to undertake that the land be maintained in its primitive condition for all time with unrestricted access to the public'. The views in question are –

1. That 'primitive' means not less primitive than the existing state.
2. That sheep farming and cattle grazing may continue, but that deer stalking must cease, and no sport of any kind carried on, or sporting

rights sold or let; any use of the property for sport being wholly incompatible with the intention that the public should have unrestricted access and use. It is understood, however, that deer may have to be shot, as that may be necessary to keep down numbers and so prevent damage, but for that purpose alone.

3. That the word 'unrestricted' does not exclude regulations, but implies that regulations, if any, should be limited to such as may in future be found absolutely necessary, and be in sympathy with the views expressed herein.

4. That the hills should not be made easier or safer to climb.

5. That no facilities should be introduced for mechanical transport; that paths should not be extended or improved; and that new paths should not be made.

6. That no directional or other signs, whether signposts, paint marks, cairns or of any other kind whatsoever, should be allowed; with the exception of such signs as may be necessary to indicate that the land is the property of the Trust, and to give effect to the requirement in the Provisional Order of 1935 that bylaws must be exhibited.

7. That should a demand spring up for hotels or hostels it is possible that it may have to be satisfied to a limited extent. If so, they should only be built alongside the public roads, and should be subject to control by the Trust; and it is suggested that no hotels or hostels should be built in Glencoe itself, or on any other part of the property, except perhaps in the lower reaches of the Trust property in Glen Etive. It is hoped that the Trust may be able to come to an understanding with the neighbouring proprietors as to corresponding restrictions being maintained in regard to land near to that held by the Trust.

8. That no other facilities should be afforded for obtaining lodging, shelter, food or drink; and especially, that no shelters of any kind be built on the hills.

9. It is hoped that the design of any buildings which may be necessary will be carefully considered by the Trust; and that, where possible, trees will be planted in their vicinity.

10. In conclusion, it is suggested that the whole question of the management of the Trust properties in Glen Etive and Glencoe should receive special attention, in view of the possibility that the policy adopted by the National Trust for Scotland in the present instance may create a precedent for similar areas in other mountainous districts, not only in Scotland, but also in England and Wales.

P. J. H. Unna
President, Scottish Mountaineering Club

Appendix II: Designations

Biosphere Reserve

These are existing NNRs (and therefore SSSIs) designated by the United Nations Educational, Scientific and Cultural Organisation (UNESCO). Each Biosphere Reserve 'conserves examples of characteristic ecosystems of one of the world's natural regions'. Biosphere Reserves aim to conserve, gather, analyse, communicate and employ information for the purpose of sustaining natural and managed ecosystems.

Council of Europe Diploma Site

This designation is awarded by the Committee of Ministers of the Council of Europe on advice from the Steering Committee for the Conservation and Management of the Environment and Natural Habitats. In the case of Fair Isle (1985) it is awarded under Category C: areas which combine the protection of 'social and recreational functions of the area with maintenance of its biological or aesthetic characteristics'. The award is for five-year periods, renewable for successive periods of five years, but only if the Committee's recommendations are fulfilled. There are two sites in Scotland. It carries no direct financial benefits.

Environmentally Sensitive Area (ESA)

ESAs were established under the Agriculture Act (1986) in order to protect areas where traditional farming practices supported distinctive landscapes and maintained valuable wildlife habitats, historic and cultural features. Farmers and crofters within an ESA can enter into a voluntary management agreement and obtain grants to carry out work to enhance or extend these features. There are more than 10 covering approximately 20 per cent of Scotland.

Marine Consultation Area (MCA)

These are non-statutory marine areas that were identified in 1990 to protect them in the face of the rapid development of fish-farming in the mid-1980s. They were identified by the Nature Conservancy Council (now SNH) as 'deserving particular distinction in respect of the quality and sensitivity of their marine environment', to assist and guide the Crown Estate Commissioners in their role as the approving body for developments on the shore and just offshore. There are approximately 30 in Scotland.

Marine Nature Reserve (MNR)

Allowance for the establishment of MNRs was made under the Wildlife & Countryside Act (1981) for the purpose of 'conserving marine flora and fauna or geological or physiographical features of special interest'. Unlike an

NNR, the establishment of an MNR requires 100 per cent consensus of all interested parties and is therefore very difficult to designate. There is only one in Scotland at the moment.

National Nature Reserve (NNR)

NNRs are in effect special SSSIs, very often large and spectacular and having management agreements between SNH and the owners, who may be private owners or approved bodies such as the Trust, SWT, RSPB or others, allowing public access, educational and research use. A very few are actually owned by SNH. Very often the management agreement includes an element of financial support, which may be substantial, for the owner to carry out positive conservation management and sometimes to support Rangers or Wardens. There are around 70, covering approximately 1.5 per cent of Scotland.

National Scenic Area (NSA)

The NSA is a national landscape designation, established in 1978 by the then Countryside Commission for Scotland (now SNH) and covering areas of national scenic significance representative of the best of Scotland's characteristic landscapes. Local planning authorities are required to consult with SNH for specified categories of development likely to have a significant effect on the scenic interest. There are 40, covering around 12% of Scotland.

Ramsar sites

These are existing SSSIs identified under the Ramsar Convention (at Ramsar in Iran) and ratified by Britain in 1976. They are wetland areas of nature conservation value designated to protect them and their wildlife.

Site of Special Scientific Interest (SSSI)

This is the principal nature conservation designation in Great Britain and covers around 10 per cent of Scotland. The SSSI designation provides the basic legal protection mechanism that underpins NNRs, SPAs, SACs and Ramsar sites. SSSIs are designated by SNH, the government's advisory body on the natural heritage. The designation requires the owner to consult with SNH before carrying out any changes to management that may affect the SSSI interest and the local planning authority to consult regarding planning applications. Management agreements can be made with SNH and financial support given to environmentally positive actions.

Special Protection Area (SPA) and Special Area for Conservation (SAC)

The European Commission (EC) Wild Birds Directive (1979) and Habitats and Species Directive (1992), establishing the SPA and SAC respectively, are laws of the European Union applying across all the member states. SPAs should 'ensure the favourable conservation status of 175 particularly vulnerable bird species and sub-species' and 'other migratory species'; while SACs should 'maintain or restore natural habitats and species of European interest' with 'special priority to be given to over 200 habitats and the sites of 193 animal species and over 300 plant species' (IUCN). Together the designations are intended to form an ecological network called Natura 2000. When completed there will be thousands of such sites right across Europe. Candidate (c) sites are sites under consideration. Before they can be designated in Britain these sites have to be SSSIs. The EC Directives requires more than just the maintenance of the *status quo* however and forbids developments that might damage the integrity of the site unless for reasons 'of overriding public interest'.

World Heritage Site
Designated by the World Heritage Committee of UNESCO under the Convention Concerning the Protection of the World Culture and Natural Heritage, to protect sites which it considers 'as having outstanding universal values'. The designation imposes no additional constraints on owners other than existing national designations. In the case of St Kilda (1986) it was already an SSSI and more recently both an SPA and SAC and is listed under the category of natural, rather than cultural, heritage. This is the highest accolade that can be awarded for the natural heritage. It presupposes complete protection, including the marine area, and the development of monitoring and research.

Appendix III: Abbreviations

Biosp.	Biosphere Reserve
BP	Before Present
CBT	Chris Brasher Trust
CC	Crofters Commission
CCS	Countryside Commission for Scotland
C. Europe	Council of Europe
CF	Crofter Forestry
COSLA	Council of Scottish Local Authorities
CPS	Countryside Premium Scheme
DCS	Deer Commission for Scotland
ESA	Environmentally Sensitive Area
EU	European Union

FA	Forest Authority
FC	Forestry Commission
FE	Forest Enterprise
FIBOT	Fair Isle Bird Observatory Trust
FICCA	Fair Isle Committee and Community Association
FIMETI	Fair Isle Marine Environment and Tourism Initiative
FIMP	Fair Isle Marine Partnership
GMP	Grazing Management Plan
HIE	Highlands and Islands Enterprise
ITE	Institute of Terrestrial Ecology
IUCN	International Union for the Conservation of Nature
JMT	John Muir Trust
JNCC	Joint Nature Conservation Committee
LARG	Large Animal Research Group
LRPG	Land Reform Policy Group
MNR	Marine Nature Reserve
MCA	Marine Conservation Area
MFS	Millennium Forest for Scotland
MLURI	Macaulay Land Use Research Institute
MoD	Ministry of Defence
MP	Management Plan
NC	Nature Conservancy
NCC	Nature Conservancy Council
NHMF	National Heritage Memorial Fund
NNR	National Nature Reserve
NP	National Park
NRA	Nature Reserve Agreement
NSA	National Scenic Area
NTS	National Trust for Scotland
RCAHMS	Royal Commission on the Ancient and Historical Monuments of Scotland
RCWG	Report of the Crofting Working Group
RDC	Red Deer Commission
RSPB	Royal Society for the Protection of Birds

(c)SAC	(candidate) Special Area of Conservation
SMC	Scottish Mountaineering Club
SNH	Scottish Natural Heritage
SOAEFD	Scottish Office Agriculture, Environment and Fisheries Department
SPA	Special Protection Area
SSSI	Site of Special Scientific Interest
SWT	Scottish Wildlife Trust
SYHA	Scottish Youth Hostel Association
TFL	Trees for Life
UNESCO	United Nations Educational, Scientific and Cultural Organisation
WCA	Wildlife and Countryside Act (1981)
WGS	Woodland Grant Scheme
WHS	World Heritage Site
WT	Woodland Trust

Appendix IV: Conversion Tables

Length

1 metre	=	3.28 feet
1 kilometre	=	0.62 mile

Area

1 hectare	=	2.47 acres
100 hectares	=	1 square kilometre

Selected Bibliography

Aitken, R. (1985) *Scottish Mountain Footpaths*. Perth: Countryside Commission.

Boyd, J. M, (1990) *The Hebrides*. London: Collins.

Callander, R. F. and Mackenzie, N. A. (1991) *The Management of Wild Red Deer in Scotland*. Perth: Rural Forum.

Campbell, J. L. (1984) *Canna. The Story of a Hebridean Island*. Edinburgh: Canongate Press.

Clutton-Brock, T. H. and Albon, S. D. (1989) *Red Deer in the Highlands*. Oxford: BSP Professional Books.

Clutton-Brock, T. H., Guinness, F. E. and Albon, S. D. (1982) *Red Deer: Behaviour and Ecology of Two Sexes*. Edinburgh: University Press.

Conroy, J. W. H., Watson, A. and Gunson, A. R. (1990) *Caring for the High Mountains – Conservation of the Cairngorms*. Aberdeen: Centre for Scottish Studies.

Countryside Commission for Scotland (1990) *The Mountain Areas of Scotland*. Battleby.

Crofters Commission (1998) *The Role of Crofters in Rural Communities*. Inverness.

Darling, F. F. (1955) *West Highland Survey: An Essay in Human Ecology*. Oxford: Oxford University Press.

Darling, F. F. and Boyd, J. M. (1964) *The Highlands and Islands*. London: Collins.

Donaldson, Lord (1994) *Safer Ships, Cleaner Seas. Report of the Inquiry into the Prevention of Pollution from Merchant Shipping*. London: HMSO.

Hunter, J. (1995) *On the Other Side of Sorrow*. Edinburgh: Mainstream.

Hurd, R. (1939) *Scotland Under Trust*. London: Adam and Charles Black.

Jewell, P. A., Milner, L. and Boyd, J. M. (eds) (1974) *Island Survivors. The Ecology of the Soay Sheep of St Kilda*. London: Athlone Press, University of London.

JNCC (various dates and editors) *Red Data Books*. Peterborough.

Land Reform Policy Group (1999) *Recommendations for Action*. Edinburgh: Scottish Office.

Macnally, L. (1993) *Torridon: Life and Wildlife in the Scottish Highlands*. Shrewbury: Swan Hill Press.

Marchant, J. H., Hudson, R., Carter, S. P. and Whittington, P. (1990) *Population Trends in British Breeding Birds*. Tring: BTO.

Mather, A. S. and Gunson, A. R. (1995) A Review of Biogeographical Zones in Scotland, *Scottish Natural Heritage Review*, No. 40. Battleby.

Nethersole-Thompson, D. and Watson, A. (1974) *The Cairngorms*. London: Collins.

Pearsall, W. H. (1950) *Mountains and Moorlands*. London: Collins.

Riddiford, N. J. (1999) *Safeguarding Our Heritage, The Fair Isle Marine Resource: A Community Proposal for its Sustainable Management*. Edinburgh: FIBOT, FICCA, NTS, RSPB.

Scottish Natural Heritage (1994) *Red Deer and the Natural Heritage*. Edinburgh: SNH.

Steel, T. (1962) *The Life and Death of St Kilda*. Edinburgh: NTS.

Steven, H. M. and Carlisle, A. (1959) *The Native Pinewoods of Scotland*. Edinburgh and London: Oliver and Boyd.

Tayside Native Woodlands (1995) *The Future for Tayside's Native Woodlands*. Perth.

Usher, M. B. and Thompson, D. B. A. (eds) (1988) *Ecological Change in the Uplands*. British Ecological Society. Edinburgh: Blackwell.

Wickham-Jones, C. R. (1994) *Scotland's First Settlers*. London: Batsford/ Historic Scotland.

Wightman, A. (1996) *Who Owns Scotland*. Edinburgh: Canongate.